On Feuerstein's Instrumental Enrichment

A Collection

Edited by
Meir Ben-Hur

SkyLight

TRAINING AND PUBLISHING, INC.

Arlington Heights, Illinois

On Feuerstein's Instrumental Enrichment: A Collection

Published by IRI/SkyLight Training and Publishing, Inc.
2626 S. Clearbrook Dr.
Arlington Heights, IL 60005
Phone 800-348-4474, 847-290-6600
FAX 847-290-6609
info@iriskylight.com
http://www.iriskylight.com

Creative Director: Robin Fogarty
Editors: Liesl Banks-Stiegman, Heidi Ray
Type Compositor: Donna Ramirez
Book Designers: Michael Melasi, Bruce Leckie
Production Coordinators: David Stockman, Amy Behrens

Printed in the United States of America
ISBN 0-932935-76-1

LCCCN 94-78544

1306D-3-97McN
Item number 1256
06 05 04 03 02 01 00 99 98 97   15 14 13 12 11 10 9 8 7 6 5 4

Table of Contents

On Feuerstein's Instrumental Enrichment
A Collection

WHO IS THIS BOOK DESIGNED FOR?
One of the critical implementation issues of Instrumental Enrichment is teacher preparation. Proponents and opponents of Feuerstein's Instrumental Enrichment agree that the training required for Instrumental Enrichment is extensive. Teachers who have not had extensive training and do not understand Instrumental Enrichment's underlying postulates may find themselves easily disheartened. In the absence of immediate results, they may return to more traditional methods. However, by having a true understanding of Feuerstein's theory and its applications, teachers will see lasting results. The key is preparation.

This collection of critical reading material on the theoretical, applied, and empirical issues cannot replace, but may support teacher preparation efforts in Instrumental Enrichment. I hope it will substitute for the traditional hand-out "paradigms," articles which are often outdated and lost in empty lecture halls.

This book is not a complete collection. Over the past four decades thousands of sources have accumulated on issues concerning this topic, including books, book chapters, journal articles, doctoral dissertations, paper presentations, and audio and audiovisual materials. This book cannot possibly attempt to present them all. Instead, this book may be defined as a "selection."

As a selection, this book suffers from the problems inherent in most, if not all, selections. Editors always "forget" to include important items, and often include some that could have been omitted. Such books rarely satisfy all experts. I wish that space limitation was my only excuse for the exclusion of important articles from this book, but this is not the case. Previously published articles can only be included with the publisher's permission. This permission was unavailable in many of my "first priorities." I was left with little choice, but with a great responsibility of making the correct judgment regarding the inclusion of articles from those released for reprint. This book includes articles that in my, perhaps idiosyncratic judgment, will help the teacher understand the theoretical, practical, and empirical aspects of Mediated Learning Experience as represented in Feuerstein's Instrumental Enrichment.

The articles in this collection were written independently of the book, by different authors, for different audiences, and at different times; therefore, some of the content is repetitious. Some articles are more difficult to read than others and there are slight differences in terminology throughout. My introductions to the chapters of this book attempt to offer a partial solution to this problem, as well as a conceptual framework for the integration of the points of views presented in them.

WHAT DOES THIS BOOK GENERALLY SAY?

The current belief that cognitive development can be enhanced and should constitute a primary goal of education is owed to the fact that the need to improve cognitive abilities is now more urgent than ever before. The assumption that it can be done provides a liberating force for optimists. Others, such as Arthur Jensen, continue to argue that this assumption limits and obstructs advancements in education. Believers must continue to practice, develop, and study humans' cognitive modifiability in order to substantiate this assumption and change skeptical minds. By doing so they will shape the future of education. Feuerstein has made a significant contribution to this optimistic alternative, both in theory and applied systems.

Feuerstein advocates education systems that consider intellectual power as their end rather than their means. He was the first to promulgate the concept of the Mediated Learning Experience (MLE) as the most critical modality of human learning and a critical factor in the variation in cognitive performance within and between individuals. His assumption that intelligence is modifiable by MLE regardless of age, level of functioning, or organic condition offers the quintessential icon for the optimistic educator. It implies a reciprocal relationship between the propensity to educate and the propensity to learn.

Feuerstein's theoretical work has been conceived from a broad scope of observations and clinical experiences. His theory of Structural Cognitive Modifiability (SCM) reports the *regularity* that he and many of his associates have found in their clinical work. In the process, Feuerstein and his colleagues have remarkably improved the lives of many children and adults from a broad range of socioeconomic strata who possess various forms of mental retardation, learning disability, emotional distress, and underachievement. A visitor to Feuerstein's world is first greeted by many of his excited patients, then struck by a feeling of inspiration.

Feuerstein's Instrument Enrichment is perhaps the best known of the available systematic cognitive education programs. It is certainly the most documented and widely used. Thirty years ago, publications on the effects of Instrumental Enrichment fueled the debate over SCM. At the same time it stimulated the development of other thinking skills curricula. Today, hundreds of such programs are available around the world, all offering Mediated Learning Experience. One way these programs differ is in their relationship with subject matter–that is, whether they are subject-matter-based (content based) or subject-matter-free (general). Content-based types vary in degree of immersion with content knowledge and general types vary in the way they consider practice in meaningful learning. Instrumental Enrichment represents Feuerstein's liberal side by being a "content-free" program and his conservative side by strongly emphasizing practice. In other words, Instrumental Enrichment exercises are designed carefully to provide enough practice for the establishment, crystallization, and automatization of cognitive behaviors while avoiding, as much as possible, the academic context.

Most thinking curricula have materialized only in recent years, and little can be known at this time about their effects.

However, it is interesting to compare the conceptual advantages and disadvantages of these approaches. The key conceptual difference among these approaches relates to the transfer of learning. Where does the approach espoused by Instrumental Enrichment stand with regard to this question?

The fundamental assumption of the general thinking approach is that there exists a significant set of cognitive skills and processes common to all thinking beings. Feuerstein's cognitive map and his list of cognitive functions offer his account for this assumption. If this assumption is true, then two strong arguments favor the general thinking approach. First, content knowledge and lack thereof may interfere with learning. Second, contextualized (content-based) learning is less likely to be transferred to different contexts than decontextualized (content-free) learning. If, however, thinking skills are not general, or if general thinking skills constitute only an insignificant part of the cognitive system, then it would appear that teaching thinking should necessarily be done in context.

Instrumental Enrichment has been in existence long enough to offer insight into this general thinking skills question. Empirical evidence from studies on the effects of Instrumental Enrichment is consistent in several areas: to the extent that IQ tests are accurate, Instrumental Enrichment appears to result in the learning of general thinking skills. These skills appear to be transferable to academic contexts. Instructional skills and dispositions relevant to SCM improve markedly as a result of Instrumental Enrichment teacher training and these skills and dispositions appear to be transferable to the teaching of academics. Transfer depends on factors that are yet to be examined.

Empirical results on transfer from Instrumental Enrichment appear to have a positive correlation not only with the quality of bridging exercises *within* Instrumental Enrichment, but also the bridging exercises *between* Instrumental Enrichment and the academic curricula. These results seem to indicate that skills and dispositions acquired by students and teachers through Instrumental Enrichment are appropriately challenged in the academic context. It also appears that while Instrumental Enrichment is a powerful tool for the mediation of cognitive performance, its effects on academic achievements depend on the way SCM is approached by the educational environment in which it is applied.

I believe, as my colleagues do, that teacher training in Instrumental Enrichment may be used as a powerful facilitator of cognitive-modifying schools. This phenomena seems to explain the success of the program throughout Israel as well as in the United States at the Flanegan Alternative High School in Omaha, the Taunton Public Schools, the Detroit school systems, and many other places.

HOW IS THIS BOOK ORGANIZED?

The first section of this book discusses the contribution of two important theorists, Reuven Feuerstein and Lev Vygotsky, to the concept of cognitive development. Reuven Feuerstein's discussion of his theory of Structural Cognitive Modifiability and Mediated Learning Experience is followed by a comparison of this theory to Vygotsky's approach to instruction. This section also offers a brief account of the theoretical foundations of the Instrumental Enrichment program.

The second section begins with a review of the research on the effects of Instrumental Enrichment and seeks to explain what the research reveals.

The third section addresses the implementation of Instrumental Enrichment. A critical issue of implementation is the need for a system of structural modifiability that supports cognitive growth in individuals and facilitates transfer of cognitive education across contexts. A theoretical discussion of this need is offered by Barbara Presseisen, Barbara Smey-Richman, and Francine Beyer. It is followed by a motivating report by Jane Williams and William Kopp of system implementation efforts in the Taunton Public Schools.

I hope the practitioner will find this book to be an effective tool for understanding the need for cognitive education, the promise it offers, and the success achieved through Feuerstein's Instrumental Enrichment.

Cognitive Modifiability: What Is It All About?

P rofessor Reuven Feuerstein's discussion of cognitive development is presented in the first part of this chapter. In this discussion Feuerstein defines intelligence as adaptability or cognitive modifiability. He argues that intelligence should be viewed as a dynamic construct; that the human cognitive facility is flexible, not fixed. Feuerstein's view of cognitive development is rooted in this theory of Mediated Learning Experience (MLE).

This modality of learning entails learning "through" a human mediator as opposed to direct learning. The "mediator" controls when learning takes place, what is learned, how it is perceived, and what meaning is abstracted in the learner's mind from the learning experience. The mediator often attempts to change the learner's psychological state, the nature of the stimuli and/or even herself in order to produce a learning experience. These changes can include the learner's state of alertness, interest, and awareness; the stimuli's appearance in time, place, intensity, and its background; and the mediator's tone of voice, appearance, and body language. Without such changes the reality is grasped episodically and learning is random. Ultimately the mediator interprets the intended meaning of the learning experience for the learner and establishes in the student a state of expectation for relevant future exposures.

Feuerstein perceives cognitive functions not as components of ability in the factor analytic sense (e.g., mathematical reasoning, logical reasoning, spatial visual abilities, verbal abilities, musical abilities, etc.), but as general native abilities, and dispositions. His developmental theory describes a structural process through which these cognitive functions are learned.

Feuerstein's critical argument is that deficient cognitive functions that result from a limited or lack of Mediated Learning Experience can be corrected or learned by formal and intensive instruction irrespective of age, etiology, or level of functioning. Feuerstein's discussion culminates in a research report which explains his distinction of low performance due to the effects of cultural differences from cultural deprivation.

An interesting comparison between Reuven Feuerstein's and Lev Vygotsky's theoretical and applied work is presented by Barbara Presseisen and Alexander Kozulin in the second part of this section. She argues that both these thinkers significantly impacted the fields of socio-cultural psychology. According to her analysis, both Feuerstein and Vygotsky distinguish between mediated and direct exposure to reality. The first tenet of both theories is that reality is mediated by meaning. The second is that meaning is instilled in the human mind through social interaction. They both argue that the major function of all cultures is to provide humans with the tools for the interpretation of reality. Human mediation represents the conduit for the transmission of these tools from one generation to the next. For both, cognitive development represents a structural process of increased mastery of cognitive abilities.

Presseisen and Kozulin's discussion culminates in reports on specific applications of Vygotsky's applied system in Israel with adult immigrants from Russia and Instrumental Enrichment conducted with elementary and middle school children in the Philadelphia School District.

Intervention Programs for Low Performers: Goals, Means, and Expected Outcomes

by Reuven Feuerstein, Mildred B. Hoffman, Moshe Egozi, and Nilly Ben Shachar-Segev

Social services have long been plagued with "creaming up." Creaming up introduces inequities in the access to well-intentioned programs of social intervention due to their methods of helping the needy. This inequity is most clearly reflected in the fact that those individuals and groups who need help less are helped more, whereas those who are most in need of help are either not helped at all or are helped in a very limited and unsatisfactory way.

The creaming-up phenomenon, initially described in social welfare, is strongly paralleled in the field of education, in general, and in the development of programs that aim at the enhancement of intelligence, in particular. A number of programs oriented to various dimensions of thinking (e.g., problem solving, critical thinking, creative thinking) have been developed for generalized use with relatively advantaged students. These students simply need to learn to make better use of the opportunities offered to them within the traditional public school system. Among the better known of

> Creaming up introduces inequities in the access to well-intentioned programs of social intervention due to their methods of helping the needy.

Excerpted from *Educational Values and Cognitive Instruction: Implications for Reform* (North Central Regional Educational Laboratory , 1991). Reprinted with permission.

these programs are Meeker's Structure of the Intellect (1969); de Bono's CORT (1973); Philosophy in the Classroom developed by Lipman, Sharp, and Oscanyan (1980); Whimbey and Lockhead's Problem Solving and Comprehension (1980); Harvard University's Odyssey (1983); Marzano and Arrendondo's Tactics of Thinking (1986); and Sternberg's (1986) program for developing practical intelligence. These programs have been structured in a way that makes their accessibility contingent upon a number of prerequisites: cognitive, emotional, motivation, and functional basic school skills. The absence of these prerequisites in a given individual or group of individuals makes these intervention programs inaccessible to them. Yet the very absence of the prerequisites is often the determinant of the individual's failure to learn and therefore makes an intervention program even more necessary.

We begin this chapter by giving several examples of the creaming-up phenomenon to show its persuasiveness. The remainder of the chapter is devoted to providing guidelines for developing programs that do address the cognitive and metacognitive prerequisites for low-functioning performers. Thus, this chapter is not intended to be a systematic, comprehensive review of thinking skills programs or of existing programs for retarded performers; rather, the purpose of the chapter is to provide a broad-stroke discussion of the creaming-up phenomenon, generally, and then a framework for analyzing current instructional programs and developing new ones. This framework emerges from over 20 years of clinical research and experience with retarded performers. In our use of the term "retarded performance," we differentiate between the manifest level of performance and the potential for learning that has not yet been actualized. It is the performance that is labeled "retarded," not the individual.

THE CREAMING-UP PHENOMENON IN EDUCATION
In Bourdieu and Passeron (1964), French sociologists, analyzed the effects of the open-gate policy that was instituted by the French higher educational authorities. This open-gate policy allowed individuals who usually would not have access to the university to enroll in courses there. Their findings pointed out that only a few of the students from the disadvantaged popula-

tion were able to benefit from this policy; those who made best use of it were those who would have "made it" in any case. The limited success of this program, designed to help individuals and groups in need of social promotion, was due to the lack of prerequisites possessed by the participants, which would have enabled them to benefit from the program. Accordingly, Bourdieu and Passeron (1964) concluded that an open-gate policy to higher education, unsupported by adequate measures to render it effective, only gives rise to pessimism about the role that education can play in the promotion of the disadvantaged. As the limited benefit of the opportunities offered to the disadvantaged becomes more evident the finger points to heredity as the major determinant of achievement. Indeed, Bourdieu and Passeron called their book Les Heritiers, hinting at the emphasis placed by certain behavioral scientists on the decisive role attributed to heredity as compared with the role played by education.

Similarly, a large number of intervention programs require that an individual show a minimal degree of initiative and resourcefulness in order to have access to them. However, the truly needy often lack this minimal capacity to create and persistently maintain conditions of inaccessibility to such programs. Thus, they are unable to make use of them. As with organisms under extreme conditions of hunger, they remain passive and in a state of torpidity that is not easily overcome, even at the sight of the most appealing food. A frequent observed reaction of many of the individuals and groups is the programs are too late to be as helpful to them as to those whose conditions may make them less eligible, but whose power, motivation, and knowledge turn them into "up-and-comers."

> A large number of intervention programs require that an individual show a minimal degree of initiative and resourcefulness in order to have access to them.

Thus, for example, it is said that remedial programs for reading are not effective with retarded individuals. Remedial programs are structured to be useful for the learning-disabled, intelligent individual. Paradoxically enough, according to the clinical definition of retardation, the retarded performer does not suffer from learning disability. This view has kept thousands of children and youngsters out of remediational reading programs. Instead, they are offered some very inadequate and highly ineffective reading programs that are not considered (even by those who implement them) as giving these children a real chance to acquire reading skills. So, the most needy are once again left out. This is true for many other programs that, from the very beginning, serve only those persons who have the prerequisites necessary to benefit from them, rather than being constructed so as to accommodate various individual conditions. Thus, these programs are not helpful to all who might benefit from them.

In a recent paper on improving thinking through instruction, Raymond Nickerson (in press) asserted that programs that address problem solving have as their major goal the *improvement* of thinking, rather than its *development*. Nickerson considers thinking as a spontaneously elicited process that therefore does not have to be produced; however, it must be improved. In his words, "While we do not have to be taught to think, most of us could use some help in learning to think better than we typically do. When we say we want to teach students to think, we really mean that we want to improve the quality of their thinking" (p. 2). This quotation makes clear the view that many programs designed for critical thinking, problem solving, and creative thinking serve individuals who possess these functions but make little or inefficient use of them.

Further evidence of this view may be found in Nickerson's (in press) analysis of the areas of thinking typically covered by researchers in their efforts to teach thinking: basic operations or processes, domain-specific knowledge, knowledge of normative principles of reasoning, knowledge of informal principles and tools of thought, wills, attitudes, dispositions, styles, and beliefs.

ASSUMPTION OF PREREQUISITE COGNITIVE PROCESSES IN THINKING PROGRAMS

Many of these areas of thinking cover the content of mental functioning but do not emphasize the prerequisite cognitive and metacognitive conditions that make this kind of thinking possible. These conditions are taken for granted, just as Piaget, in his search for conservation of matter, took for granted the presence of the process of comparative behavior. The success or failure of programs teaching these thinking operations are rarely explained by the presence or absence of these prerequisite conditions. Similar comments may be made of the framework for dimensions of thinking developed by Marzano and colleagues (1988), which covers parallel aspects of thinking.

This point can also be made for the work of Piaget. The authors did not find the Piagetian concept of conservation of matter as a developmental, maturational phenomenon in the functioning of Moroccan children, despite the fact that they were 4 or 5 years older than the age suggested for this achievement in a Genevan population. When we started to look into the process responsible for this difficulty and to manipulate the assessment procedure, it became evident that the most important component of this mental operation—namely, comparative behavior—was missing, and therefore the conservation of matter could not be achieved. Assuming that this activity at this stage of the child's development was universally present, the absence of conservation seemed like a pathological phenomenon. However, when we oriented the children to compare the variations in the form of the plasticine with the constancy of its weight, we found that once this elementary cognitive prerequisite was established, the conservation of matter and even the conservation of volume (which represents an even higher level of operation) were acquired and adequately used (Feuerstein & Richelle, 1963).

Educational systems and intervention programs are replete with false assumptions as to universal and obligatory presence of certain prerequisites of thinking.

Educational systems and intervention programs are replete with false assumptions as to the universal and obligatory presence of certain prerequisites of thinking. Conversely, whenever an inaccessibility to a given program is established or even anticipated, program planners conclude that the cognitive functions addressed in this program are simply not appropriate, not designed, or not necessary for the person who does not respond to them. One can see the circular nature of this assumption. On a most simple level, these programs are not made available as a matter of choice. Some educators even invoke the noble need to protect the children from the undue pressure with which they will be confronted if they are faced with a program whose set of goals is too high, and therefore their accessibility to the program is denied.

The senior author remembers the negative reaction of teachers and supervisors of Educable Mentally Retarded children when it was suggested that they introduce one of the Instrumental Enrichment program instruments that requires a high level of spatial functioning and hand-eye coordination. Teachers did not criticize the instrument for requiring a high level of information processing, but for requiring a level of visual-motor skills that was assumed to present particular difficulties for the Educable Mentally Retarded child. This did not prove to be true. The fact that, after adequate mediation, these children mastered the tasks on the instrument became proof to many teachers that indeed these children were much more modifiable in their cognitive performance than had been expected.

In order to make such modes of thinking available to the disadvantaged and to make them able to achieve what such programs require, a system-oriented approach must be implemented. Much more is required than offering some specific skills or mental operations. In a system-oriented approach, a single school system or school district is totally involved in (a) assessing the students' characteristics and their level of modifiability more dynamically; (b) offering the information obtained through this assessment to policy makers, teachers, parents, and last, but not least, to the children themselves; and then (c) establishing guidelines for intervention based on the preferred modes for increasing modifiability, as derived from the results of a dynamic assessment. In a system-oriented approach, emphasis is placed on the system that is the target for change, rather than on the individual. The environment is shaped so that it becomes a modifying environment. Ultimately, however, with the shaping of the environment, the modifiability of the individuals is increased.

In their thorough review, Resnick and Resnick (1977) pointed out that the current movement to teach thinking is distinctive in no longer addressing a small elite as in the past, but rather in its attempt to serve all learners in a truly democratic educational system. The question is: To what extent have the programs in current use been designed to make them accessible and beneficial to the masses of persons in need of development? It is our belief that these masses have been largely unable to benefit from whatever the school system offered them in curricular, content-oriented programs because they have been unprepared for this confrontation and limited in their use of cognitive skills necessary for mastering the curriculum (see chapter 9, this volume). These disadvantaged students were even less able to derive from their acquisition of basic school skills either higher mental processes or "good" thinking behaviors. To some extent, this failure is true even among students who are well prepared for their schooling and have benefited from instruction by becoming better achievers in school, although not necessarily better thinkers. This position accords with Nickerson's (in press) view: "In the aggregate, the findings from these studies force the conclusion that it is possible to finish 12 or 13 years of public education in the USA without developing much competence as a thinker" (p. 3).

> Feuerstein and his colleagues (1980) have emphasized the decisive role played by the presence of prerequisites of thinking in the capacity of the learner to benefit from learning opportunities.

PREREQUISITES FOR LEARNING: TARGETS FOR INTERVENTION

Feuerstein and his colleagues (1980) have emphasized the decisive role played by the presence of prerequisites of thinking in the capacity of the learner to benefit from learning opportunities. Specifically, three levels of cognitive deficiencies found in retarded performers have been defined. Input level deficiencies concern the quantity and quality of data gathered by the individual. Elaboration level deficiencies include those factors that impede efficient use of available data and existing cues. Output level deficiencies include those factors that lead to an inadequate communication of final solutions. Examples of deficiencies at each level are shown in Table 5.1. Deficiencies at the input, elaboration, and output levels markedly reduce the accessibility of the content of thinking. We explain what this means for each level of deficiency.

The Effects of Input Deficiencies

A blurred perception that renders the gathering of data laborious, fragmented, partial, and imprecise will set strict limits on the individual's interaction with stimuli, necessary for the process of thinking itself. Similarly, a lack of systematic exploration of the data at the input level will expose the individual to the hazards of a probabilistic perceptual encounter with stimuli and will not be conducive to the elaboration of all of the available data. Failure to use two or more sources of information will limit the individual's cognitive processes to the simple act of recognition and will not be conducive to the higher order conceptual thinking. The various objects that are thus perceived will not be coordinated. Such deficient functions on the input level will both affect and be affected by inadequate elaborative processes. Inadequate elaboration will follow an inadequacy in perceiving and registering a problem, because the individual will not ascertain the incompatibility between the stimuli that are perceived.

Table 5.1
Deficient Cognitive Functions on Input,
Elaboration, and Output Levels

Impaired cognitive functions affecting the Input level include those impairments concerning the quantity and quality of data gathered by the individual as he or she is confronted by a given problem, object, or experience. They include:

(1) Blurred and sweeping perception.

(2) Unplanned, impulsive, and unsystematic exploratory behavior.

(3) Lack of, or impaired, receptive verbal tools that affect discrimination (e.g., objects, events, relationships, etc. do not have appropriate labels).

(4) Lack of, or impaired, spatial orientation; the lack of stable systems of reference impairs the establishment of topological and Euclidian organization of space.

(5) Lack of, or impaired, temporal concepts.

(6) Lack of, or impaired, conservation of constancies (size, shape, quantity, orientation) across variation in these factors.

(7) Lack of, or deficient, need for precision and accuracy in data gathering.

(8) Lack of capacity for considering two or more sources of information at once; this is reflected in dealing with data in a piecemeal fashion, rather than as a unit of organized facts.

Impaired cognitive functions affecting the Elaborational level include those factors that impede the efficient use of available data and existing cues:

(1) Inadequacy in the perception of the existence and definition of an actual problem.

(2) Inability to select relevant versus nonrelevant cues in defining a problem.

(3) Lack of spontaneous comparative behavior or limitation of its application by a restricted need system.

(4) Narrowness of the mental field.

(5) Episodic grasp of reality.

(6) Lack of, or impaired, need for pursuing logical evidence.

(7) Lack of, or impaired, interiorization.

(8) Lack of, or impaired, inferential-hypothetical, "iffy" thinking.

(9) Lack of, or impaired, strategies for hypothesis testing.

(10) Lack of, or impaired, ability to define the framework necessary for problem-solving behavior.

(11) Lack of, or impaired, planning behavior.

(12) Non-elaboration of certain cognitive categories because the verbal concepts are not a part of the individual's verbal inventory on a receptive level, or they are not mobilized at the expressive level.

Impaired cognitive functions on the Output level include those factors that lead to an inadequate communication of final solutions. It should be noted that even adequately perceived data and appropriate elaboration can be expressed as an incorrect or haphazard solution of difficulties exist at this level.

(1) Egocentric communicational modalities.

(2)   Difficulties in projecting virtual relationships.
(3)   Blocking.
(4)   Trial and error responses.
(5)   Lack of, or impaired, tools for communicating adequately elaborated responses.
(6)   Lack of, or impaired, need for precision and accuracy in communicating one's response.
(7)   Deficiency of visual transport.
(8)   Impulsive, acting-out behavior.

Note: The three disparate levels were conceived so as to bring some order into the array of impaired cognitive functions seen in the culturally deprived. Yet, there is interaction occurring between and among the levels that is of vital significance in understanding the extent and pervasiveness of cognitive impairment.

The failure to adequately register and define a problem, which may be due to blurred perception or to a lack of relevant data (with consequent insufficient information processing about the characteristics of the stimuli), will meaningfully limit any motivation to search for additional data. As a consequence, the learner will not experience the disequilibrium produced by a perceived incompleteness, incompatibility, or controversiality of data. A lack of curiosity, reflecting a lack of motivation to know more, is often the outcome of a deficiency on the input level.

The Effects of Elaborative Deficiencies
In many cases, deficiencies on the elaborative level, such as lack of need for logical evidence or a lack of need to compare, are responsible for a lack of critical thinking behavior. In turn, elaborative deficiencies often create insufficiency in the input processes. Gathering data not only determines the nature of thinking but, to a very large extent, is determined by it. The goals set by elaboration for the perceptual apparatus during the input phase—such as creating relationships between discrete units of information through their comparison, creating substitutes, or producing groups through categorization—all these operations and elaborative activities result in a greater need for accuracy

and precision, a more systematic exploration, and a meaningful reduction in the individual's impulsivity. These conditions of thinking itself that affect the disposition and orientation of an individual's interaction with reality, with external or internal sources of information, and with formal or informal opportunities to learn. As a result, the individual benefits from experiences by developing higher level cognitive processes. Presenting low-functioning individuals with tasks that aim at producing problem-solving behaviors, strategic thinking, and critical thinking without equipping them with the prerequisites of thinking leaves their deficiencies uncorrected and will necessarily render these efforts inefficient. Intervention programs that do not include the correction of these deficient functions are, of necessity, inaccessible to individuals with such deficiencies.

The Effects of Output Deficiencies

The output level, that phase the mental act in which individuals communicate the product of their thoughts, also largely determines the efficiency of the mental processes. Impulsive responses and egocentricity (in the Piagetian sense of the term) may leave even an adequately elaborated answer without the attributes necessary to make it acceptable. Furthermore, imprecision, or the lack of need for precision on the output level, may, but need not always, result in limited needs for precision on the input or elaborational levels of the low-functioning individual. All mental processes will be affected by the confrontation with tasks to which the individual has not learned to respond with the required degree of precision. The result will be a failure to use such tasks for the development of meaningful learning processes.

GOALS OF REMEDIAL PROGRAMS

A number of goals can serve as guidelines in the selection and production of tasks to include in programs designed to develop cognitive processes, problem-solving behavior, creative thinking, critical thinking, philosophical modes of thinking, or even lateral thinking (such as is present in the de Bono program, 1973) when they are addressed to retarded performers, regardless of the distal determinants of their low functioning. In order to benefit from any program, students must have the capacity to learn from experiences, whether those experiences are intentionally produced for developing thinking or emerge from informal circumstances that individuals may be exposed to in their daily life. The capacity to learn cannot be considered as universally and equally present in all individuals. Some people benefit from each exposure, be it accidental or incidental, no matter how organized the experience is or whether or not it is meant to be a learning situation. Others have an extremely limited capacity to benefit from such learning opportunities. These individuals are exposed to experiences, are confronted with many and often powerful sources of stimuli, and yet are affected by them very little. For disadvantaged learners, it is not sufficient to make these stimuli available; they need to help in rendering stimuli accessible to them.

> In order to benefit from any program, students must have the capacity to learn from experiences, whether those experiences are intentionally produced for developing thinking or emerge from informal circumstances that individuals may be exposed to in their daily life.

These individuals need to enhance their propensity to use their encounters with stimuli in order to become modified and more experienced by this exposure. They must be rendered more flexible so that their previous ways of thinking and the established schemata can interact with the new data by new ways of perceiving them, new modes of elaborating them, and new and more adequate ways of responding to them. Through this process of assimilating the novel and the more complex and becoming modified by this very process of assimilation in the direction of a better accommodation to the new situation, they will become better able to benefit from experience. Without this process of enhanced assimilation and accommodation, the simple presentation of data will affect the population of low-functioning individuals very little, if at all.

In other words, the first goal of a program that aims at enriching low-functioning individuals will be to render them permeable to the program by creating in them the prerequisites for learning, that is by increasing their modifiability. To this end, a number of subgoals are necessary. These subgoals must guide the construction of the program and the selection of its materials and its content. Even more, they must be considered in determining the program's presentation, didactics, and techniques that shape the interaction between the teacher (turned mediator) and the learner (turned mediatee). In the following subsections, we present the six subgoals that we chose as the basis for an intervention program whose major goal is to enable individuals to better learn what is being offered them by life or by education.

Correction of Deficient Cognitive Functions

The first subgoal is to correct the deficient cognitive functions referred to previously (see Table 5.1). What we presented as prerequisites of learning we now define as goals. The overarching goal aims at correcting the deficient functions that characterize the individual with learning problems and reduced modifiability. This goal requires that the program be designed and applied both implicitly, in the way that tasks are structured, and explicitly, in the way the tasks are presented. The program is, therefore, designed to correct those deficient cognitive functions that are responsible for the reduced learning propensity of the individual.

Thus, in the Instrumental Enrichment program, tasks are shaped so as to compel the learner to invest much more meaningfully in their perception. For instance, the learner is compelled to search at great length for a given figure in a cloud of dots in which the figure is superimposed among others. The act of segregating a given shape in a cloud of dots requires that the perceptual activity be regulated, that impulsivity be inhibited, and that the number of dots identified as belonging to the sought- after shape be kept constant until the other dots that belong to it are found. Learners will have to look for strategies to facilitate their search, such as keeping their fingers on two of the dots while looking for the other two missing dots of the square, or finding certain systems of references that facilitate greater efficiency in the process of searching. Perception must be much more accurate than when it is confronted with unequivocal stimuli. Furthermore, by making the task require more than sheer perceptual processes, the learner must actively use cognitive processes to solve the problem.

Thus, in the search for the hidden square, individuals will have to gather more precise data about the model figure. The square's attributes will have to be compared with the attributes of a triangle or quadrangle. For this end, learners will have to use numerical criteria, such as four sides and four angles. The concept of equilaterality will have to be applied, as opposed to the differences in size of the sides of the rectangle. They will have to use the concepts of distance, length, and size. The constancy of the object across changes in its orientation will have to be maintained. From the presence of a given set of dots, the presence of another set must be inferred. From the absence of one particular dot, conclusions will be reached as to the inadequacy of the set under consideration (see Fig. 5.1).

The elaborational process is initiated by confrontation with incompatibilities inherent in the task, which are intended to produce a state of disequilibrium. The immediate feedback of the outcome of their activities will correct many deficiencies on the output level and will create a greater readiness in individuals to control their mpulsivity and to check on their hypotheses, restructuring them according to the outcomes of previous trials. Instrumental Enrichment has been shaped by this need to confront the learners with stimuli, experiences, and tasks that correct their specific deficient functions. The list of deficient cognitive functions has been very important in the development of tasks designed to reach this particular goal (see Table 5.1).

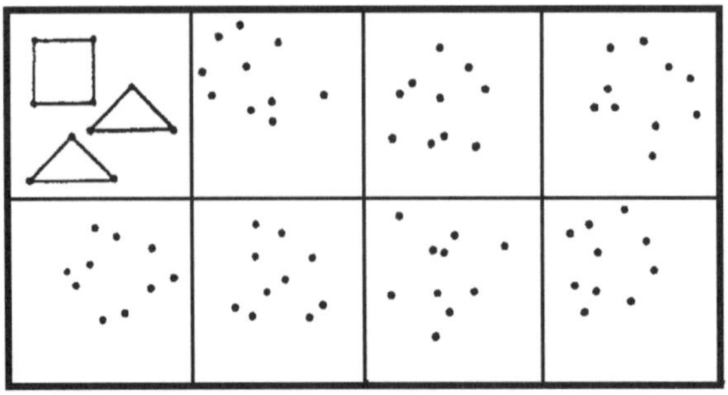

FIG. 5.1 Selected tasks from Organization of Dots, page 2. The individual must seek the necessary dots in an irregular, amorphous cloud so as to project figures identical in size and form to the given model. Successful completion involves segregation of the dots and articulation of the field. Tasks of Organization of Dots become more difficult with increased density of dots, complexity of figures, overlapping, and changes in orientation.

Acquisition of Prerequisite Repertoire

The second subgoal is to equip learners systematically and intentionally with the prerequisite information, verbal labels, types of relationships, and modes of operation that they need to do the exercises. Terms such as *square, triangle, parallel, equilateral, central, peripheral, before, after, simultaneous, identical, similar,* and *opposite* are necessary prerequisites whose presence in the individual's repertoire should not be taken for granted, even though, in practice, there may be evidence of their application even by the most low-functioning individual (Bryant, 1974). For purposes of learning and generalizing, however, the explicit meaning of such terms is a precondition for adequate learning. Similarly, operations such as analogical reasoning, logical multiplication, permutations, substitutions, and elisions will have to become active and explicit components of the repertoire of the individual's mental functioning (see Fig. 52.).

This second subgoal is achieved mostly through the active intervention of teachers/mediators who interpose themselves between the learner and the task and, according to their knowledge of the individual's need, introduce the vocabulary, operations, and strategies necessary for the mastery of the tasks. This subgoal should not be seen as the specific content of learning, even though it represents the content aspect of the program, which itself is not content-oriented.

Production of Generalization and Transfer

The third subgoal is to build into the program itself a propensity for generalization and transfer as a dimension of the learning process. This subgoal, the most neglected in many other programs, is mainly achieved through the creation of insight and opportunities to activate this propensity immediately. Teachers/mediators interpose themselves between the learners and the tasks and help in the analysis of the processes involved in solving a specific task. The mediator interprets to the learners the meaning of these processes and the way such processes can be applied in a variety of situations. Insight enables the learner to recognize that the functions that have been applied in a given task are relevant and applicable in others. Insight is also oriented towards discovering (through a self-reflective process) the kinds of changes produced in one's own cognitive structure by exposure to given experiences. These will be the source of new strategies applicable to other situations. Thus, insight will become an effective and powerful tool in producing transfer of the acquired elements and their generalization over situations differing from those to which the individual has been exposed.

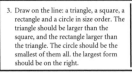

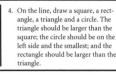

3. Draw on the line: a triangle, a square, a rectangle and a circle in size order. The triangle should be larger than the square, and the rectangle larger than the triangle. The circle should be the smallest of them all. the largest form should be on the right.

4. On the line, draw a square, a rectangle, a triangle and a circle. The triangle should be larger than the square; the circle should be on the left side and the smallest; and the rectangle should be larger than the triangle.

FIG. 5.2. Selected tasks from Instructions, page 11. Vocabulary, concepts, and relationships previously acquired in earlier instruments are applied in the tasks of later instruments. Operations, such as inferential thinking and logical reasoning, are elicited in Instructions. Tasks require encoding, decoding, and translation from a verbal to a graphic modality.

Insightful learning, leading to generalization and transfer, relies heavily on the concept of transcendence, taken from the mediated learning experience. Mediators do not interact with the learner only to the extent that the current task requires; they go beyond the immediacy of the needs of the current situation into other areas of functioning that the individual may be called upon to fulfill. Many of the programs that fail to generalize and transfer to other tasks have failed because there was no provision for those elements that would ensure that such generalization and transfer would occur; they relied heavily on what the processes themselves would do. It was supposed that individuals who were given a set of principles would apply them spontaneously, by themselves, because development was assumed to be spontaneous and from within, outwards. The social origins of generalization and transfer have been neglected very badly. They originate in a mediated orientation toward such processes. Through the transcendent nature of their interactions, the mediators orient individuals toward a process of generalization.

> **Many of the programs that fail to generalize and transfer to other tasks have failed because there was no provision for those elements that would ensure that such generalization and transfer would occur...**

In Instrumental Enrichment, for instance, the passage from learned rules, principles, strategies, and habits to other areas that are unrelated to the initial task is accomplished through what we refer to as *bridging*. The process of bridging consists in creating a certain orientation of the individual's mental activities. The individual is constantly oriented to seek areas of affinity between situations that warrant the application of the same principle. Transfer is ensured by the individual's acquired propensity toward comparing situations in terms of their commonality and difference; by an orientation toward facilitating problem-solving behavior by referring to previous experiences; by the use of the solutions of previous experiences; and by the selection of specific strategies, or modes, or styles (see Fig. 5.3).

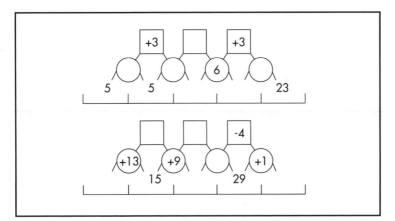

FIG. 5.3. *Selected tasks from Numerical Progressions, page 21. The tasks of Numerical Progressions, presented in a numerical and graphic modality, deal with establishing the rule governing the relationship between objects and events and using that rule to explain the past and anticipate the future. The preceding tasks illustrate higher order relationships that are not readily discerned. The principle that is revealed is readily bridged to family relationships, or divisions of the atom, or the phenomenon of chain letters.*

The teacher as mediator not only activates one particular individual in the classroom, but enriches that person's propensity to generalize through the participation of the whole group, which offers the variety and diversity of its particular experiences, thus fostering divergent thinking. Insight, defined here largely as metacognition, orients the individual toward the search for the mental process to master a given task. This metacognitive activity, involving self-reflection and control, leads to activating a variety of cognitive processes that will enhance meaningfully the structural nature of the changes produced by learning. For example, the current task may be compared to a past task in which difficulty was experienced. Following this comparative behavior, the current task will be solved more easily by the application of a strategy that was found to be efficient in the previous situation.

Development of Intrinsic Motivation

The development of an intrinsic motivational system is the fourth subgoal that must be kept in mind in developing programs for the disadvantaged learner. This intrinsic motivation is necessary in order to ensure that the learner will apply those learned rules, principles, sets, strategies, and problem-solving behaviors to situations in which there is no explicit demand to do so, as in the classroom (in particular), or in life situations (in general), it is not enough to know that there is a strategy. In order for it to be applied, one must also be motivated to use it. Such motivation may be extrinsic, as when one is specifically asked to implement the strategy; but such situations are rarely present in the life of disadvantaged individuals, whose encounters with situations that demand higher order thinking may be very limited (at least as long as they function as disadvantaged, both in school and at home).

The motivation to use adequate cognitive processes may become possible through an internalization and an intrinsically determined activation of part of the repertoire of functioning. One disadvantage of many available programs is that intrinsic motivation as a determinant of behavior is not addressed. Producing intrinsic motivation is especially important for disadvantaged learners. The great problem is how intrinsic motivation can be produced where it does not exist. The disadvantaged learner is often very much of a "realist," seeking types of skills or information that can best serve in immediate encounters with situations. When it comes to intellectual higher order mental processes, internal needs rarely animate. There is a pragmatism in grasping at the easiest way to perform and achieve immediate goals.

How, then, can we produce intrinsic motivation towards types of functioning that are not always needed and not necessarily economical? What types of investment are required in order to endow the low-functioning individual with a motivation that is detached from the immediately experienced, extrinsically generated need? To deal directly with low-functioning individuals, we must confront this question. Our answer is that intrinsic motivation can be equated with habit formation. A habit is an intrinsic way of determining behavior. In certain cases, the habit is not contingent on any situational constraints. In some extreme cases, it is even incompatible with extrinsic needs. When we are habituated to do something, we do not do it because it is necessary; but because we have the habit of doing it. The habit itself makes it necessary that an act be performed in a specific way.

> The question, therefore, is to what extent should rote, mechanical learning be used in order to form habits of thinking and functioning?

Habit formation has been badly neglected in an era when everything has had to rely on internal reconstruction, on discovery learning, and on a spontaneous and fluid kind of approach. Many educators have fought against habit formation, which has been considered—and rightly so—as too mechanical, less thought-through, and as having no requirement for the fluid intelligence that is applied in operational thinking. Habit formation, therefore, has been totally neglected in programs in which thinking rules and problem solving are the major goals. Principles that are taught are applied to a situation in the immediate experience episodically and spuriously, leaving place for another principle to be taught. All that is taught remains on the level of fluid intelligence. There is no purposeful, intentional way of producing a crystallized form of thinking in the learner.

Habit formation usually relies heavily on a repetitive, rote type of learning. It requires repeating the same thing until it gets applied mechanically. The question, therefore, is to what extent should rote, mechanical learning be used in order to form habits of thinking and functioning? The damage that may be produced in the motivation of individuals (in having them do things they do not like to do), and to the fluidity of their thinking (by making them do things without having to think) may be greater than the benefit derived from forming habits of cognitive functioning.

In attempting to solve this problem, which sounds very much like "squaring the circle," we have used a Piagetian concept initially termed by Baldwin (1925) as the "circular reactions." We have made sure that habit formation through repetition of the same principle will never become purely mechanical. We achieved this by designing tasks that repeat themselves in one or two of the parameters they have in common but change in other parameters. A need has always been created to rediscover the familiar, the mastered part of certain skills in situations that constantly become different, more complex, more novel. Even when the same rule is applied, it will always be done with the help of more fluid types of thinking, by rediscovery, and by shaping the known element so it will fit the situation that was previously unknown. This need to create habits is addressed in Instrumental Enrichment by producing numerous repetitions of the same principle, but never applying it mechanically or blindly nor using exactly the same situation. The repetitive tasks require a great effort of discovery and restructuring. The goal of producing intrinsic motivation through habit formation makes the program require more time than does a usual enrichment program in which principles and rules are taught in a hit-and-run fashion, with hopes that by hitting and running the goal will be attained (see Fig. 5.4).

The need to crystallize the acquired cognitive processes is felt mostly in the input and output phases of the mental act, which are more resistant to change than the elaborative phase and, therefore, require much more investment in order to reach higher levels so automatization and efficiency. Thus, in order to make individuals with blurred, sweeping perception invest more and focus longer in order to reach a greater level of clarity and accuracy in the perceived, many situations must be created in which this will be imposed by the nature of the task. The same is true in the output phase. Inhibiting impulsivity in the

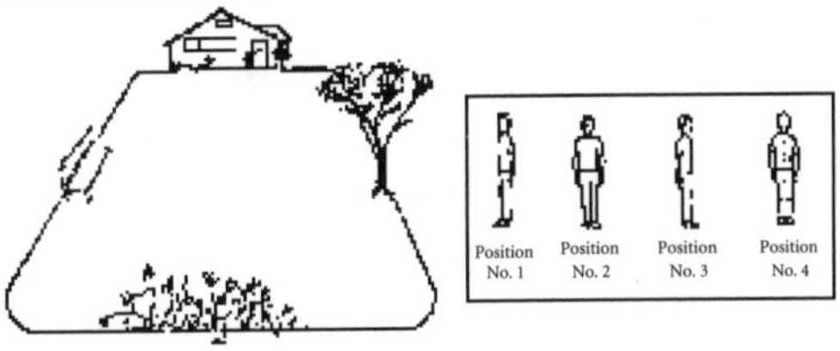

Fill in what is missing:

Position	Object	Direction in Relation to the Boy
1	The tree	
4		right
2		back
	The house	front
3	The bench	
2	The house	
	The tree	left
4		back
	The bench	
		left
3		back
4	The tree	
		right

FIG. 5.4. Orientation in Space I, page 5. The preceding task illustrates the controlled repetition of the same principle. The field must be constantly restructured for mastery. The instrument, Orientation in Space I, introduces a personal, stable system of reference by which to describe spatial relationships. It also seeks to develop and enhance the use of representation and the ability "to put oneself in the shoes of the other." A transcendent goal of the instrument is to develop an understanding and tolerance for ideas and attitudes that stem from perspectives different from one's own.

output level is not achieved by imparting to the individual the meaning of control of impulsivity. It will require a neutralization of the original determinant of impulsivity and then the undoing of the habit that has become established through long years of practice. Undoing a habit is best achieved by substituting another and more desirable one for it. Formation of a new habit requires more effort and is spread over longer periods of time.

Follow-up research (Rand, Mintzker, Miller, & Hoffman, 1981) found an increase in the effects of Instrumental Enrichment with time elapsed after cessation of the program, a fact at least partially explained by the process of consolidation and crystallization of the cognitive habits. Time has thus acted as a reinforcer rather than as a weakening determinant of the acquired cognitive functions (see Fig. 5.5).

Habit formation adds the dimension of efficiency to the mental act. Efficiency (defined later as the "rapidity-precision" complex and the feeling of ease by which a given task is performed) is strongly dependent on whether the program allows for habit formation. The more habit formation, the greater the efficiency. The greater the efficiency, the more chances that the individual will use the acquired cognitive functions, because it will be easier, require less investment, and hence be more economical.

Instrumental Enrichment: Follow-Up Study

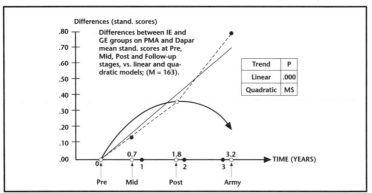

FIG. 5.5. *Divergent Effects of Instrumental Enrichment. Differences between Instrumental Enrichment and general enrichment groups on PMA and Army Dapar mean standard scores at pre, mid, post, and follow-up stages indicate that nearly 2 years after the cessation of intervention, the positive effects of IE intervention continue to grow. Differences between the two groups closely resemble a linear, rather than a quadratic, model.*

The Piagetian concept of assimilation and accommodation has been used in shaping the formation of habits. We create a schema through repetitive behavior. But then, in order to make this schema able to accommodate to the new elements that the schema assimilates, we create conditions by which to keep the schema flexible and plastic. Thus, in Instrumental Enrichment, we have made sure that the rules and principles, strategies, modes of search, and the various subgoals that deal with the correction of cognitive deficiencies will be spread over the whole program, and that individuals will again and again have the opportunities to apply what they have learned to other areas and in a large variety of tasks. Bridging and insight will render explicit the applicability of certain automatized strategies implicit in other situations (see Fig. 5.6).

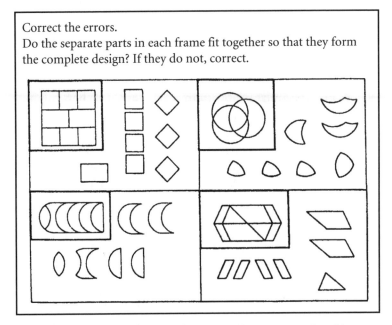

FIG. 5.6. Selected tasks from Analytic Perception, page 10. Cognitive operations, such as identification, differentiation, discrimination, categorization, representation, hypothetical thinking, and logical reasoning are elicited by tasks in Analytic Perception and will be used over and over in coping with tasks of other instruments. The sources of errors of commission and omission illustrated in the preceding tasks will be discussed and bridged into errors occurring in academic and vocational areas, daily life experiences, world affairs, and interpersonal relationships.

Development of Task-Intrinsic Motivation

The fifth subgoal is the creation of task-intrinsic motivation. This requires producing types of tasks that will entice the disadvantaged learner and stimulate a readiness to act in response to the appeal of the task itself. To be stimulating, Instrumental Enrichment uses rather complex and difficult tasks. Instrumental Enrichment makes these tasks accessible to learners by offering them the necessary mediation, carefully gauged to individual needs, to help them succeed. Once the learners are successful, the mediator leaves them to work independently. The task may be complex, but the learners' competency is not based on their previous experiences. We have carefully avoided making success contingent on previously known units of information. The complexity of the task relates only to the mental act that the individual will have to perform to solve the problem, with very little reference to previous experiences. Of course, some individuals will be more advantaged when confronted with these tasks because of their greater generalized or specific experience. However, even the advantaged must invest again and again when they are confronted with the same task. Teachers themselves must invest and make an effort when presented with our materials. In certain cases, their effort is even accompanied by their feeling, "How is it possible that I cannot do what the children are supposed to learn, and I must make an effort to do what the children will have to learn with ease?" Usually, programs used in training for problem-solving behavior are easily mastered by the teachers themselves. By the nature of the complexity of its tasks, and its independence from demands for previous learning, this program becomes a target worthy of mastery by individuals with a proficient education, as well as being interesting and appealing to the disadvantaged who have had very little or very inefficient modes of learning (see Fig. 5.7).

This task-intrinsic motivation, which is produced by the very nature of the tasks, has both a substantive and a social aspect. The substantive aspect is, of course, the nature of the mental operation in which the individual becomes engaged while doing the tasks, which tends to become "addictive" because it is both challenging and a source of success. Some of the children cannot stop doing the exercises. Some adults, as well, experience this because of the challenge of the exercise and the pros-

Look at the sample. In each of the two frames, make a drawing that is the same as the sample ONLY in those aspects indicated by the encircled words.

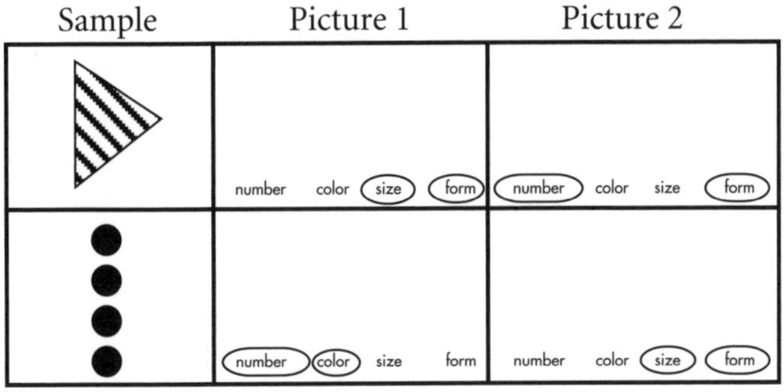

FIG. 5.7. Selected tasks from Comparisons, page 12. The preceding exercises from Comparisons illustrate the level of difficulty posed by the tasks for even advantaged learners. In order to draw items that are similar to the given model in only a few aspects, it is necessary to process information from several sources simultaneously and to devise a strategy for checking the completed work. The instrument, Comparisons, teaches the student to find and describe the similarities and differences between two or more objects or events. It also aims at enriching the verbal repertoire of parameters to direct clear, precise and accurate perception.

pects of success. In many instances, low-functioning individuals may initially be frustrated when they see themselves caught in a task in which they have to invest, because they have never done anything requiring from them more than a very fleeting, sweeping kind of perception and attention. They may actually tear up the page of exercises. But if the mediator has enabled them to experience a first success, they come back slowly, so that what was initially a source of frustration becomes enticing. Then the task-intrinsic motivation and the curiosity emerge, not only about the task but also about themselves ("How will I be able to do?", "How much better will I be able to do it at a later stage?," "How much more difficult will the tasks be that I will be able to do later?"). Indeed, some of the learners, having once experienced success, request more difficult tasks. This kind of task-intrinsic motivation is very seldom experienced with disadvantaged, dysfunctional learners. They usually avoid learning. They also avoid anything that is new because of the difficulties it presents to them. This behavior is followed by the evasion and lack of persistence that so strongly mark the disabled learner.

Another positive aspects of task-intrinsic motivation is the social meaning that the mastery of such tasks bears for the learner. The learner—child or adult—learns the worth of this type of activity as a socially valued and appreciated experience. Many of the children in the classroom situation who have experienced constant failure learn through Instrumental Enrichment for the first time that they can do as well as the more successful students do in subject-matter areas. Furthermore, the nature of the tasks is such that they require a constant rediscovery when they are presented to even initiated, experienced learners, including the teacher, who have performed the tasks before. A constant need exists for investment each time they are confronted with similar tasks. Even if, admittedly, they will need less investment, nevertheless they will not be able to perform just by looking at the task. Learners cannot solve the problem by simple recognition, they must restructure and rediscover the problem. The tasks have been shaped in a way that will make such discover possible, but it requires a reinvestment. Teachers and students then realize that they are very close to each other in doing these tasks and that the relationship in the teacher/mediator–task–student triangle is much more equilateral than in any other instructional experience (see Fig. 5.8).

A new social status emerges when a disadvantaged student becomes involved in Instrumental Enrichment. Opportunities are created for the individual to succeed and to feel competent in areas in which even adults have to work hard in order to succeed. Students feel an attraction to tasks that are so effective in changing their status.

Changing the Role of the Learner

The sixth subgoal, probably the most important in dealing with the disadvantaged, is to create a feeling of not being just passive reproducers of units of information that are offered to them ready-made, but as people who are called on to generate new information that would not come into existence without their direct contribution. In many instances, deficiencies in the func-

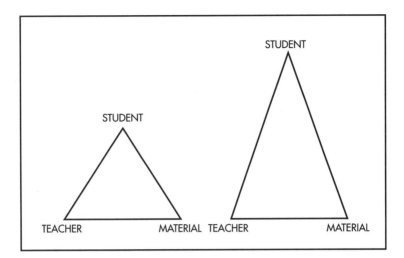

FIG. 5.8. Teacher-Student-Material Relationship. In teaching curriculum material, the teacher is usually very familiar with the lesson's content. Students perceive the teacher and material as a unit and feel very distant from both. In Instrumental Enrichment, however, the teacher-mediator and student confront the tasks together. This cooperative relationship makes the distance from the material the same for both. The teacher–student–material interactions more closely resemble an equilateral triangle.

tioning of the disadvantaged, deficiencies in their learning process, are the direct result of a view of themselves as the recipients of information and, at best, the reproducers of the received information, without any pretense or even readiness to see themselves in the role of those who are called on and able to produce information. In many instances, programs designed to create higher mental processes offer the learner problems that are matched to the presumed repertoire of prerequisites of thinking, the componential skills, and the motivation to solve them.

Success in such programs is built on the conditions for solving the tasks, which presuppose certain prerequisites. However, low-functioning learners do not possess these prerequisites. They will not be able to solve such problems unless they are properly and systematically prepared for them and unless they are equipped, through previous focused intervention, with the necessary conditions for such problem-solving behavior. Presenting tasks that require the production of new modes of thinking, new strategies, and the discovery of rules in situations not previously experienced leads toward their perception and awareness of themselves as generators and creators of new information, which is essential in solving problems (see Fig. 5.9). Many of the individuals experience this change as having a significant impact on their lives.

Low-functioning students often attribute their failure to that to which they have not been exposed. If they do not function properly, they comment: "I have never learned it. Nobody taught me. I have never been told to learn it," as if everything one knows depends on external sources of information. It is noteworthy that outer-directedness is described by Zigler and Butterfield (1986) as a typical phenomenon of the mentally disadvantaged individual. This affects the output phase of the mental act, turning even a properly elaborated problem into a failing response, just because the students do not dare think they will ever be able to respond to something about which they have never been told. Programs addressing themselves to low-functioning learners have to create the situations, the modes of presentation, and the interpretation that will convey to that learner, "Yes, you are the generator of information and thereby can be engaged in the processes of discovery and creativity, and in more efficient learning." Processes of generalization and transfer to situations other than those that have been learned will then take place.

THE DILEMMA: EMBEDDING OR ISOLATION

The literature is replete with questions about the nature of a program aimed at developing cognitive processes or enhancing problem-solving skills. Should it be given as an independent type of activity? Or should the ingredients and components of the program be intermingled and entwined as interstitial tissues in an otherwise content-oriented academic studies curriculum? (Resnick, 1987; Jones, Palincsar, Ogle, & Carr, 1987).

Those who advocate the latter approach would say that teaching intelligence without a specific content to which it is applied may leave it totally isolated from the areas of performance in which the individual is called to function. What is learned may remain isolated without any effect on the performance of the individual in a real-life or academic situation.

Every day Joan bought a tuna sandwich and a cup of coffee for lunch. She usually ate at Joe's Cafe, but one day she decided to eat at Tip's Tea Room, a place that had just opened. The total bill for her egg sandwich and cup of tea was exactly the same as it usually was at Joe's for her regular lunch; however, she noticed that the price of the sandwich at Tip's was higher than at Joe's. She immediately concluded that:

The coffee at Joe's ☐ the tea at Tip's Tea Room

When A + B $=$ C + D   When A + B $=$ C + D

And   A $<$ C   And   A $>$ C

Then   B $>$ D   Then   B $<$ D

FIG. 5.9. *Selected task from Transitive Relations, page 17. The transivity of the relationships in the preceding task permits students to generate information and arrive at conclusions otherwise unavailable to them. The instrument deals with logicoverbal reasoning and requires the use of functions, operations, and strategies acquired in earlier instruments.*

Other arguments pertain to the structure of the intellect and to some theoretical considerations about the specificity of certain modes and types of thinking operations that are not considered to be freely and easily generalized, but must be taught, learned, and applied to specific content. The question is, therefore, to what extent will creating cognitive skills outside of, or free from, specific content be as efficient as when they are taught within their specific context? This argument is, of course, valid when we deal with higher mental processes in a direct way. However, it cannot be considered a valid argument once we deal with prerequisites of thinking, such as adequate data gathering on the input level through proper focusing, through sharpened perception, through prolonged and persistent investment, and through systematic search for data. It is not valid when we must equip the individual with the most elementary type of mental functions, such as comparative behavior, or when we deal with the episodic grasp of reality that is characteristic of the learning disabled. An episodic grasp of reality hampers the individuals' orientation and readiness to create relationships between things, and keeps them from organizing the experienced events in a sequence that permits the perception of causal relationships, the means-and-goal relationship, or the types of associations that are necessary when one is involved in such higher order thought processes as categorization and inductive and deductive reasoning.

> An episodic grasp of reality hampers the individuals' orientation and readiness to create relationships between things, and keeps them from organizing the experienced events in a sequence that permits the perception of causal relationships.

When one deals with elementary cognitive functions that have not been established, for whatever reason, in the individual's cognitive apparatus, then the issue of specificity is much less important. These basic cognitive functions have to be mediated and consolidated in order to render them efficient, especially when dealing with the peripheral phases of the mental act (the input and the output phases; see Table 5.1). They must be dealt with in a very focused way in situations that permit the exercise of these functions in a systematic, repetitive, and crystallizing way. This cannot be done when one deals with the curricular content-oriented programs that require a particular strategy or a particular type of function. Therefore, in attempting to increase the cognitive modifiability of the low-functioning individual with deficient cognitive functions on the input, elaboration, and output levels, the usefulness of the curricular, content-oriented approach is very doubtful.

The controversy around the question as to which is the preferable approach to the development of cognitive skills is best resolved when one refers to the broader goal of learning to learn, notably to increase the modifiability of individuals by rendering them more sensitive to opportunities for learning in a formal and informal manner. Learning to learn may then become the source of the acquisition of new strategies, the development of specific cognitive skills, the acquisition and retention of information, and the organization of sets or units of information in a way that will permit easy access and retrievability whenever required. This goal is to be considered as a precondition for any attempt to involve low-functioning individuals in more specific types of objectives that would render them accessible to content-oriented goals of learning.

REASONS FOR CONTENT-FREE PROGRAMS
In addition to the preceding arguments, four specific reasons in favor of using a specially designed content-free program for these goals, rather than making them a derivative of curricular content-oriented approach are as follows.

Resistance of the Student
The first difficulty in using curriculum materials for creating prerequisites of thinking resides in the resistance of the student. When these students are involved in learning and acquiring units of information of any nature, they usually show very little readiness to allow themselves to be "led off" or "taken away" from the subject matter with which they are dealing in order to elaborate on the relationship between units of information to which they are exposed or to deal with certain molecular components of the mental act. Low-functioning learners are often marked by a materialistic approach. They want to master the presented material. They are not interested in going beyond the stimuli, the data, or the events with which they are dealing in order to speak about the relationship between these events, the way they are organized, the way they are grouped, substituted, generalized, and conceptualized as accomplished by using higher mental processes. Some of the learners claim their right to finish a given number of pages or a given number of exercises. Never mind how much comprehension accompanies this "mastery." Teachers who attempt to derive from the acquired information the supraordinate inferences (the "moral of the story") are met with the resistance of the learners whose orientation is focused very little on the relationship and much more on the facts themselves.

The detachment from the content to the more formal aspects of thinking that can be derived from it is to be considered as an end product of a process of mediation and training, rather than as a primary goal. It is only after the program has created a state of accessibility in the disadvantaged learners that they will be able to use content-oriented learning, as well as any other event they directly experience as a source of rule learning and conceptualization. The two programs, content-laden and content-free, have to run parallel to each other with the teacher as mediator, building bridges between the two streams of learning. In this way, the resistance of the learner will be more neutralized. Once equipped with the orientation and the proper tools for the acquired information, there are much greater chances that the learner will be ready to invest in organizing, planning, encoding, categorizing, judging situational conflicts, searching for criteria for truth and falsehood and the "objective" logical evidence within it. Hopefully, then, the way of learning the curriculum content materials will prove to be much more effective and mean more than when the learning is devoid of the principles, rules, and efficient modes of input and output.

Resistance of the Teacher

A second source of resistance to the use of curriculum learning for training toward higher mental processes (such as critical thinking and problem solving) are the teachers. The teachers' materialistic orientation is encouraged by the educational system and its supervisors as well as by the children themselves. Teachers become very reluctant to spend too much time on formal aspects of learning, because this interferes with the possibility of dispensing the amount of information the learners are supposed to acquire during a given period in their school activities. Teachers often jealously guard the time allocated for teaching content even when they know how little of what is offered the children reaches them. Asking teachers to stop the flow of information or the learning of basic school skills in favor of teaching formal elements of thinking is considered to be a true loss of time, especially if they do not believe in the modifiability of the learner and when their teaching efforts are not found to lead to measurable, palpable academic achievements.

Teacher resistance is even more difficult to counteract, because teachers are little aware of the prerequisites of thinking that are responsible for adequate cognitive processes. This lack of awareness is due to their training or orientation, or their interest and motivation. They take for granted certain conditions of thinking that do not necessarily exist in each student; or, even when they exist, they are not always used efficiently by the student. Thus, teachers base their instructional strategies on false assumptions.

For all these reasons, teachers trained in the traditional manner do not use the content of their teaching for the broader goal of teaching how to learn. However, according to our experience, a program that uses mediational interaction and "bridging" to content is more acceptable to teachers. When the program's major goals and subgoals focus on the learning-to-learn strategies, teachers will be more likely to use even content-oriented learning in a way that is compatible with this broader objective of education.

Resistance of the Subject Matter

A third reason for not combining instruction in prerequisite skills with subject-matter instruction is that the structure of the subject matter may compete with the enhancement of the process of learning. The subject matter (e.g., literature, geography, history, biology, mathematics, physics) resists the imposition of a structure of learning that is alien to the content's nature. For example, consider an attempt to use a poem written in an associative way in order to derive from it the cognitive dimensions of organization and succession. Trying to create types of grouping of events that are totally inadequate in order to learn categorization or classification may render the learning of the content extremely difficult, if not impossible. Changing the flow of a given set of data in order to reflect upon it, as required by the more formal goals of learning, may again seriously disturb the learning of the subject matter. This may result in a double loss, with the subject matter and the process of learning neutralizing, rather than reinforcing, each other.

As previously described, a program designed to produce the prerequisites of thinking has its own rhythm and rationale, and cannot follow the natural succession of the events required by the subject matter. Indeed, some programs fuse the two goals, with the consequence being that neither one is adequately reached. Therefore, we consider it much more appropriate to keep the programs of teaching subject matter and teaching thinking parallel to each other, rather than to have them mixed and integrated. The two streams of learning can be integrated by the active interpretation of the teacher and amplified by the participation of the students in the classroom.

> Another danger in the use of content-oriented material lies in the fact that some of this content was experienced as a source of failure and negative experiences by many of the dysfunctional students.

Resistance Associated with Failure

Finally, another danger in the use of content-oriented material lies in the fact that some of this content was experienced as a source of failure and negative experiences by many of the dysfunctional students. Any attempt, therefore, to use this content as the way to provide a more positive, more optimistic experience may be met with great student resistance. Some of them say quite openly, "I won't try again," "I have failed so many times to learn this," "I give up." The use of a neutral program that is not content-oriented is much less conducive to such negative attitudes.

Even difficult tasks, but those that the students have no reason to believe they are supposed to know without learning, are more appealing and easier for the learners than engaging in something with which they have a repeated history of failure. The conditions of mediation that accompany the Instrumental Enrichment program ensure successful mastery by varying the amount and nature of the mediation that is offered. This may offset the negative orientation and enhance in the learners a readiness to re-engage in the process that they previously adamantly rejected.

In conclusion, a program mainly designed to help students acquire the prerequisites of learning will be required to make accessible to individuals those cognitive processes that are necessary for their greater adaptability.

EXPECTED OUTCOMES OF INTERVENTION

Another consideration in constructing programs for low-functioning individuals is deciding upon which areas to place the greatest emphasis. Such decisions cannot be made simply as a function of the individual's greater or lesser strengths. Because the goal of an intervention program is to create a greater facility for benefiting from learning processes, the decision as to which dimensions to choose for greater investment must be guided by conceptual, theoretical considerations.

Our own work has been guided by the "cognitive map," a conceptual framework that has enabled us to analyze tasks that require mental operations. That cognitive map is not limited to the construction of intervention programs, but it is an important tool for understanding the differential responses of individuals to different tasks in various universes of information and domains of skills. Through its parameters, it is possible to analyze and pinpoint the anticipated sources of failure inherent in the nature and characteristics of a particular task. With this information, a teacher or mediator is able to devise strategies and techniques by which to overcome or bypass the difficulties a particular individual (with a specific cognitive structure and level of information) will encounter.

The cognitive map, as opposed to the list of deficient cognitive functions, does not describe the individual; it describes the tasks and its requisites. Analysis of tasks according to the cognitive map contributes significantly to the teaching of all curricular materials. It not only permits a differential diagnosis of possible pitfalls, it also orients the teacher to the particular elements students must acquire in order to cope efficiently with the demands of the material of a lesson. It also becomes a powerful guide in decisions concerning the choice of one or another type of task, or mode of presentation, as suitable for attaining the goals set by a program.

Each cognitive task, each mental activity, can be analyzed by the following seven dimensions:

1. Universe of content.
2. Language of presentation.
3. Phase of mental act.
4. Type of operation.
5. Level of abstraction.
6. Level of complexity.
7. Degree of efficiency.

Universe of Content

The first, the universe of content, is the least relevant to the area of cognitive functions and operations. Categorization, permutation, or logical multiplication can be literally applied to any universe of information. A task's content has the least relevance to the individual's mental capacity and also probably the least influence on the nature of teaching. A very simple story may illustrate an elaborate array, and the most complex content may be used to reach a very pedestrian, illogical, irrational understanding.

Although each universe may have its own rules, they are not necessarily exclusive. Therefore, when we deal with the prerequisites of thinking, content learning should be the last component of concern. To a certain extent, anchoring the thinking process in a specific content may either cause too strong an attachment to it or narrow it too much.

As previously mentioned, this is one of the reasons why we suggest making the intervention program as content-free as possible. This means choosing the content that is best fitted to teaching a given principle or mode of thinking, rather than choosing the latter and adapting it to a given content. In evaluating functioning, one must be extremely careful not to judge an individual on the basis of a content that, for a variety of reasons, may be unfamiliar. By the same token, teaching thinking (or reading) with content that is too familiar may become so boring that it obstructs learning, because the necessary orientating process and alertness are not produced.

Language of Presentation

The second parameter of the "cognitive map," the language of presentation, is also a relatively peripheral component as compared to the cognitive processes. Of course, verbal language is the most economical and adequate modality for conceptual, abstract thinking. However, there are many languages by which problems and concepts can be presented for learning and elaboration. Symbolic language (symbols and signs as in algebraic and mathematical thinking) or figural, spatial elements may be woven into a logical network no less complex than when words are used as the major modality of presentation and communication. Failing in one modality may not necessarily obstruct the more successful use of another.

A linguistic modality may be better for training individuals who may then be able to apply what they have learned in another modality. In one of our research studies, we offered training of analogies in a figural modality; then we looked for the effects of this training in the verbal modality of presentation (Feuerstein, Rand & Hoffman, 1979).

In planning a program for an individual or a group with certain deficiencies, one must consider using a language that will not, at least in the beginning, arouse too many resistances on the part of the learners because of their specific deficiencies. Thus, the first instruments of Instrumental Enrichment require very little, if any, literacy. Verbal components are introduced only following a thorough preparation with nonverbal exercises. Similar planning decisions may be necessary in dealing with people with low levels of literacy, reading comprehension, and decoding ability. To wait until they are literate before they acquire the prerequisites of thinking and of learning may result in a very costly delay that will negatively affect their learning capacity and achievement.

> In planning a program for an individual or a group with certain deficiencies, one must consider using a language that will not, at least in the beginning, arouse too many resistances on the part of the learners because of their specific deficiencies.

Too many intervention programs and measurements of intelligence and achievement use verbal, literate behavior as the sole criterion for success and totally neglect other modalities of communication, interaction, comprehension, and problem solving. This does not mean that the verbal element should not be given a very important role in the education processes; however, it should be considered as a goal to be achieved through intervention, rather than as a means.

Phase of Mental Act

The third parameter is the phase of the mental act. As previously mentioned, we used the information-processing model of input, elaboration, and output as the major phases of the mental act. The choice of a program for the disadvantaged learner or its development should clearly define its goals at a given stage of intervention in order to choose deficient functions in one or two of the three phases for special emphasis.

The elaborative phase, responsible for the data's transformation, their categorization, classification, labeling, and other operations by which new information is generated, is certainly the essential goal of a program that aims at developing thought processes. However, for increasing the individual's capacity to learn through a learning-to-learn program, mediating the input (i.e., increasing the efficiency by which the individual gathers the data, makes use of the perceptual apparatus, and registers information) and, at a later stage, the output level (i.e., defining the results of elaboration in order to convey them to oneself or to a partner) may be crucial. Choosing programs that emphasize only the elaboration of data may not necessarily enhance the learning process. In certain cases, they may even miss the major goal itself if the peripheral input and output phases have not been corrected through adequate investment.

> A certain number of basic operations, monitored by a taxonomy of operations requisite for further learning, must be imparted to the learner in the course of any enrichment program.

Instrumental Enrichment emphasizes correcting deficiencies on the input and output levels, and exercises are structured so as to confront the learners with the need to gather data systematically and to be precise and to elaborate events using a spatiotemporal grid. Through the nature of the task and the mediated learning experience, which is the prevalent mode of interaction, learners search for modalities of presentation, learners search for modalities of presentation that are most responsive to the need for logical evidence as the way to make the conveyed response acceptable to partners. If the elaboration phase represents the core of the thought processes, the peripheral phases of input and output represent those means that make the elaboration possible and the output acceptable.

Analyzing the mental act according to phases permits the ascription of a differential weight to the success or failure of functioning and achievement instead of the global evaluation that results from a product-oriented measurement.

Type of Operation

The type of operation is the fourth parameter to be considered when constructing tasks of an intervention program. Operations may range from purely perceptual and reproductive, such as the process employed in "re-cognition," or may reach the upper levels of formal and abstract thinking, such as inferential, inductive, and deductive reasoning. A certain number of basic operations, monitored by a taxonomy of operations requisite for further learning, must be imparted to the learner in the course of any enrichment program.

In Instrumental Enrichment, a number of such operations have been dispersed over the entire program. These operations include tasks that can only be accomplished by representational thinking, tasks that require inferential and hypothetical thinking, seriation of events according to rules transitive relationships, logical multiplication, analogical thinking, education of rules, deductive and inductive processes, and so on. Whenever the operations are not explicit, they are evoked and shaped in the mediational interaction of the classroom. Thus, inferring the presence of a little square from a cluster of dots allows us also to infer the presence of other figures intermingled in an amorphous cloud (see Fig. 5.1). The co-existence of two conditions permits us to infer the existence of one condition from the presence of the other. The same is true for inductive and deductive modes of thinking and transitive relationships (see Fig. 5.9). It is most interesting to see how operations from hierarchically higher levels of thinking can be implemented in programs that address otherwise low-functioning individuals. This is done by choosing appropriate content, language, and phase without necessarily renouncing the operation itself.

Level of Abstraction

The fifth parameter that must be considered in choosing or constructing a program is its level of abstraction. The level of abstraction is a very ambiguous concept, especially when it is used by educators to define certain tasks and the failure to achieve them. Thus, the ability to count or to compute is considered a higher level of abstraction, although we know that learning to compute may be based on a purely reproductive, technical memorization process and serial learning and need not rely on abstract thinking. By the same token, certain verbal interactions are considered abstract when very little operational thinking is either necessary or used during their generation.

It is, therefore, necessary to define the level of abstraction operationally (very much in line with the Piagetian approach) as the distance between a mental act and its concrete component. Piaget, who relates to mental behavior as an interaction ("conduit"), describes the sensorial concrete interaction as marked by a zero distance between the act/"conduit"/behavior and the reality upon which it is effected. Touching a table represents an interaction of zero distance between organism and the object. Zero distance also defines an interaction between a star and the eye that sees it. It does not really matter whether the light of the star reaches the eye or whether the finger touches the table. In both examples, the interaction is limited to a sensorial experience, and the distance is zero.

Calling an object "a table" immediately sets a great distance between the object itself and the mental act that results in its labeling. Think of the considerable differences in size, color, material, function, and so forth that are included in "table." From what distance will the labeler perceive the common traits of all these objects and be able to ignore the number of differences among them? The distance is increased even more when two objects that exist in isolation are brought together by a mental act and grouped by the words, "two tables." When "furniture" is used, conceptualizers climb up a number of steps, and the distance between them and the specific objects to which they relate is increased even more. The concept of distance is very useful in gauging the modalities by which abstract thinking can be introduced and evaluated.

Thus analyzed, the mental acts of various levels of retarded performers may actually be far more abstract than one would tend to believe, so that barriers considered as unsurpassable are actually much less so. Abstract thinking may be considered more accessible and, wherever necessary, more economical to the individual's adaptation.

Level of Complexity

The level of complexity is also a parameter that must be borne in mind in attaining a well-defined goal of creating the prerequisites of thinking. We define the level of complexity as the number of units of information required to elaborate a given task. The absolute number may be corrected and even reduced significantly by certain cognitive processes. Categorizing a list of units or bytes of information may reduce the number by simply using categories instead of units. By the same token, the degree of an individual's familiarity with certain units of information may reduce the level of complexity of certain tasks. Deciding and selecting the desirable level of complexity at a given point in the development of an individual or a program may have an important bearing on the efficiency of the intervention.

It is clear that disadvantaged learners are accustomed to dealing with very limited levels of complexity. In certain cases, due to their episodic grasp of reality, they ignore whatever is beyond their threshold. Therefore, it is important to endow them with adequate cognitive strategies to enlarge their capacity to deal with complexity, teaching them how to group, to categorize, to generalize, and to use other cognitive approaches.

It is clear that disadvantaged learners are accustomed to dealing with very limited levels of complexity. In certain cases, due to their episodic grasp of reality, they ignore whatever is beyond their threshold.

Level of Efficiency

The seventh parameter, and probably the most controversial one, is the level of efficiency. The reader must take note that the concept of efficiency refers to the level of efficiency required for a given task to be mastered; it is neither the individuals nor their functioning that is the target of analysis. Tasks differ in the amount and degree of efficiency required for their mastery.

Efficiency is defined by two measurable dimensions. One is referred to as the "rapidity-precision" complex. The other, an imponderable but still important dimension, is the subjectively experienced effort involved in working on a given task. Rapidity can be measured by the time required to do the task. Precision can be scored by simply counting the number of errors. The effort can be evaluated indirectly by the statements of subjects about their feelings, their readiness to continue, their fatigue, or from other cues. Tasks that require efficiency for their mastery may require special investment, lest the achievement be very poor.

Efficiency may best be acquired through automatization and habit formation, which, in turn, are produced by repetitive, mechanical, rote kinds of learning. Any reluctance to use rote repetitive learning may deleteriously affect the mastery of tasks that strongly depend on high levels of efficiency. By illustration, reading is one of the activities whose mastery depends mostly on efficiency. Somebody who reads too slowly may understand very little of what has been read because of a broke gestalt and an overload on the mnemonic functions due to the dispersion of the data over time. Somebody who takes a year to read a book may have very little understanding of the basic denouement of the story because the beginning may have been forgotten by the time the end is reached. This also occurs with sentences. Children who have difficulty in decoding forget the beginning of a sentence by the time they reach its end. Also, without a satisfactory level of precision in reading, comprehension will be very limited. Rapidity attained at the expense of precision, or precision to the detriment of rapidity, may render reading extremely inefficient. By the same token, when accompanied by a subjective feeling of effort, reading will be very limited, even if it is rapid and precise. Efficiency, therefore, is a dimension that must be purposefully, systematically developed, particularly with tasks that require efficiency as a precondition.

Certain new modes of learning, such as discovery learning and critical thinking, have totally ignored the development of efficiency. We suspect that many of the difficulties in learning may be due to the inefficiency of individuals in their interactions with the new elements they must learn.

In summary, as described by both the discussions of the deficient cognitive functions and the cognitive map, the types of tasks to be offered in a program designed to increase the modifiability of individuals, that is, to render them more sensitive to learning experiences, must be guided and purposefully related to the combined needs of the learner and the tasks.

TEACHER TRAINING

Another characteristic of programs addressing disadvantaged and low-functioning individuals is their strong dependence on training the teacher to act as a mediator and not merely as a dispenser of information. Mediated Learning Experience (MLE), a pivotal component of the theory of Structural Cognitive Modifiability, is defined as a quality of the organism—environment interactions that are characteristic of human beings and responsible for their modifiability. It serves as a powerful guideline for structuring programs for the enhancement of Structural Cognitive Modifiability.

To turn teachers into mediators instead of conveyors and dispensers of units of information requires a very meaningful change in both the perception of the child as a modifiable entity and in the belief that, indeed, education can play a significant role in this process. Furthermore, turning teachers into mediators means equipping them with the skills and motivation to produce such changes. Additionally, teachers must reach mastery of the program they offer the child, a mastery that will be buffered by a good knowledge of its theory and a full understanding of the "whys, the hows, the whens, and the when nots." The more theoretically based the teaching activity, the more modifying the interactions and the greater the degree of freedom teachers will have in structuring the learning experiences of their students.

> To turn teachers into mediators instead of conveyors and dispensers of units of information requires a very meaningful change in both the perception of the child as a modifiable entity and the belief that, indeed, education can play a significant role in this process.

MLE is characterized by closing the loop between the teacher as an emitter of a message (the proximal partner of the interaction), the receiver of the message (the distal partner of the interaction), and finally, the emitted message itself. The three partners involved in the interaction (mediator, stimuli/message, and mediatee) are manipulated and transformed so that, indeed, the emitted message will be received and have the desired effort on the receiver.

By way of contrast, consider the regular modality of teaching. The teacher emits a message, presents a unit of information to a classroom of children or even to a single individual, and is contented with the process of emission, without considering the need to ensure that what was transmitted was truly registered, received, and eventually integrated into the receiver's system. Regular teaching often neglects to ensure that the communication loop is closed. In many cases, teachers ignore the need to change all three partners in this interaction so as to guarantee that the mediational process has been accomplished.

The intention of the mediators is recognized by the way they transform the message, amplifying it, detailing it, substituting language to make it better understood, and increasing its appeal so that it will penetrate the system of the mediatee. By manipulating the mediatee's state and rendering them more attention, more eager, more affected by the unit of information, they are transformed and rendered more accessible and sensitive to the particular element mediated to them. By the same token, mediators are changed by their intention to mediate to the child. By the intentionality of the mediators, the teaching interaction receives the quality of a mediational experience (see Fig. 5.10).

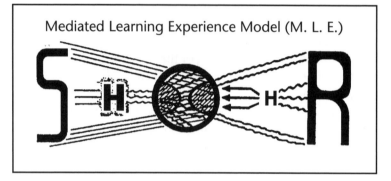

FIG. 5.10. *Mediated Learning Experience. The human mediator (H) interposes himself/herself the stimulus (S) and the organism (O) and between the organism and the response (R) in order to change the quality of the interaction. In MLE there is a change in the nature of the stimulus, an increased vigilance and alertness on the part of the organism, and change in the mediator as well. As illustrated, the mediator does not block out stimuli that reach the organism by direct exposure, nor does he/she control all response to stimuli. One of the mediator's functions is to filter, frame, and focus incoming stimuli in the input phase. At the output level, among other functions, the mediator attempts to restrain impulsivity or to help initiate a response.*

It is for these reasons that teacher training is a condition sine qua non for making any program accessible to the disadvantaged. We consider that teacher training is a necessary condition for many of the required qualities of any instruction. However, programs for advantaged individuals whose functioning allows them to benefit from direct exposure to stimuli and learning opportunities are less dependent on Mediated Learning Experience interactions. On the other hand, disadvantaged learners can benefit very little from even the most powerful programs if there is not adequate mediation. Teacher training, though it may be costly and problematic logistically, should therefore be considered as an integral quality of the program. Without it, the program's value may be extremely limited, even though it may be attractive and easy to implement.

Many evaluators of intervention programs consider dependence on teacher training as a costly burden and, to a certain extent, a negative feature. We contend, however, that programs that are carried out without teacher training as a condition of their application may do more damage than good, even if they show some effects. As strong as this assertion sounds, it highlights our belief that disadvantaged learners do not simply need tasks to master nor principles to learn. A disposition must be produced in them that will change their cognitive structure, their way of interacting with new aspects of information, and the way they perceive themselves as changing entities affected by experience in the direction of a higher level of efficiency. Exercises and activity alone, even if they are efficient and very meaningful, do not always lead to this state of awareness. People may repetitively experience certain events, become familiar with them, and even reach mastery, and still have a feeling of incompetence unless a mediator interprets this behavior to them and turns it into a source of their self-perception of being producers of information through processes of inference, of being decision makers through planned exploration of alternatives, and of choosing among priorities by comparing various processes. In fact, they must perceive themselves as contributors to reality rather than as being subdued by it.

For this end, direct experience is not enough. This is borne out by the great number of people who do not derive these cognitive and emotional structures from their direct experience. A mediator is needed for much of what makes us human. The fact that we are independent on mediators does not reduce our status as independent autonomous thinkers. It only interprets the story of our autonomy as a product of millennia of cultural transmission through our Mediated Learning Experiences. Teacher must be mediators. To turn teachers into people who believe and who are sufficiently skilled, training is a must. In addition to its role in increasing the efficiency of any program, a vital by-product of teacher training is the large body of information on human modifiability and the most efficacious ways in which it can be achieved. Through such training, a teacher will acquire a better understanding of cognitive processes, the prerequisites of learning, and the deficient cognitive functions responsible for learning disabilities, thereby becoming more aware of the skills by which to turn the student into a willing and efficient learner.

SUMMARY

In this chapter, we have attempted to show that the tendency today is to produce programs with built-in conditions for accessibility, but that the conditions do not exist in the most needy population. The "creaming up" phenomenon then becomes a natural selection process that renders those who cannot "make it" unable to benefit from such programs. We have outlined a number of conditions that may make programs accessible and beneficial to such individuals, even when their own conditions seem to show no promise of benefit. These suggested conditions become especially useful for programs deemed essential to modify the individual's course of life. The modifiability of individuals, in turn, is dependent on the cognitive processes, their capacity to learn from formal and informal experiences, and their disposition or readiness to adapt to more novel and complicated life situations.

The mass of disadvantaged learners represent an untapped reservoir of human resources. In these days when life requires a constant adaptation through the process of learning, we cannot afford to turn these neglected human resources into a danger to themselves or society, nor to offer them a menial, restrictive life. Investment in intervention and enrichment programs must not be considered a luxury but a vital instrument for personal and societal progress.

REFERENCES

Baldwin, J. M. (1925). *Mental development in the child and the race.* London: Macmillan.

Bourdieu, P., & Passeron, J. C. (1964). *Les heritiers: Les etudiants el culture.* Paris: Les Editions de Minuit.

Bryant, P. E. (1974). *Perception and understanding in young children.* London: Methuen.

de Bono, E. (1973). *CORT thinking.* New York: Pergamon Press.

Feuerstein, R., Rand, Y., Hoffman, M. B. (1979). The dynamic assessment of retarded performers. In R. Feuerstein, Y. Rand, & M. B. Hoffman (Eds.), *The Learning Potential Assessment Device: Instruments and techniques.* Baltimore: University Park Press.

Feuerstein, R., Rand, Y., Hoffman, M. B., & Miller, R. (1980). *Instrumental Enrichment: An intervention program for cognitive modifiability.* Baltimore: University Park Press.

Feuerstein, R., & Richelle, M. (1963). *Children of the Mellah.* Jerusalem: Mossad Szold Press.

Harvard University; Bolt, Beranek and Newman, Inc.; & The Ministry of Education of the Republic of Venezuela. (1983). *Odyssey: A curriculum for thinking (Foundations of reasoning, understanding language; verbal reasoning; problem solving; decision making; innovative thinking).* Watertown, MA: Mastery Education.

Jones, B. F., Palincsar, A. S., Ogle, D. S., & Carr, E. G. (Eds.) (1987). *Strategic thinking and learning: Cognitive instruction in the content areas.* Alexandria, VA and Elmhurst, IL: Association for Supervision and Curriculum Development in cooperation with the North Central Regional Educational Laboratory.

Lipman, M., Sharp, A. M., & Oscanyan, F. S. (1980). *Philosophy in the classroom.* Philadelphia, PA: Temple University Press.

Marzano, R. J., & Arrendondo, D. E. (1986). *Tactics for thinking.* Aurora, CO: Mid-continental Regional Educational Laboratory.

Marzano, R. J., Brandt, R. S., Hughes, C. W., Jones, B. F., Presseisen, B. Z., Rankin, S. C., & Suhor, C. (1988). *Dimensions of thinking: A framework for curriculum and instruction.* Aurora, CO: Association for the Supervision and Curriculum Development in cooperation with the Mid-Continental Regional Educational Laboratory.

Meeker, M. N. (1969). *The structure of the intellect: Its interpretation and uses.* Columbus, OH: Charles Merrill.

Nickerson, R. (in press). On improving thinking through instruction. *Review of Research in Education.*

Rand, Y., Mintzker, Y., Miller, R., & Hoffman, M. B. (1981). *Instrumental Enrichment: Immediate and long-term effects.* In P. Mittler (Ed.), Frontiers of knowledge in mental retardation: Vol. 1 (pp. 141–152). Baltimore: University Park Press.

Resnick, D. P. and Resnick, L. B. (1977). The nature of literacy: A historical explanation. *Harvard Educational Review, 47,* 370–385.

Resnick, L. B. (1987). *Education and learning to think.* Washington, DC: National Academy Press.

Sternberg, R. J. (1986). *Intelligence applied.* New York: Harcourt Brace Jovanovich.

Whimbey, A., & Lockhead, J. (1980). *Problem solving and comprehension: A short course in analytical reasoning*. Philadelphia, PA: Franklin Institute Press.

Zigler, E., & Butterfield, E. C. (1986). Motivational aspects of changes in IQ test performances of culturally deprived nursery school children. *Child Development, 39,* 1–14.

Mediated Learning: The Contributions of Vygotsky and Feuerstein in Theory and Practice

by Barbara Presseisen and Alex Kozulin

T he dynamic involvement of the learner in the construction of his/her own knowledge system is not just a recent goal of educational reform. Various theorists in the history of twentieth century psychology have made contributions to the approaches and research supporting this view (Belmont, 1989; Piaget, 1973; Sternberg, 1990). This study examines the concept of **mediated learning**, the subtle, social interaction between the teacher and the learner in the enrichment of the student's learning experience. It focuses on the work of two major figures of socio-cultural psychology, Lev Vygotsky (1896-1934) and Reuven Feuerstein (b. 1921). First, their theoretical positions are examined, followed by the review of a recent, practical application of each man's work. Finally, mediated learning is discussed in terms of its relationship to current, educational change.

INTRODUCTION OF THE STUDY

Theoretically, and in terms of recent classroom practice, both Vygotsky's and Feuerstein's research are significant influences on the ways students are being instructed all over the world.

From a paper presented at the Annual Meeting of the American Educational Research Association, April 23, 1992, San Francisco, CA.

Tharp and Gallimore (1991) suggest that Vygotsky's socio-historical approach is profoundly affecting education's understanding of teaching, learning, and student cognitive development. Sternberg (1990) maintains that both theorists underline the importance of socialization for intelligence and its development. In Feuerstein's "mediated learning experience," he proposes, the process by which Vygotsky's internalization of higher psychological functions occurs is actually described. The questions central to this study emerge from this general relationship

• What is mediated learning for Vygotsky and Feuerstein?

• Of what significance is mediation for effective instruction?

• What implications does mediation have for different populations of learners?

• How does mediated learning extend the cognitive psychologist's new paradigm for education?

Initially, it is useful to consider these questions from a historic understanding of mediated learning in socio-cognitive theory.

Natural to Human Distinctions

The acknowledgment of mediated learning changes perspectives in both animal and human behavior. Consider first how children or animals learn to avoid dangerous objects. According to a classical, behavioristic paradigm, such learning must include a number of direct exposures of the child to a dangerous stimulus (e.g., a hot object), which in due time results in the formation of a conditioned avoidance reflex. This mechanism, which indeed can be studied in animals under experimental laboratory conditions, seems to have a very low ecological validity. Ethological studies suggest that avoidance of harmful stimuli is achieved in quite a different way (Bronson, 1968). Young animals tend to avoid all objects which have not previously been encountered in the presence of the mother. Learning, therefore, is achieved not through direct exposure, but through the indirect experience or mediation provided by the presence (or absence) of the mother.

> **The acknowledgment of mediated learning changes perspectives in both animal and human behavior.**

The role of mediation becomes even more pronounced in human learning. Aside from cases of severe social-cultural deprivation (to be discussed later), the human child does not learn about harmful stimuli through direct exposure to them. Instead, a complex process of mediated learning takes place, with the mother or another caretaker inserting him/herself "between" the stimuli and the child. The caretaker *indicates* to the child which objects are dangerous. Sometimes, the caretaker deliberately *exposes* a child to a dangerous or unpleasant stimulus under controlled conditions, creating the equivalent of a psychological "vaccination." The caretaker *explains* to the child the *meaning* of dangerous situations. Finally, the caretaker stimulates *generalization*, creating in the child the notions of a dangerous situation and a possible response to it.

The above example suggests that there is a **qualitative** difference between learning based on the direct exposure to stimuli and learning **mediated** by another human being. Before presenting the psychological theory of mediated learning for either Vygotsky or Feuerstein, it seems relevant to discuss briefly the philosophical, sociological, and linguistic aspects of mediated interaction.

The Roots of Mediated Learning: Philosophical, Sociological, and Linguistic

On the philosophical plane, the notion of mediation (*Vermittlung*) constitutes one of the cornerstones of the Hegelian philosophical system. Both directly and indirectly, particularly through Marx, this notion influenced Vygotsky's theory, as well as the work of his followers such as Leontiev (1978) and Luria (1976).

According to Hegel, the very existence of a human type of activity depends on the transition from the immediate, animal type of satisfaction of needs, which coincides with the ability of the individual animal, to the human satisfaction of needs dependent on the activity of others. Human beings satisfy their needs indirectly through work with end products which are intended not for the producer him/herself, but for others.

> The being that acts to satisfy its *own* instincts, which - as such - are always *natural*, does not rise above Nature: it remains a *natural* being, an animal. But by acting to satisfy an instinct that is *not*

my own, I am acting in relation to what is not - for me - instinct. I am acting in a relation to an *idea*, a *non*biological end. (Kojeve, 1986, p. 42)

Hegel links the emergence of human consciousness and self-consciousness to this process of mediated activity which is work. The philosophical notion of mediation already suggests a whole range of possible mediating agents. First, work presupposes material tools interposed between the human individual and the natural object. These tools, though directed at natural objects, also have a reciprocal influence on the individual, changing his/her type of activity and cognition. Secondly, since work is nearly always work for somebody else, then social and psychological characteristics of the other person also enter the equation. Finally, since work is impossible without symbolic representations, they and the means of their transmission become two additional mediatory agents.

> The interaction between the individual and the environment is never immediate, it is always mediated by meanings which originate "outside" the individual—in the world of social relations.

On the sociological plane, the issue of mediatory mechanisms embedded in the structure of human society was raised by G.H. Mead (1974). Mead made an important distinction between stimuli and objects. Instead of just perceiving and responding to stimuli, he suggested objects are not given — they are "constructed." The *construction* of objects becomes possible only because stimuli of the environment take on certain *meanings* in the course of human activity which is social in nature. Mead's ideas influenced others.

The meaning of a thing for a person grows out of the ways in which other persons act toward the person with regard to the thing… Their actions operate to define the thing for the person. Thus, symbolic interactionism sees meanings as social products, as creations that are formed in and through the defining activities of people as they interact. (Blumer, 1969, pp. 4–5)

The interaction between the individual and the environment is never immediate, it is always mediated by meanings which originate "outside" the individual — in the world of social relations. Moreover, unlike animals, human beings are capable of becoming objects to themselves.

Feuerstein (Feuerstein & Feuerstein, 1991) has broadly defined Mediated Learning Experience (MLE) very much in this sociological framework. MLE is the interaction of the organism with its environment via a human mediator (p. 3). From this relationship, then, it seems an essential feature of human cognition is that it is based on the internalized forms of what originally appeared as **social interactions**. Internalized *gestures*, verbal as well as nonverbal, become significant symbols whose meaning is shared by a group of individuals, say the child's family. The role play of a child who addresses him/herself as a teacher, or arrests him/herself as a police person, is an example of an early experience of being another to one's self.

Many of these same problems were independently formulated in the context of language and literature studies. A pioneering effort was made by the Russian literary scholar and philosopher, Mikhail Bakhtin (1986). Bakhtin argued that instead of starting with individual speech (understood as a natural phenomenon) and proceeding toward written forms of language, it might be more advantageous to start at the highest point of language development — a literary text — and to look, from this vantage point, at the less complex forms of verbal activity. Language, as it reveals itself in literary discourse, he proposed, offers a paradigm for any human action to the extent that this action is addressed and interpreted. Individual oral speech and verbal thought can thus be comprehended as "degenerate" or "underdeveloped" forms of literary discourse.

The quality of literary discourse, for example, often depends on the writer's ability to manipulate different genres of speech within a given text. Mediation suggests *the use* of the language is significant. As Bruner (1966) noted years ago when searching for a theory of instruction, "…it is obviously not the language per se that makes the difference; rather, it seems to be the use of language as an instrument of thinking that matters, its internalization, to use an apt but puzzling word" (p. 14). This same linguistic skill is needed in ordinary life, not only for using appropriate greetings or words or condolences, but also for the development of one's free, creative narratives. A study of genres in individual speech returns to the already-mentioned problem of mediation through social roles. Though empirically observable in individual speech, speech genres belong to the social realm; they are **super**-individual. Human speech, therefore, is not a free combination of permitted linguistic forms, but involves much bigger units which are genre-specific utterances. What on the social-psychological level is identified as role, position, status, or attitude, on the linguistic level finds its expression in the genre-specificity of individual speech.

Only recently have these ideas on mediation become adopted by psychologists and led to inquiries into the influence of the narrative style on the individual's description and comprehension of his/her own life (Bruner, 1987). Similarly, only in the last decade or so has the concept of learning that is mediated been seriously examined as a construct for a better understanding of cognitive development in the classroom (Belmont, 1989; Goldenberg, 1991; Palincsar & Brown, 1984; Tharp & Gallimore, 1991).

ELABORATION ON THEORY

Mediated learning is part of a larger movement in the development of psychology that has seen the replacement of the behaviorist's model by a more cognitive conception of human intelligence and learning (Gardner, 1985). Both Feuerstein (1980) and Vygotsky (1986) developed their theories under strong influence of Jean Piaget, who can legitimately be called the "father" of cognitive developmental psychology. However, both of them were dissatisfied with certain aspects of the Piagetian approach. For Vygotsky, there was concern about epistemological individualism in Piaget's theory and the neglect of social mediation.

> Mediation assumes a changing nature to human intelligence, a pliability and a dynamic quality in contrast to behaviorism's static definition.

For Feuerstein, there was the issue of the concrete mechanisms of learning through the mediation of another human being. Mediation assumes a changing nature to human intelligence, a pliability and a dynamic quality in contrast to behaviorism's static definition. Indeed, the problem of **inert** knowledge, says Bransford and his associates (1986), with its corollary of passive learning, are central concerns today for building a meaningful curriculum in the classroom.

Mediation also stresses the communal understanding of knowledge, not only in the collaborative sharing of experience but in the sorting or categorizing of ideas. The mediator helps the learner "frame, filter, and schedule stimuli," says Feuerstein (1980), and, ultimately, influences the potential ways that transfer of knowledge occurs in the student's thinking (Perkins & Salomon, 1988). Mediation assumes that instruction is more concerned with **going beyond** the information given, with connecting the present with both the past and the anticipation of the future, than with mastering specific bits of here-and-now data.

The approach of mediated learning suggests a new paradigm for education, one in which intelligence itself is redefined and conceived. What is intelligence, asks Feuerstein? The ability to learn and change. Intelligence is now much more broadly understood than a narrow, static I.Q. test presumes. In fact, according to current researchers (Detterman & Sternberg, 1982; Diamond, 1988), reflective, intelligent behavior can actually be enhanced. Understanding the work of Vygotsky and Feuerstein is to begin to discover what the new educational paradigm is all about.

Vygotsky's Approach to Mediated Learning

Vygotsky (1978; 1986) proposed that higher mental processes can be considered as functions of mediated activity. He suggested three major classes of mediators: material tools, "psychological tools," and other human beings (see Kozulin, 1990a). Material tools have only indirect influence on human psychological processes, because they are directed at the processes in nature. Nevertheless, the use of material tools puts new demands on human mental processes. Vygotsky suggested that the historical progress of tool-mediated activity from the primitive to more advanced forms should be taken into account in a study of comparative human cognition (Vygotsky & Luria, 1930).

Materials tools do not exist as individual implements; they presuppose collective use, interpersonal communication, and symbolic representation. This symbolic aspect of the tool-mediated activity gives rise to a new and important class of mediators, which Vygotsky designated as "psychological tools." While material tools are directed at the objects of nature, psychological tools mediate humans' own psychological processes. Among the most ancient psychological tools Vygotsky (1978) mentioned are such psychological "fossils" as "casting lots, tying knots, and counting fingers" (p. 127). Casting lots appears in a situation when the uncertainty of decision caused by the presence of two equipotent and opposing stimuli is resolved by an application of the artificial and arbitrary stimulus — dice aimed at the subject's own psychological processes. Tying knots exemplifies the introduction of an elementary, external mnemonic device to ensure the retrievel of information from memory. Finger counting is the adaptation of an always-available "tool" for the organization of higher mental processes involved in elementary arithmetic operations.

Beyond these primitive "tools" lies the vast area of higher order symbolic mediators which include natural and artificial languages, discourses and cultural-symbolic systems of different epochs and nations. One of the major goals of Vygotsky's theory was to develop a typology of higher mental processes which would reflect historical transition from one system of psychological tools to another. An empirical study of such a transition and its psychological consequences was undertaken by Vygotsky and Luria in the context of cultural change in Soviet Central Asia in the early 1930's (Luria, 1976). On the ontogenetic plane, Vygotsky's (1986) contribution was primarily in studying changes in conceptual reasoning of children produced by the growing sophistication of verbal mediation.

As to mediation through another individual, Vygotsky (1978) suggested two possible approaches. The first was expressed in the famous statement that "every function in the child's cultural development appears twice: first, *between* people (*interpsychological*), and then *inside* the child (*intrapsychological*) (p. 57). As an illustration, Vygotsky cited the phenomenon that was first noticed by J. M. Baldwin and later investigated by Jean Piaget, namely that a child's ability to consider different points of view on the mental plane depends on actual arguments between children. More recently, this phenomenon was discussed by Miller (1987).

The second approach focuses on the role of the other individual as a mediator of meaning. An illustrative example here is the development of indicatory gesticulation in the child. According to Vygotsky (1978), gesture first appears as a natural attempt to grasp an object. The grasping movement is interpreted by an adult as a gesture; thus the human meaning of the natural act is supplied to the child from "outside" by the adult. The addressee of the movement accordingly changes from that of the object to that of a human subject. Movement itself becomes transformed and reduced — it "starts" as a grasping attempt and "becomes" a real gesture. Later, such gestures are internalized and form the child's inner commands to himself or herself. The meaning of one's own activity is thus formed by mediation through another individual. Vygotsky (1983) believed that this principle holds for the entire personality as well: "One may say that only through the other do we become ourselves, this rule applies to each psychological function as well as to the personality as a whole" (p. 144). In recent years, these ideas of Vygotsky were amplified, but also challenged at certain points, by Trevarthen's (1978, 1988) notion of "secondary intersubjectivity," Rogoff's (1990) theme of "guided participation," Wertsch and Minick's (1990) notion of the "negotiation of sense," and Tharp and Gallimore's (1991) concept of "assisted performance."

> ...mediation through another individual is closely linked in Vygotsky's theory to the notion of symbolic function.

For the purpose of the present discussion, it is important to emphasize that mediation through another individual is closely linked in Vygotsky's theory to the notion of symbolic function. A human individual as a mediator appeared first and foremost as a carrier of signs, symbols, and meanings. In terms of educational application, the most popular of Vygotskian ideas in the West became the "Zone of Proximal Development" (ZPD) (Rogoff & Wertsch, 1984). Operationally, ZPD is defined as a difference in the child's achievement in assisted versus unassisted performance. Vygotsky (1986) argued that assisted performance reveals those capacities of the child which are not manifest yet, but which have already undergone inner development. The child with wider ZPD has a better chance to succeed in school learning. Learning in the ZPD, according to Vygotsky, is also associated with an interaction between spontaneous concepts of the child and systematic, "scientific" concepts introduced by the teacher.

In Vygotsky's theory, no attempt was made to differentiate between human mediators beyond their function as vehicles of symbolic mediation. As mentioned elsewhere (Kozulin, 1990a), Vygotsky only declared that concept formation and communication have one common, vital point — word meaning. But, while the hierarchy of concept formation was explored in considerable detail by Vygotsky (1986), the corresponding study of communicative situations was not elaborated beyond a general counterposition of classroom instruction and spontaneous everyday learning. This left considerable lacunae or missing parts in Vygotsky's theory of mediation. These lacunae, ultimately, have been addressed by the work of other psychologists and educators — notably by Reuven Feuerstein and his colleagues. In understanding the contributions of both Vygotsky and Feuerstein to mediated learning theory, many issues related to this important topic can be seen in a new light.

Feuerstein's Approach to Mediated Learning

Mediated learning experience, or MLE according to Feuerstein, is broadly seen as the interaction between the human being and its socio-cultural environment. But MLE does not include all interactions — rather, MLE is concerned with experiences that influence the individual's "propensity to learn," the quality of interaction that helps the learner "become modified by exposure to stimuli in the direction of higher and more efficient levels of functioning and adaptation" (Feuerstein & Feuerstein, 1991, p. 5). The central question which Feuerstein's MLE theory attempts to answer is: What is the cause of differential cognitive development? The central aspect of mediation is the change that qualitatively influences the learner and enables him/her to develop cognitive prerequisites for learning on his/her own from direct stimuli (Kozulin, 1991).

Feuerstein (1990) maintains that different learners have different capacities to benefit from mediated experience. Every individual exhibits differences in terms of their cognitive structure, their knowledge base, and their operational functioning. Given the same stimuli, different learners can show considerable variations in the degrees of rapidity, generalizability, and permanence of changes with which they respond to instruction. For some, a slight change in color, shape, or size might neutralize the effects of a previously learned response — and require a new process of learning, as if a lesson were totally new and unfamiliar. Feuerstein's point is that MLE, as a quality of interaction, is responsible for two major phenomena unique to human beings: modifiability and diversity. These two phenomena are closely intertwined and contribute to every human learner's considerable cognitive plasticity and flexibility. It is the existence of these two phenomena which Feuerstein maintains is unexplained in earlier theories of cognitive development.

What are the parameters or criteria of MLE? Feuerstein (1990) distinguishes twelve major criteria of MLE. The first three criteria need to be accounted for in every learning exchange that constitutes MLE, they are universals. These criteria include: mediation of intentionality and reciprocity, mediation of transcendence, and mediation of meaning. The remaining nine criteria are not to be considered exhaustive, but are seen rather as a first selection of qualities of interaction that may — but need not — appear in each interaction in order to turn it into a mediating experience. Feuerstein considers the presence of any of these secondary parameters is situationally determined and varies greatly according to societal, environmental, and cultural factors. These nine criteria include: mediation of a feeling of competence; mediation of regulation and control of behavior; mediation of sharing behavior; mediation of individuation and psychological differentiation; mediation of goal-seeking, goal-setting, planning, and goal-achieving behavior; mediation for challenge: the search for novelty and complexity; mediation of an awareness of the human as a changing entity; mediation of the search for an optimistic alternative; and mediation of the feeling of belonging.

The criterion of intentionality turns the interactive situation from a random, incidental experience into one that is intentional. This intentionality has two foci: one is the object of the learning, the other is the child or learner. Some characteristics of the object — such as location, brightness, or arrangement — are transformed by the adult in order to ensure its registration by the learner. The intention thus changes the learner's "state of mind, level of vigilance, and alertness," (Feuerstein,

1990, p. 97). These physical transformations are accompanied by direct statements from the adult informing the learner of the goals of mediation. The mediating teacher thus alters the instructional role; instead of being a mere provider of information, of data, of verbal directions, he/she has become a source of constant affirmation that objects or information involved are cognitively important to the learning, the capacity building, of the student (Kozulin, 1991).

The reciprocity aspect of Feuerstein's first criterion underlines the fact that it is not the object but the child's very cognitive processes that are the primary target of mediation. By constantly focusing on the learner's state of attention, the strategies that he/she is using, even mistakes and insights that may not yet seem directly relevant to a task, the adult shows the child that his/her response is what is really important. A reciprocity develops; mediated learning becomes a two-way street. Not only are the stimuli transformed by the first criterion, but the mental, emotional, and motivational states of the learner are transformed, as well (Feuerstein & Feuerstein, 1991).

The second parameter of universal quality is the mediation of transcendence, to go beyond the goals of the particular interaction. Feuerstein (1990) points out that a mediator does not limit the length and breadth of an interaction to those parts of the situation that have originally initiated the exchange. Rather, he/she widens the scope of the interaction to goals that are at the moment more remote to the learner. For example, if a child points to an orange and asks what it is, merely to provide a label to name the object would be an *un*mediated response. A transcendent interaction would offer a broader definition, one that indicates categorical classification ("It's the fruit of a plant, a tree.") and provide other references to taste, smell, etc., in order to help the learner make further connections. Transcendence as a mediating criterion provides not only for the anticipated widening of cognitive factors in the information under question, but assumes the constant enlargement of the learner's own need system and his/her dynamic, continuous change.

One interesting aspect of the criterion of transcendence is pointed out by Kozulin (1991). To be effective, transcendence need not necessarily be either conscious or deliberate. Many parents skillfully employ mediation leading to transcendence without being aware of it. Much of this is provided through cultural development and transmission. By contrast, Feuerstein (1990) notes that transcendence is seldom, if ever, observed among animals who rather model behavior of particular and discrete intentions alone, very much limited by the organism's primary instinctual needs. Transcendence, for Feuerstein, is the most humanizing of the universal parameters.

> To be effective, transcendence need not necessarily be either conscious or deliberate. Many parents skillfully employ mediation leading to transcendence without being aware of it.

The third universal parameter of mediation is the mediation of meaning. In this criterion, Feuerstein (1991) finds the generator of the emotional, motivational, attitudinal, and value-oriented behaviors of the individual. It is the energetic dimension of an interaction; meaning deals with the questions of why, what for, and other reasons for which something is to happen or be done. The goal of this parameter is to make explicit those didactic or parental understandings that all-too-often are only implicit in exchanges with children. Sometimes they begin with kinesthetics and preverbal mimesis or gestures that express a parent's joy and encouragement. Gradually, later verbal exchanges are internalized by the learner who develops an "orientation" toward the search for such meaning, an expectation that reaches beyond the specific learning exchange.

Feuerstein emphasizes the importance of mediation of meaning in the context of cultural transmission. He notes that in the context of the modern world, where dialogues between parent and child and teacher and student are much too few, there is all-the-more a paucity of exchanges about meaning. This situation has grave consequences of both immediate and long-term concern:

> A parent who is reluctant to impart to his children the 'meaning' of existence impoverishes their lives, not only by certain contents, values, and motivations, but by denying them the very faculty and need to search and even construct for themselves the meanings of their lives and their activities. In the absence of these meanings, any substitute, no matter how noxious, comes to fill up the void and becomes acceptable even if it is self-destructive. (Feuerstein & Feuerstein, 1991, p. 27)

At the same time, in emphasizing that the three universal parameters together make possible the essence of what it is to be human, Feuerstein proposes that modifiability and flexibility are possible for any subject, at any time in their lives. Kozulin (1991) notes there are two major causes for the lack of MLE: the absence of mediation — the failure to understand and to provide such experiences — and those conditions which render a normal amount or type of mediation insufficient or inadequate. Feuerstein's theory, says Kozulin (1991), is absolutely incompatible with certain behavioristic principles and practices which leave meaning beyond the sphere of psychological analysis and modification. It is easy to see, however, when applied to all learners, the consistency between Feuerstein's approach to mediation and the new paradigm for education.

Mediated Learning and Educational Application

Over the past two decades, Vygotsky and Feuerstein's theories of mediation have been applied to a multitude of educational practices and research. The work of Brown & Ferrara (1985), Goldenberg (1991), Kozulin (1990b), Rogoff (1990), Rogoff & Wertsch (1984), and Tharp & Gallimore (1988) report on specific applications of Vygotsky's concepts with learners from early childhood to adulthood, with subjects of limited language ability and various cultural backgrounds. Similarly, Feuerstein's theory has had extensive application with varied populations through the worldwide implementation of both an instructional program, *Instrumental Enrichment* (IE) (Emerson, 1991; Kaniel & Feuerstein, 1989; Link, 1985; Sharron, 1987), and an assessment technique, the *Learning Potential Assessment Device* (LPAD) (Haywood & Tzuriel, 1991; Lidz, 1987; Missiuna & Samuels, 1988). These studies are significant today in explicating the dimensions of the new cognitive paradigm for education.

> ... Feuerstein's theory has had extensive application with varied populations through the worldwide implementation of both an instructional program, *Instrumental Enrichment* ... and an assessment technique, the *Learning Potential Assessment Device* ...

While it is not the goal of this study to review extensively the findings of numerous researchers who have sought to apply

Vygotsky and Feuerstein's theories, it is important to examine the work of the two socio-cultural psychologists in terms of the meanings of particular applications regarding mediation. Discussion in the next section reviews a practical study of each theorist's concept of mediated learning in terms of the objectives set in his own writings. This discussion is followed by an examination of the outcomes of the specific applications in light of what has been learned in the "grand leap" from theory to practice.

IMPLEMENTATIONS OF MEDIATED LEARNING

How do the seminal ideas of Vygotsky and Feuerstein play out in the real world? In practical application of each theorist's approach, what happens when mediated learning intentionally directs instruction and how is it received by various types of learner populations and their teachers? Given the so-called cognitive revolution in education (Baars, 1986; Gardner, 1985), what are the possible changes in schooling that might take place if the goals of each of these socio-cultural psychologists are attempted and, to some extent, actualized? An examination of an application of each theorist's view of mediation was completed in the course of this study. These experiments are described herein.

A Vygotsky-based Study of Contradictions among Adult Russian Immigrants

In Vygotskian theory, cognitive progress is determined by the increased mastery of the individual over his/her own psychological processes through the use of psychological tools. Within this paradigm, the successful introduction of a psychological tool always brings about an advance in cognitive functioning. This paradigm has been challenged in the first application in this study which focused on the discovery of contradictions in a written text (Kozulin, 1990b). Subjects in the study, a group of American students and young professionals, read the text which was plausible as prose, but which contained statements contradicting simple laws of physics ("river flowing uphill"). After their ability to detect contradictions spontaneously was established, the subjects were given verbal (multiple choice) and pictorial tools which, according to the Vygotskian model, are supposed to improve the subjects' performance. Surprisingly, neither the multiple choice activity nor the pictorial tools were effective in evoking the memory of contradictions. Only 12% of the subjects reported contradictory statements after these types of mediation were applied. Moreover, from the subjects' narratives and their manipulations of a picture kit, it became clear that some subjects turned this kit into an instrument for rendering the cognitively dissonant information neutral.

These results may have a direct bearing on the problem of mediated experience as an integral component of learning activity. The failure of multiple choice items to serve as a means for the discovery of the contradictions indicates that even the choice of correct answers does not guarantee a fully conscious comprehension of the information involved. This underscores the difference between Feuerstein's understanding of mediation and both the Piagetian and the "activity theory" approaches. According to Piaget (1980), contradiction engenders cognitive conflict or disequilibrium which, in its turn, leads to insight. The problem that arises is that in order to be productive, contradiction should be experienced as such, and this does not necessarily always happen. Activity theory, proposed by Leontiev (1978), advanced the idea that in order to bring contradiction to consciousness some form of relevant activity needs to be organized. Our findings, however, indicate that even such a highly relevant activity as multiple choice assessment may have no effect on the subjects — if there is no **mediation of meaning**. According to Feuerstein, the simple presence of an activity or of a tool related to both the task and the corresponding cognitive function does not yet constitute a mediated learning situation. For mediation to occur, the transmission of meaning, among other conditions, *must* take place.

In addition to testing the Vygotskian hypothesis concerning psychological tools, this study also inquired into possible cross-cultural differences in the spontaneous discovery of contradictions. For that reason, stimulus material (a text that included statements contradicting elementary laws of physics) was adopted from the Soviet study by Tikhomirov and Klochko (1981), for young American subjects. It was reasoned that an extremely low level of spontaneous discovery of contradictions (3.8%) in the Soviet sample may reflect the lack of mediation of challenge in recent Soviet education. Therefore, in a course of study, if a student is not encouraged to look for novel and challenging features of the material, he/she will be unable to explore the material critically. The data obtained demonstrated that, indeed, spontaneous reporting of contradictions was much higher among American students and young professionals than among their Soviet peers (28% compared to 3.8%).

The problem remains, whether it is possible to teach cognitive strategies that will help a student discover contradictory information. This question has both general and more specific aspects. The general aspect concerns the effectiveness of Feuerstein's *Instrumental Enrichment* (IE) program used as a tool for the enhancement of analytic capacities in students. The specific cross-cultural aspect concerns the low level of spontaneous exploratory behavior identified in recent immigrants from the former Soviet Union. From clinical work with this population, initial impressions suggest that these immigrants display a high level of authoritarianism, low ambiguity of tolerance, and insufficient spontaneous exploratory behavior. In addition, it seems worthwhile to explore the relationships between cognitive strategies nurtured by the IE training and the content knowledge necessary for the identification of contradictory information.

The following pilot study is part of a larger research project being conducted in Israel with recent adult immigrants from Russia. The pilot study was designed to answer the questions of whether the IE training can serve as a tool for the enhancement of analytic and exploratory strategies among these subjects, and how these cognitive strategies interact with content knowledge.

Subjects. The subjects in the study included 19 special education teachers, all new immigrants from Russia, who were enrolled in a retraining program that leads to their licensing as teachers in Israel.

Methods. In the pretest, subjects were presented with pictures of different physical situations and asked to explain which situations are possible and which are impossible under any conditions. The problems closely resembled those used by Piaget (1980) in his study of contradictions. Each student received four problems depicting physically possible and impossible situations.

The instructional phase included weekly training in the IE program over a period of four months, for the total of 50 hours. The following IE instruments were used: *Organization of Dots,*

Orientation in Space, Comparisons, Analytic Perception, and *Illustrations* (Feuerstein, 1980). The IE training was part of the students' regular curriculum. The nature of the instruments and their teaching were such that they fostered a critical approach, exploratory behavior, and attention to contradictory information. At the same time, the IE instruments contained no cues that could be used in the solution of the posttest. The subjects received no training in physics nor in any other natural science content.

For the posttest, four problems similar — but not identical — to those in the pretest were used.

Results. Discovery of contradictions in the pretest was lower than expected. Only one student correctly identified all the impossible situations and correctly commented on contradictory material. Two students failed to discover even one contradictory point. The average success rate was 55%.

In the posttest, the average success rate was only slightly higher: 65%. At the same time, the pattern of responses changed significantly. Four subjects correctly identified all impossible situations, and no student scored a total failure. Moreover, all students whose success rate at the pretest was 25% or lower, improved their performance. Their average success rate became: 62.5%.

> **Short-term IE training seems to be effective in improving analytic, exploratory, and contradiction identification strategies in poorly performing adult learners.**

The average success rate for the group as a whole remained modest because some of the subjects who performed well on the pre-test performed less successfully on the posttest.

The analysis of subjects' comments and reasons for declaring certain situations possible or impossible revealed an interesting interaction between subjects' cognitive strategies and their content knowledge. Frequently, subjects' lack of elementary scientific knowledge and their reliance on quotidian experience prevented them from distinguishing between possible and impossible situations.

Conclusion. Short-term IE training seems to be effective in improving analytic, exploratory, and contradiction identification strategies in poorly performing adult learners. The effectiveness of cognitive strategies is limited by a subject's reliance on non-scientific, everyday experience in particular content areas.

A Feuerstein-based Study of Thinking with American Minority Students

During the 1989-1990 school year, the Philadelphia School District, in collaboration with the Pennsylvania Department of Education, trained a group of educators (teachers, principals, supervisors, and school psychologists) from middle and elementary schools in two subdistricts of the city in the first level of Feuerstein's instructional intervention program, *Instrumental Enrichment* (IE). Nine teachers who had been trained and were using the materials with their middle-grade classes volunteered to be part of a study conducted between January and June, 1991. The objective of the study was to examine the effects of the IE materials and their instruction on the thinking of middle school students in these teachers' classes. Students were mainly of Latino and African American backgrounds. Seven teachers and a total of 161 students, of regular and special education status, participated fully in the project. Results were reported on a non-verbal measure of students' intelligence, the *Standard Progressive Matrices* test which was pre- and posttested (Raven, 1958); on students' report card marks; and on students' city-wide test scores obtained from a standardized, nationally-normed reading and mathematics instrument (Offenberg, 1992). The goals, methods, and outcomes of this study are reviewed in the following discussion.

Goals. The goals of the IE program seek to correct deficiencies in a student's cognitive development. Feuerstein and his associates (Feuerstein, Jensen, Hoffman, & Rand, 1985) identify the need to enhance the capacity of a low-functioning adolescent "to become modified as a result of exposure to new experiences" (p. 59), the IE lessons are those experiences. The deficiencies referred to are categorized in three phases: the quantity and quality of data gathered by the student, the efficient use of data available to the student, and communication by the student of the outcome of elaborative processes. Obviously, students need to focus on the cognitive behaviors required to complete the various "instruments" in the first level of the IE program. This includes the concepts, labels, operations, and an understanding of relationships, strategies, and skills embedded in the content-free materials, particularly in the first two units or instruments introduced, *Organization of Dots* and *Comparisons*.

The IE program also seeks to change students from passive recipients of information to confident, active learners. Improved habit formation, particularly relative to intrinsic motivation on the student's part, is a focus of the program. "IE strives to help learners consolidate and internalize new operations, principles, and skills so fully that they are used as a result of an internal need and because of the economy that results from greater efficiency" (Feuerstein, Jensen, Hoffman, & Rand, 1985, p. 60). Feuerstein sees the controlled repetition and organization of activities in IE as approximating the mediated learning experience that is required for student internalization of ability; the learner spontaneously and fluently becomes able to be in control of the material on his/her own. Involved in this development is the student's own insight and the awareness of his/her own work as part of the (meta) cognitive functioning. Ultimately, Feuerstein hopes that students will become interested in the material for its own novelty, challenge, and inspiration. Although all the instruments are not necessarily capable of this outcome, it is nevertheless a general goal of the IE program. In the end, Feuerstein proposes that learners will develop a different view of their own perception of themselves as learners. With the sounder success of mediated learning experience, he and his colleagues anticipate that students who master IE will become active generators of new information, problem solvers, and proactive thinkers.

The IE program also expects that students' standardized test scores will improve. Thus, in the Philadelphia study, the Reading/English/Language Arts, the Mathematics Computation, and the Mathematics Concepts and Application sub-tests of the City-Wide Testing Program (CWT) were tracked on the participating students during the course of the project.

Subjects/Methods. The first phase of the project involved the training of the district teachers and staff in the IE materials. This occurred during 1989-1990 and involved the four instruments included in Level One: *Organization of Dots, Orientation in Space, Comparisons,* and *Analytic Perception.* Fifty-five educators from eleven schools in two subdistricts took part in this training. Eventually, seven of nine teachers who volunteered to be part of the research effort committed one class of students each for the study. These classes included 161 students who were in the fifth through seventh grades; they were mainly from Latino and African American backgrounds. Twenty-nine of the students were in two special education (mixed-category, mildly handicapped) classes. This group of 161 students constituted the population upon which the entire study was completed between January and June, 1991.

Early in 1991, three researchers from Research for Better Schools — who were trained in both levels of the IE program — were engaged to observe the teachers instructing the IE material. They used a common observation protocol and made uniform observation and testing arrangements with six of the participating teachers. These researchers also conducted the pre- and posttest of a sample of the students with the *Standardized Progressive Matrices* test. Prior to the posttesting of the Raven instrument, these same researchers coached a subsample of the students on test-related skills. They used a common coaching and testing protocol based on a plan provided by the Office of Assessment of the school district. Following the close of school in June, 1991, school district staff tracked the academic grade records of the students in the study. They also kept record of these students' scores on city-wide testing in Reading/English/Language Arts, Mathematics Computation, and Mathematics Concepts and Application subtests.

There were five types of data generated in the study. The *Standard Progressive Matrices* pretest was administered to 73 students across the nine experimental classes. When students who were absent from the second testing and classes that were dropped from the study were eliminated, a sample of 47 students evenly distributed among seven classes remained. The pre-tests were given in March and April 1991, the posttests were administered in May and June 1991. Two students from each of seven classes were included in the coached subsample on the Raven posttest. Report card marks in English/language arts, reading, mathematics, science, and social studies were tracked for June 1990 and June 1991 for all students, in order to measure the effect of IE on the students' becoming successful learners in the eyes of their teachers. Letter grades on the report cards were turned into a numerical scale similar to ones used for computing grade-point averages. Scores on the city-wide test as of Spring 1990 and Spring 1991 were tracked on three subtests noted to measure the effect of IE on students' performance on a nationally-normed measure. Normal Curve Equivalent (NCE) scores, based on the publisher's (CTB McGraw Hill for the School District of Philadelphia) national norms were used for this study. Teacher questionnaires were employed to identify the students in the study, the amount of IE instruction that had been conducted by each instructor, and the particular instruments taught to the classes involved. And finally, classroom observations documented over the course of the study were used to provide contextual information about the instructional program as implemented.

Analyses of the various data were completed by the end of 1991. The study was based on the assumption that there would be naturally occurring variation in the number of occasions that an experimental class would have had IE instruction, and that more IE sessions would result in greater individual student gains. The evaluation strategy was to relate students' exposure through IE sessions to the three measures of student attainment: *Standard Progressive Matrices* test scores, marks in their regular subject matter courses, and city-wide test scores. Pre-values of the student attainment measures, grade level, and participation in special education, were used to distinguish pre-existing individual differences among students from the effects of IE. Specialized forms of the pre-values were used to explore effects which were strong initially, but then diminished (curvilinear effects), or to explore the ways that IE effected student subgroups (interaction effects). Regression analyses relating the number of IE sessions to the outcome variables were used to evaluate the data. This technique was used in lieu of experimental group-control group comparisons, because there were many teachers who did not volunteer for the study although they had been trained in IE and had received the IE materials. Many students who might have been considered for a potential control group may actually have had IE instruction in these teachers' classes.

> The study was based on the assumption that there would be naturally occurring variation in the number of occasions that an experimental class would have had IE instruction, and that more IE sessions would result in greater individual student gains.

Results. The average number of IE sessions between the *Standard Progressive Matrices* pretesting and posttesting was 14.8 sessions. During this period, the average score for students in the study went from 31.3 to 34.4 raw score points, an average gain of 3.1. Analysis of the test results showed several statistically reliable trends (Offenberg, 1992, p. 10): (1) Regular education students' scores were increased as a result of participating in IE sessions. The more sessions they participated in, the higher their posttest scores, when the effects of other variables (pretest scores, coaching, and special education participation) were removed. (2) The rate of growth of special education students on this measure was not as marked as the growth rate of regular students. This finding is considered to be tentative because the special education students had more IE sessions than any regular students, making it impossible to separate the effect of IE sessions from the effect of having been designated special education. (3) Coaching improved the posttest scores of students with low *Standard Progressive Matrices* pretest scores more than the scores with high pretest scores. However, coaching students did not improve the ability of the Raven test to detect the effects of IE.

In terms of the examination of students' report card marks in English/language arts, reading, mathematics, science, and social studies between spring 1990 and spring 1991, the findings focused on the five regular education classes for whom end-of-the-year letter grades were consistently reported. There were 115 students in these classes; their instruction consisted of approximately 21 to 58 sessions of IE. From spring 1990 to spring 1991, students' average marks declined in each of the major subjects. This trend is similar to one found in middle grades of the school district as a whole (Offenberg, 1992, p. 11). For students who received up to 35 IE sessions, the decline of marks was moderated in the following subjects: English/language arts, reading, science, and social studies. One regular class had more than 35 IE sessions. It seems to have affected student marks less in this class than in the classes that had fewer sessions. Finally, the study showed IE instruction did not affect students' mathematics grades.

In terms of the city-wide test scores on nationally-normed portions of the spring test in Reading/English/Language Arts, Mathematics Computation, and Mathematics Concepts and

Applications, the normal-curve equivalent (NCE) test scores of the five regular education classes in the study were examined. Special education classes were excluded because they did not participate in the City-Wide Testing Program (CTW). It was found that program participants' Mathematics Computation NCE scores improved. However, Reading/English/Language Arts and Mathematics Concepts and Applications NCE scores declined between spring 1990 and spring 1991. Participation in IE sessions appears to be correlated with lower NCE scores; the greater the number of IE sessions, the lower the test scores. "It is not known whether IE instruction interferes with teaching the skills measured by these tests, or whether there is some other cause for this finding" (Offenberg, 1992, p. 21).

Conclusion. The Philadelphia schools study suggests that IE is a valuable instructional program that shows positive effects for urban adolescents' learning. In less than a school year, despite the fact that observation reports indicate that extensive bridging between the innovative program and traditional classroom instruction did not generally occur, IE had positive effects for minority, middle-grade students. These effects were evident in two types of outcomes: better marks in language-based subjects and improved non-verbal measures of intelligence. These results suggest that students improved in areas where teachers were able to mediate more successfully and on an assessment instrument that is similar to the particular IE materials. Student performance on the city-wide, standardized test needs to be examined further, especially with regard to how instruction and testing are related to aspects of mediated learning such as content bridging.

> The Philadelphia schools study suggests that IE is a valuable instructional program that shows positive effects for urban adolescents' learning.

IMPLICATIONS OF THE RESEARCH

The Vygotskian study highlights the fact that the ability to identify and to deal with contradictory information is essential for successful learning. At the same time, it shows that even educated adults seem to be ill-prepared for this task when it needs to be carried out outside their narrow area of specialization.

The study also shows that spontaneous discovery of contradiction, even when it lies completely within the framework of everyday experience, is rare. The usefulness of verbal and pictorial tools-mediators, explored in the Vygotskian tradition, is limited if there is no mediation of meaning.

The IE program developed by Feuerstein and his associates may serve as a useful technique for enhancing analytical, exploratory, and contradiction identification strategies in poor performers. The effectiveness of these strategies, however, depends on interaction with the subject's content knowledge. It seems that the Vygotskian distinction between "scientific" and "everyday" concepts is appropriate here. If a subject's content knowledge is organized around non-scientific, everyday experiences, his/her ability to utilize cognitive strategies remains limited. Everyday experience interferes with the logical train of thought that may eventually lead to the correct identification of contradiction.

Two lines of future research can be suggested from this study. One of them is the exploration of how the mediation of meaning can be incorporated into the Vygotskian psychological tools paradigm. The second concerns the development of "bridging" techniques within the IE program in such a way that cognitive strategies are linked to the content knowledge areas such as physics, biology, or mathematics. The latter attempt may produce a synthesis between the Vygotskian notion of "scientific" concepts and Feuerstein's emphasis on the development of cognitive strategies.

The Philadelphia study shows that Feuerstein's innovative instructional program can influence adolescent students' thinking in a relatively short period of time. As an intervention tool of learning, IE materials were effective in changing the ways students work in middle grade classrooms. The gains in student performance on the *Standard Progressive Matrices* test seemed most directly related to the new classroom experience provided by IE, especially on the *Organization of Dots* exercises. The growth in language-based subject areas, as reported by report card grades, suggest that the goals of IE instruction carried over to student performance in those particular content areas beyond the Feuerstein program. The question of how to bridge classroom IE experience to mathematics construct learning appears to be a topic of needed future research, but the fact that student learning requires such integration seems to be obvious. Were the middle-grades students influenced by greater mediation? The success of the coaching subsample on the posttest of the Raven test, especially for lower performing students, suggest that indeed they were.

Although this middle grades study provides some interesting data about student change in this large city school district, it also raises some interesting questions about teacher change. Teachers' questionnaire comments indicate that, after initial use of the innovative program, they began to see some of their students in a different perspective. Some students seemed more motivated by the IE materials than by the traditional instruction; some youngsters showed greater spontaneity and curiosity about their work. Some students appeared more engaged in the learning; they seemed to persist longer at tasks, even at taking the Raven posttest. Had the students changed and/or the teachers? Had only mediation of meaning developed, or, as Feuerstein advocates, had intentionality/reciprocity and transcendance also occurred? The results of this large school district study suggest some areas of significant, future research concerning mediation, particularly in terms of specific, classroom interactions and long-term change among students and teachers.

> ... they see humans born with relatively few inherited instincts, but they note that "the human parent can teach not only by example, but also by precept."

CONCLUSION

Returning to the four questions that began this study, much has been revealed about both Vygotsky's and Feuerstein's contribution to the concept of mediated learning. Both theorists take a strong sociological approach to the development of intelligence and cognition. They both see such development as a dynamic process; they concur that human modification is gradual, as well as natural. From the thirties, when Vygotsky wrote, to Feuerstein's views today, their socio-cultural psychology seeks to place human beings in a larger biological context, but also in a unique position. Like Childe (1951), they see humans born with relatively few inherited instincts, but they note that "the human parent can teach not only by example, but also by precept" (p. 29). In that symbolic world, mediation for learning is an important key to survival and success.

Vygotsky's and Feuerstein's approaches do not always perfectly match. Kozulin (1991) points out that Feuerstein makes an important, though not fully elaborated, distinction between *functions* (Vygotsky's concept) which serve as prerequisites of cognition, and cognitive *operations* which correspond more or less to the Piagetian notion of intellectual operations. Thus, classification, to the Israeli psychologist, is an operation which might be ineffective because the function of using two different sources of information is deficient. At the same time, an absence of a specific type of hypothetical reasoning in a culturally different individual may be merely a result of his/her particular experience and not a sign of deficiency, as long as the prerequisites for such an operation are present. In one sense, Feuerstein designed his IE program to develop such prerequisites for learning among low achieving performers.

Of what significance is mediated learning for effective instruction? It seems to have been a key ingredient in both field implementations studied. Perhaps, its first important role showed that the prerequisite of mediated learning helps a teacher focus on what is significant to the success of the learner. At the same time, both Vygotsky and Feuerstein are not surprised at the diversity and variation among learners. They agree that the learner's needs and abilities are the central issue of planning effective instruction. Along with many researchers today (Campione, Brown, Ferrara & Bryant, 1984; Goldenberg & Gallimore, 1991), their mediated learning best includes a dynamic approach to classroom diagnosis and assessment and a learner-centered orientation to curriculum and instruction, especially for individual concerns. Similarly, for the needs of particularly disadvantaged groups of youngsters, such as those described in the large city school district experiment, addressing group needs may be another essential aspect of sound, effective instruction as well as large scale intervention (Presseisen, 1992).

In both the empirical studies, the use of significant tools of instruction, embedded in the scaffolding or apprenticeship models of learning as described in Vygotskian terms, seemed to highlight the tasks of internalization of ability through mediation among differing populations of learners. Whether adult immigrants from another country or low-achieving adolescents with backgrounds different from the mainstream culture, the social interaction involved in learning the Feuerstein instruments became the "tool" for transcending the cognitive limitations within these different groups. In that respect, mediated learning holds unique hope for the improvement of different populations of students all over the world. Finding the appropriate tools and planning their use in an effective sequence of instruction may also be an important aspect of sound teacher preparation.

Finally, how might mediated learning extend cognitive psychology's new paradigm for education? First, an emphasis on mediation suggests a strong theme of metacognition and mindfulness for every learning environment. The teacher's overall role may significantly shift from that of information provider to learning facilitator, but, by the same token, the student can become self-regulated, independent, and creative. Secondly, mediation provides a useful link between thinking processes and concepts of content. The emphasis here is that of meaningfulness and significance—in making the ideas of a discipline come to life in the thoughtful classroom. And finally, mediated learning legitimizes thinking at school, as well as learning at home and in the full community. The question is not whether the student is ready for school, but rather, what can be provided in the classroom to help every learner take advantage of and progress in terms of his/her unique potential?

Vygotsky and Feuerstein provide much food for thought for the mindful educator. Like Piaget, their intellectual forebear, their work suggests there is nothing like a good theory for practice.

REFERENCES

Bears, B.J. (1986). *The cognitive revolution in psychology*. New York: Guilford Press.

Bakhtin, M. (1986). *Speech genres and other late essays*. Austin, TX: University of Texas Press.

Belmont, J.M. (1989). Cognitive strategies and strategic learning: The socio-instructional approach. *American Psychologist, 44*(2), 142-148.

Blumer, H. (1969). *Symbolic interactionism*. Englewood Cliffs, NJ: Prentice Hall.

Bransford, J.; Sherwood, R.; Vye, N.; & Riser, J. (1986). Teaching thinking and problem solving: Research foundations. *American Psychologist, 41*(10), 1078-1089.

Bronson, G.W. (1968). The development of fear in man and other animals. *Child Development, 39*, 409-430.

Brown, A.L. & Ferrara, R.A. (1985). Diagnosing zones of proximal development. In J.V. Wertsch, (Ed.), *Culture, communication, and cognition.* New York: Cambridge University Press.

Bruner, J. (1987). Life as narrative. *Social Research, 54*, 11-32.

Bruner, J. (1966). *Toward a theory of instruction.* Cambridge, MA: Belknap Press.

Campione, J.C.; Brown, A.L.; Ferrara, R.A.; & Bryant, N.R. (1984). The Zone of Proximal Development: Implications for individual differences in learning. In B. Rogoff & J.V. Wertsch (Eds.), *Children's learning in the "Zone of Proximal Development".* New Directions for Child Development No. 23. San Francisco: Jossey-Bass.

Childe, V.G. (1951). *Man makes himself.* New York: New American Library.

Detterman, D.K. & Sternberg, R. J. (Eds) (1982). *How and how much can intelligence be increased.* Norwood, NJ: Ablex Publishing.

Diamond, M.C. (1988). *Enriching heredity: The impact of the environment on the anatomy of the brain.* New York: The Free Press.

Emerson, L.W. (1991). MLE and American Indian Education. Chapter 6 in R. Feuerstein, P. S. Klein, & A. J. Tannenbaum (Eds), *Mediated learning experience (MLE): Theoretical, psychosocial and learning implications.* London: Freund Publishing House.

Feuerstein, R. (1990). The theory of structural cognitive modifiability. Chapter 4 in B.Z. Presseisen, R.J. Sternberg, K.W. Fischer, C.C. Knight & R. Feuerstein, *Learning and thinking styles: Classroom interaction.* Washington, DC: National Education Association.

Feuerstein, R. (1980). *Instrumental enrichment: An intervention program for cognitive modifiability.* In collaboration with Y. Rand, M.B. Hoffman, & R. Miller. Baltimore, MD: University Park Press.

Feuerstein, R. & Feuerstein, S. (1991). Mediated learning experience: A theoretical review. Chapter 1 in R. Feuerstein, P.S. Klein, & A.J. Tannenbaum, *Mediated learning experience (MLE): Theoretical, psychological and learning implications.* London: Freund Publishing House.

Feuerstein, R.; Jensen, M.R.; Hoffman, M.B. & Rand, Y. (1985). Instrumental Enrichment, an intervention program for structural cognitive modifiability: Theory and practice. In J.W. Segal, S.F. Chipman, & R. Glaser (Eds), *Thinking and learning skills.* Vol. I *Relating instruction to research.* Hillsdale, NJ: Lawrence Erlbaum Associates.

Gardner, H. (1985). *The mind's new science: A history of the cognitive revolution.* New York: Basic Books.

Goldenberg, C. (1991). *Instructional conversations and their classroom application.* Educational Practice Report: 2. Washington, DC: The National Center for Research on Cultural Diversity and Second Language Learning.

Goldenberg, C. & Gallimore, R. (1991). Local knowledge, research knowledge, and educational change: A case study of early Spanish reading improvement. *Educational Researcher, 20*(8), 2-14.

Haywood, H.C. & Tzuriel, D. (1992). *Interactive assessment.* New York: Springer-Verlag.

Kaniel, S. & Feuerstein, R. (1989). Special needs of children with learning difficulties. *Oxford Review of Education, 15*(2), 165-179.

Kojeve, A. (1986). *An introduction to the reading of Hegel.* Ithaca, NY: Cornell University Press.

Kozulin, A. (1991). *Mediated learning and education: Vygotsky and Feuerstein.* Philadelphia, PA: Research for Better Schools (photocopy).

Kozulin, A. (1990a). *Vygotsky's psychology: A biography of ideas.* Cambridge, MA: Harvard University Press.

Kozulin, A. (1990b). Mediation: Psychological activity and psychological tools. *International Journal of Cognitive Education and Mediated Learning, 1*(2), 151-159.

Leontiev, A.N. (1978). *Activity, consciousness, and personality.* Englewood Cliffs, NJ: Prentice Hall.

Lidz, C.S. (Ed.). (1987). *Dynamic assessment: An interactional approach to evaluating learning potential.* New York: Guilford Press.

Link, F.R. (1985). Instrumental Enrichment: A strategy for cognitive and academic improvement. In F.R. Link (Ed.), *Essays on the intellect.* Alexandria, VA: Association for Supervision and Curriculum Development.

Luria, A.R. (1976). *Cognitive development: Its cultural and social foundations.* Cambridge, MA: Harvard University Press.

Mead, G.H. (1974). *Mind, self, and society.* Chicago: University of Chicago Press.

Miller, M. (1987). Argumentation and cognition. In M. Hickman (Ed.), *Social and functional approaches to language and thought.* San Diego, CA: Academic Press.

Missiuna, C. & Samuels, M. (1988). Dynamic assessment: Review and critique. *Special Services in the Schools, 5*(1/2). Binghamton, NY: Haworth Press (reprint).

Offenberg, R.M. (1992). *A study of the effects of Instrumental Enrichment on minority middle-grade students.* Philadelphia, PA: School District of Philadelphia, Office of Assessment (photocopy).

Palincsar, A.S. & Brown, A. (1984). Reciprocal teaching of comprehension-fostering and comprehension-monitoring activities. *Cognition and instruction, 1*(2), 117-175.

Perkins, D.N. & Salomon, G. (1988). Teaching for transfer. *Educational Leadership, 46*(1), 22-32.

Piaget, J. (1980). *Experiments in contradiction.* New York: Academic Press.

Piaget, J. (1973). *To understand is to invent: The future of education.* New York: Grossman.

Piaget, J. (1969). *The psychology of intelligence.* New York: Humanities Press.

Presseisen, B.Z. (1992). *Implementing thinking in the school's curriculum.* A paper presented at the third annual meeting of the International Association for Cognitive Education, Riverside, CA (photocopy).

Raven, J.C. (1958). *Standard progressive matrices* (Sets A, B, C, D, and E). London: H.K. Lewis & Co., Ltd.

Rogoff, B. (1990). *Apprenticeship in thinking: Cognitive development in social context.* New York: Oxford University Press.

Rogoff, B. & Wertsch, J.V. (Eds.). (1984). *Children's learning in the "Zone of Proximal Development."* New Directions for Child Development No. 23. San Francisco: Jossey-Bass.

Sharron, H. (1987). *Changing children's minds: Feuerstein's revolution in the teaching of intelligence.* London: Souvenir Press.

Sternberg, R.J. (1990). *Metaphors of mind: Conceptions of the nature of intelligence.* New York: Cambridge University Press.

Tharp, R.G. & Gallimore, R. (1991). *The instructional conversation: Teaching and learning in social activity.* Research Report: 2. Washington, DC: National Center for Research on Cultural Diversity and Second Language Learning.

Tharp, R.G. & Gallimore, R. (1989). Rousing schools to life. *American Educator,* 13(2) 20-25, 46-52.

Tharp, R.G. & Gallimore, R. (1988). *Rousing minds to life: Teaching, learning, and schooling in social context.* New York: Cambridge University Press.

Tikhomirov, O. & Klochko, V. (1981). The detection of contradiction as the initial stage of problem formation, In J. Wertsch (Ed.), *The concept of activity in Soviet psychology* (pp. 341-382). Armonk, NY: Sharpe.

Trevarthen, C. (1988). Universal cooperative motives. In G. Jahoda & I.M. Lewis (Eds.), *Acquiring culture: Cross-cultural studies in child development.* London: Croom Helm.

Trevarthen, C. & Hubley, P. (1978). Secondary intersubjectivity. In A. Lock (Ed.), *Action, gesture, and symbol.* London: Academic Press.

Vygotsky, L.S. (1986). *Thought and language* (Revised edition). Cambridge, MA: MIT-Press.

Vygotsky, L.S. (1983). *Collected papers.* (Vol. 3). Moscow: Pedagogika.

Vygotsky, L.S. (1978). *Mind in society: The development of higher pscyhological processes.* Edited by M. Cole, V. John-Steiner, S. Scribner, & E. Souberman. Cambridge, MA: Harvard University Press.

Vygotsky, L.S. & Luria, A.R. (1930). *Essays in the history of behavior.* Moscow: Sozekgiz.

Wertsch, J. & Minick, N. (1990). Negotiating sense in the zone of proximal development. In M. Schwebel, C. Maher, & N. Fagley (Eds.), *Promoting cognitive growth over the life span.* Hillsdale, NJ: Lawrence Erlbaum.

What Does Research Tell Us About Feuerstein's Instrumental Enrichment?

T his section of four articles discusses studies on the effects of Instrumental Enrichment (IE). The first article is an examination of the empirical status of Instrumental Enrichment in 1986, the time the report was initially published. It is followed by more recent articles on studies conducted in the United States, Canada, France, and South Africa.

In their comprehensive examination of research done in several countries, Savell, Twohig, and Rachford highlight two issues: the nature of the effects, and the investment (the "amount" of IE) required to produce them. They report that significant gains were commonly found in nonverbal measures of intelligence, while other types of measures yielded inconsistent results. In addition, the authors report that measurable gains were discovered in studies that ensured at least one week of training for Instrumental Enrichment instructors and eighty or more hours of student exposure over a period of a year of longer. They conclude by posing eight questions for future research and offering several ways to improve research reliability and validity.

The Savell et al. research implies that the implementation of Instrumental Enrichment is only partly responsible for the program's success. Where mediation is not provided, the students are only exposed to a structured set of Instrumental Enrichment exercises. At the same time, these students do not obtain the critical aspect of IE — the opportunity to benefit from mediated learning experience. The significant gains frequently reported are likely to occur even with poor mediation. Effects on self-esteem, impulsivity, classroom behavior, academic achievement, course content, and many other areas seem to be strongly related to the mediation offered by the Instrumental Enrichment teacher. These constructs are often reported to be inconsistently affected by the program.

Rosine Debray provides insight into the nature of mediation that is needed for effective Instrumental Enrichment and the effects of this training and teaching on the attitudes of teachers and their professional practices. Debray's observations may be summarized in her statement that the Instrumental Enrichment experience "transformed their way of teaching their own subjects, since it threw light on what is involved in thinking and intelligence."

In the last two articles, Skuy and his colleagues examine the relationship between the quality of mediation offered by an Instrumental Enrichment teacher and the effects of the program on culturally deprived students. They report statistically significant differential effects of Instrumental Enrichment which are related to the quality of mediation. While they report an increase in cognitive performance irrespective of the quality of mediation, in measures of verbal and socio-emotional performance they found significant gains only where the mediation quality was higher.

Empirical Status of Feuerstein's "Instrumental Enrichment" (FIE) Technique as a Method of Teaching Thinking Skills

by Joel M. Savell, Paul T. Twohig, and Douglas L. Rachford
US Army Research Institute for the Behavioral and Social Sciences

BSTRACT
This paper examines reports of empirical research on Feuerstein's "Instrumental Enrichment" (FIE) as a method of teaching thinking skills and asks what can be concluded from these reports with respect to the following: (a) the nature and statistical reliability of observed FIE effects and, for those effects that are statistically reliable, (b) the "amount" of FIE that appears to be required for these effects to appear.

INTRODUCTION
Background and Purpose
In recent years a good deal of interest has been expressed concerning the possibility of teaching thinking skills (Detterman & Sternberg, 1982; Furth, 1970; Glaser, 1984; Lochhead & Clement, 1979; Walsh, 1984), and a number of techniques purporting to teach such skills have been developed (e.g., Bransford & Stein, 1984; Covington, Crutchfield, Davies, & Olton, 1974; DeBono, 1975; Furth & Wachs, 1975; Hayes, 1981; Lipman, Sharp, & Oscanyan, 1980; Nisbett & Ross, 1980, pp. 280-286; Vye & Bransford, 1981; Whimbey & Lochhead, 1980. For a summary, see Nickerson, 1984; Nickerson, Perkins, & Smith, 1985). In most cases, however, these techniques have been subjected little, if at all, to empirical testing by researchers

From Review of Educational Research, Winter 1986, Vol. 56, No. 4, P. 381–409. Reprinted with permission.

other than the ones who originally developed the technique; and it is often difficult to assess the claims made in their behalf. An exception to this generalization (though the data reported thus far raise a number of questions) is a technique developed by Reuven Feuerstein and his colleagues (Feuerstein, Rand, Hoffman, & Miller, 1980). This technique is sometimes referred to as "Instrumental Enrichment" (IE) and sometimes as "Feuerstein Instrumental Enrichment" (FIE), depending on whether the reference is to the technique *as a technique* (IE) or to the technique as carried out using the particular set of materials developed by Feuerstein (FIE).[1] (We have used the latter term in this review.) This technique was developed for use with culturally disadvantaged, low-performing Israeli adolescents. Feuerstein et al. (1980, p. 69) make the point, however, that although the materials were developed for use with adolescents, the principles are applicable to all age groups.

The technique has to ingredients: (a) a set of 14 (increasingly complex) paper-and-pencil exercises designed to help students identify basic principles of thinking and to practice self-monitoring with respect to the use of these principles, and (b) a set of training procedures involving teacher-guided "bridging" back and forth between the principles introduced in the exercises and various subject matters of interest. Feuerstein and his colleagues have reported that, in a 2-year field experiment, individuals exposed to FIE performed significantly better on a variety of intellectual and behavior measures than a group of matched controls (Feuerstein, Rand, Hoffman, Hoffman & Miller, 1979; Rand, Tannenbaum, & Feuerstein, 1979); and, on the measure examined, the superiority of the FIE subjects was observable several years after the experiment was over (Feuerstein, Miller, Hoffman, Rand, Mintzker, & Jensen, 1981; Rand, Mintzker, Miller, Hoffman, & Friedlander, 1981). In fact, according to these authors (Feuerstein et al., 1981; Rand et al., 1981), the difference between FIE and control scores was found not simply to have been maintained but actually to have increased.

> Feuerstein and his colleagues have reported that, in a 2-year field experiment, individuals exposed to FIE performed significantly better on a variety of intellectual and behavior measures than a group of matched controls.

Reports such as these are striking, to say the least. Based presumably on these reports, the considerable intuitive appeal of the technique's underlying theory, and the fact that a number of individuals not directly involved in this research have spoken favorably either of the technique itself or of the technique's seeming potential (Bruner, in E. Hall, 1982; Campione, Brown, & Ferrara, 1982; Chance, 1982; Glaser, 1982; Hobbs, 1980; Sternberg, 1983; Ziegler & Berman, 1983), a number of school administrators and other educators have recommended adopting the technique for use in their school districts or colleges.[2] In view of this fact, it seems an appropriate time to examine the relevant empirical research and to ask what this research has shown with respect to the technique's success in doing what its developers said it is capable of doing.

This review examines reports of empirical research on FIE—journal articles, doctoral dissertations, conference papers, and institutional reports—and asks what can be concluded from these reports with respect to the following: (a) the nature and statistical significance of FIE effects and, for those effects that are statistically significant, (b) the "amount" of FIE that appears to be required for these effects to appear. Before proceeding, however, it is desirable to indicate just how the documents reviewed here were selected, what kinds of reports are not included in the review, and (to assist the reader in assessing the relevance of negative findings) what conditions the developers of FIE believe are required for adequate implementation. Finally, although descriptions of the FIE program are available elsewhere (e.g., Feuerstein & Hoffman, 1985; Feuerstein & Jensen, 1980; Feuerstein, Rand, Hoffman & Miller, 1980), it is desirable to try to give the reader a feel for what a typical FIE session is like. Comparisons of FIE with other techniques for teaching thinking skills can be found in Bransford, Arbitman-Smith, Stein, and Vye (1985) and in Sternberg (1985).

Source of documents reviewed. We began by searching *Science Citation Index* and *Dissertation Abstracts International,* through December 1984, for publications that cited Feuerstein's major publication on FIE (Feuerstein et al., 1980). We also examined recent copies of American Psychological Association (APA) and American Educational Research Association (AERA) convention programs in search of conference papers reporting

FIE research. Finally, we obtained copies of reports cited in these sources, as well as reports we learned of from individuals to whom we had sent the first draft of this paper for comment.

Some exclusions. As indicated above, not all the reports we obtained or heard about are discussed in this review. We have not discussed reports: (a) where the study was characterized by the investigators as a pilot (Kieta, Pfohl, & Redfield, 1982; Martin, 1984a, 1984b, 1985; Messerer, Hunt, Myers, & Lerner, 1984; Russ-Eft, McLaughlin, Oxford-Carpenter, Harman, Simutis, & Baker, 1984; the first study reported in Haywood & Arbitman-Smith, 1981); (b) where the intervention was not yet complete (Redfield, 1984; Royer & Swift, 1984; Rosine Debray, personal communication, February 1, 1985; Mogens Jensen, personal communication, January 15, 1985); (c) where the study (in most cases, a pilot) did not include a comparison group (e.g., Jackson, 1984;[3] Redfield, Kieta, Pfohl, & O'Connor, 1983); (d) where the study used intervention procedures other than or in addition to the procedures ordinarily used in FIE programs (Beasley, 1984; Jackson, 1984; Waksman, Silverman & Messner, 1982 [summarized in Waksman, Silverman & Messner, 1984]); and (e) where the purpose of the study was to investigate effects of FIE on the instructors who were using it rather than on the students who were being taught (Kersh & Gehrke, 1984; Martin, 1984b). This last topic is an important one, as Feuerstein et al. (1980) have pointed out, but to date there has been very little research on it.

Conditions required for implementation. The developers of FIE (Feuerstein et al., 1980), as well as others who have been associated with them in this research (e.g., Arbitman-Smith, Haywood & Bransford, 1984; Michael Begab, personal communication, December 18, 1984; Hobbs, 1980; Link, personal communication, January 7, 1985; Abraham Tannenbaum, personal communication, January 4, 1985), have pointed out that certain minimum conditions must be provided as part of the FIE implementation before effects of any real significance can be expected. There apparently has not been much research focusing systematically on these conditions (e.g.,

> ... certain minimum conditions must be provided as part of the FIE implementation before effects of any real significance can be expected.

on the "amount" of FIE required to produce an effect of
specified magnitude in a specified population), but there
appears to be a good deal of agreement that researchers should
pay particular attention to certain things, among them the
following: (a) preliminary and subsequent training of FIE
instructors in the theory and method of FIE, as well as follow-
up supervision and consultation while the intervention is being
carried out; (b) the "dosage" of FIE given to the students,
meaning mainly the number of (increasing complex) FIE
instruments gone through but with implications for the
number of hours devoted to the implementation as a whole;
and (c) the integration of FIE and regular subject matter
instruction, which in most cases means having FIE taught by
individuals who are involved in regular classroom instruction
rather than by someone who comes in just for the FIE. In
Feuerstein's original study (see Feuerstein et al., 1980, pp. 325-
410), FIE instructors participated in a 10-day workshop before
the start of the program and in a second (12-day) workshop
before the start of the second year. In addition, throughout the
2-year period FIE instructors were supervised in their work and
given opportunities for consultation. With respect to "dosage,"
students in the experimental classes received 3-5 hours of FIE a
week for the 2 years; during this period they were exposed to 13
of the 14 available FIE instruments. With respect to
instructional integration, FIE was taught by individuals who
had the students for other subjects as well. Arbitman-Smith,
Haywood, and Bransford (1984) have said that FIE is "designed
to be taught 300 to 350 hours for a period of 2-3 years" (p. 467)
and that, in order to realize significant gains, "necessary . . .
investment may be in the range of 75-100 hours in an academic
year" (Haywood et al., 1982, p. 13). Frances Link (personal
communication, May 3, 1985) has said that what is desired is to
go through all 14 of the available instruments and that,
depending on the abilities of the students, doing this can take 1-
3 years. Bransford (personal communication, January 1985) has
made the point that ". . . the question of *who* is being taught
and tested is extremely important. It undoubtedly interacts with
the number of hours of instruction needed and perhaps even
with what it means to 'deliver effective instruction.'" More
generally, FIE researchers seem to be saying: (a) that FIE is
designed to provide a particular thing for those individuals

whose prior experience has been deficient in it— what
Feuerstein and his colleagues call "mediated learning
experience" (for a discussion, see Bransford et al., 1985, pp.
181-185; Feuerstein et al., 1980, pp. 13-70; Passow, 1980); and
(b) that to the extent that particular individuals do not have the
deficiencies addressed in FIE, they would not be expected to
show improvement after exposure to the program. In addition,
Haywood et al., (1982, p. 14) suggest that it may be useful to
spread out the program for very slow-learning students, giving
many hours of instruction on a few pages and exercises, and
taking longer to cover the whole program.

Feuerstein's Theory and the FIE Method
(This summary draws from a number of sources, e.g.,
Arbitman-Smith, Haywood, & Bransford, 1984; Bransford et
al., 1985; Feuerstein & Jensen, 1980; Feuerstein & Hoffman,
1985; Feuerstein, Rand, Hoffman & Miller, 1980; Hobbs, 1980;
Link, 1980; and Passow, 1980). Feuerstein's theory is basically a
theory of cognitive development, and the key construct of this
theory is what Feuerstein calls a "Mediated Learning
Experience" (MLE). MLE is said to occur when an individual
(typically a child) is shown or taught cognitive methods for
interpreting information, for solving problems, or for learning
something. For example, in interacting with a child an adult
might illustrate the usefulness of categorizing a particular piece
of information and then go on to demonstrate a technique for
doing this categorizing. Feuerstein, like Piaget (1954), believes
that children can learn from interacting with the environment;
but, like Vygotsky (1962), he emphasizes the importance of the
mediation of the child's learning by adults.

Feuerstein argues that enhancing a child's cognitive
abilities can have a snowballing effect in that, with these abilities
enhanced, the child is capable of learning additional and even
more complex cognitive operations and strategies. Feuerstein
has tried to measure children's potential for such enhancement
(he refers to this potential as "cognitive modifiability") by
means of a set of procedures and materials referred to
collectively as the "Learning Potential Assessment Device"
(LPAD). (See Feuerstein, Rand, & Hoffman, 1979). It is
Feuerstein's view that this potential for cognitive enhancement,
this cognitive modifiability, can be changed and that the FIE
program has the capability of accomplishing this change.

As suggested above, one of the anticipated results of providing children with MLEs is that they would become more aware of their cognitive processes and abilities, that is, they would exhibit an increase in their metacognitive activity. An increase in metacognitive awareness, in turn, would be expected to give the children greater control over their cognitive styles and thus greater consistency with respect to the patterning of their cognitive processes. Feuerstein is particularly concerned with children who exhibit an impulsive problem-solving style, since this style is so often found to be ineffective (Kagan, 1965); and he is also concerned that children should be able consistently to generalize from their experience and to adopt an abstract rather than a concrete cognitive style (Goldstein & Blackman, 1978).

Feuerstein combined this theoretical framework with generally accepted principles of learning (e.g., the value of extensive practice and of getting feedback on results), and, drawing on his own experience with the LPAD (which had led him to identify what he considered to be a key set of cognitive skills), he developed a set of classroom instructional procedures and a collateral set of 14 paper-and-pencil instruments: Organization of Dots, Orientation in Space I and III, Comparisons, Categorizations, Analytic Perception, Family Relations, Temporal Relations, Numerical Progressions, Instructions, Illustrations, Representational Stencil Design, Transitive Relations, and Syllogisms. Feuerstein believes that these procedures and instruments, when used together in the way he proposes, have the capability of significantly enhancing students' cognitive skills. The use of these procedures with the FIE instrument called "Organization of Dots" (OD) is now described.

Feuerstein argues that enhancing a child's cognitive abilities can have a snowballing effect in that, with these abilities enhanced, the child is capable of learning additional and even more complex cognitive operations and strategies.

OD, like the other instruments, is included in a single booklet, with each page typically presenting a series of problems for the student to solve. On the cover of the booklet is printed the slogan for the program, "Just a minute—let me think," with a drawing of a young man in thought. The booklet is divided into sections (not separately identified in the student's booklet), each emphasizing a particular cognitive skill (e.g., precision in problem analysis, ability to recognize recurring patterns) or strategy (e.g., a strategy for identifying errors). In the case of OD, the booklet presents the student with a set of dots; the student is asked to draw lines connecting the dots in a way that makes the resulting drawings match a model pattern that is presented (e.g., two squares and a triangle). The booklet contains a number of such sets, and the student is asked to complete as many sets as possible. Generally speaking, the problems get more difficult as the student works through the booklet, and some of the problems prove difficult even for college-educated adults. The following would be a typical classroom sequence:

• The students are asked to comment on the slogan ("Just a minute—let me think") that is printed on the cover of their booklet. The expectation here is that doing this will stimulate discussion of impulsive problem-solving styles and the desirability of not using such styles.

• The students' attention is directed to one of the pages in the booklet, and the students are asked to say what they think their task on that page will be. (FIE problems use a minimum of explicit instructions, and some aspects of the tasks must be inferred.) In the case of OD, some of the dots in the first few problems have already been connected and, as the discussion progresses and if students seem to be having difficulty, the instructor offers suggestions (more or less explicit, depending on the judged needs of the student at that moment) as to what the student might try next. For example, the instructor may call students' attention to certain critical features of the information already provided.

• Ordinarily, students work on the problems independently, but there is a provision for working in pairs or in groups, and the instructor circulates, providing probing questions or hints (e.g., "Is your triangle the same size as the model?").

• Students discuss their solutions to the problems they have been working on, and one or more students may be asked to present their solutions to the group. Mistakes, as well as what the instructor considers faulty approaches, are discussed with an eye to improving students' future problem-solving behavior and their awareness of the cognitive patterns they typically use.

• The instructor encourages induction by the students of general principles and provides them with examples of possible applications. For example, the instructor (or the students) might relate the organizing of the dots into patterns to the organizing of stars into constellations and, at a more abstract level, to the organizing of text material into paragraphs. This two-step process of inducing principles from the work they have carried out in performing the tasks and then applying these principles to some other content area is referred to as "bridging." Students are encouraged to generate their own bridges and to apply them to subject matter (including school subjects) that is of interest to them.

> Students are encouraged to generate their own bridges and to apply them to subject matter (including school subjects) that is of interest to them.

REVIEW OF FIE STUDIES
The Israel Studies
The first study, which was conducted in Israel in the early 1970s (Feuerstein, Rand, Hoffman, & Miller, 1979; Rand et al., 1979)[4], was a two-year field experiment using what Cook and Campbell (1979) call an "untreated control group design with pretest and posttest." In this design, subjects—in the present instance, *groups* of subjects—are assigned on a basis other than random to experimental and control conditions, are given a pretest, and then (after an experimental intervention) are given a posttest. Analysis of treatment effects uses either an analysis-of-covariance design (as here) or (as in some of the other studies discussed) a repeated-measure design, with "time of testing" being included in the design as an independent variable.

The experiment was carried out at two remedial/vocational education centers, one a residential center, the other a day school, that the Israeli government had established to provide special education for adolescents who, because of their special histories as well as their scores on various socioeconomic and ability measures (cf. Feuerstein et al., 1980; Peleg & Adler, 1977), had been characterized as "culturally disadvantaged." At each center two groups of classes were identified. One group (consisting of the experimental classes) was to receive approximately 45 minutes of FIE 3-5 days a week for 2 years (an estimated total of 200-300 hours) as an adjunct to "the usual

Aliyah curriculum," which the investigators refer to as "general enrichment" (GE). The other group (consisting of the control classes) was to receive only the GE. (It is not clear just what procedure was used in designating those groups as "experimental" and "control".) Over the 2-year period the experiment involved a total of 28 FIE classes, 11 at the residential center (7 the first year and 4 the second) and 17 at the day school (11 the first year and 6 the second). (The corresponding *ns* for the control group are not reported.) At one time or another during the two years of the experiment, some 515 students ages 12-15 were enrolled in these four (two FIE and two GE) groups; but, because there were some students who entered these groups after the experiment had started and because there were some who left before it was over, only 218 of the students (114 FIE and 104 GE) were present for the full 2-year period. (The reports do not provide data on drop-out rates from the original experimental and control groups.) From this set of 218 students, which Feuerstein et al. (1980) refer to as the "population," the investigators selected 114 [57 pairs matched on sex, ethnicity, and pretest score on Thurstone's Primary Mental Abilities (PMA) test] to serve as the sample for the study. It is the data from these 114 that were analyzed and reported in this first study.

The amount of training and supervision given to the FIE instructors appears to have been considerable. According to the investigators (cf. Feuerstein et al., 1980), these instructors took part in one (10-day) workshop during the first year and another (12-day) workshop during the second year. In addition, they were visited regularly for consultation and supervision throughout the 2 years of the experiment. The instructors taught their students both in the FIE classes and in other (academic subject matter) classes; in most classes the instructor got through 13 of the 14 available instruments.

Data were analyzed by means of a treatment (FIE vs. GE) x location (residential vs. day school) analysis of covariance, but since the residential-nonresidential variable produced almost no effects, it will not be considered further in the present review. For those measures that were administered both the pretest and posttest (Thurstone's PMA, Project Achievement Battery, two classroom participation scales, and the 3-factor Levidal Self-Concept Scale), the pretest score was used as the covariate; for those measures that were administered only as a posttest (Witkin Embedded Figures Test, Human Figure Drawing Test, Kuhlmann-Finch Postures Test, Lahy Test, Terman Nonverbal IQ, and the D-48 Test), the subject's pretest score on Thurstone's PMA (sometimes combined with another measure) was used as the covariate. Reliability coefficients are not reported, but the authors say (Feuerstein, Rand, Hoffman, & Miller, 1979, p. 544) that the measures "yielded satisfactory reliability coefficients that are reported elsewhere (see Feuerstein & Rand, Note 2)."

With respect to the pretest-posttest data, analysis of covariance showed that the FIE group had higher scores than the GE group on the PMA, both on the total score (approximately 173 vs. approximately 164) and on each of the eight subtest scores (the reports by Feuerstein et al., 1979, and Rand et al., 1979 give slightly different figures for two of the PMA subtests and the total). The difference is statistically significant in the case of the total score and three of the subtest scores ("Numbers," "Addition," and "Spatial Relations"). On the Project Achievement Battery, a set of specially-prepared measures of scholastic achievement in eight areas, FIE subjects scored higher than GE subjects in six of the eight areas; but only one of the measures (Bible) was statistically significant. The authors make the point that, although the FIE subjects did not perform any better than the GE subjects on the Project Achievement Battery, they performed just as well in spite of the fact that they had received some 300 fewer hours of academic instruction (the hours devoted to FIE) than the GE subjects had received (cf. Feuerstein et al., 1980, p. 369). On the two sets of classroom participation scales (Tannenbaum & Levine, 1968), the data were mixed: In one set, FIE students scored higher than GE students on all three subscales (significantly higher on two of them); but in the other set, the two groups did not differ on any of the subscales. Feuerstein, Rand, Hoffman, Hoffman, and Miller (1979) and Rand et al. (1979) do not provide reliability estimates for these subscales, but according to Abraham Tannenbaum (personal communication, January 4, 1985), one of the scales (the one that showed reliable treatment effects) has an estimated reliability of .90 whereas the other (the one that did not show reliable effects) has an estimated reliability of .79. Finally, on the Levidal Self-Concept scale, there were no significant differences between the two groups on any of the three factors (failure at school, motivation for learning, and confidence in personal success).

With respect to the posttest-only data, the analysis of covariance (PMA pretest as covariate) showed that on two measures of general intellectual ability (Terman nonverbal IQ and the D-48, which is a nonverbal analogies test) FIE subjects scored significantly higher than GE subjects; on the third measure (Porteus Maze Test) there was no significant difference between the two groups. On the measures of specific abilities (Embedded Figures Test, which is viewed as a measure of perceptual discrimination; Human Figure Drawing Test, which is viewed as a measure of psychological differentiation; Postures Test, which is viewed as a measure of spatial orientation; and the Lahy Test, which is viewed as a measure of rapidity-precision), FIE subjects performed significantly better than GE subjects in almost every instance. On the Terman Test there was, in addition to a treatment main effect, an interaction indicating that the treatment variable made more of a difference at the residential center than at the day school. On the Reading Comprehension subtest of the PMA there was also an interaction (though no main effect), but the pattern for that interaction is not described. Finally, a subscale from one of the two classroom interaction scales (the one that showed no main effects of FIE) showed an interaction; but his interaction is not described either.

Approximately two years after the conclusion of the study, Feuerstein and his colleagues (Feuerstein et al., 1981; Rand et al., 1981)[5] analyzed some test scores that the Army provided for 184 individuals from the original population who now were in the Army. [The authors do not say how many of the 114 [57 matched pairs) who provided the data for the original study are included in the 184]. One of the tests for which scores were provided was the Dapar, which the authors describe as a 2-part instrument consisting of "(1) a verbal intelligence test similar to the . . . Army Alpha Test and (2) a figural intelligence test similar to the Raven's Matrices Test" (Rand et al., 1981, p. 143).[6] Using subjects' scores on the Dapar as a dependent measure (separate scores for verbal and nonverbal parts are not reported), the authors performed a series of three analyses.

In the first analysis the subject's earlier PMA pretest score was used as a covariance, and the investigators performed a covariate analysis on the Dapar test scores and found that those who had been in the FIE group scored significantly higher (about two-thirds of a standard deviation higher, on the average) than the ones who had been in the GE group.

In the second analysis, the investigators cast the total group into a 2 x 2 x 2 matrix according to (a) whether they had been through FIE or GE; (b) whether their pretest PMA scores were above or below the median for the group as a whole; and (c) whether their Army Dapar scores were above or below the Armywide mean (93 were above, 91 were below), which was also the cutoff point for selecting individuals to become officers. A chi square analysis of the cell frequencies indicated that significantly more experimentals than controls were in the top half of the Dapar distribution, and this was the case both for those who were in the top half of the (PMA) pretest distribution and for those who were in the bottom half. Of the GE students who were in the top group on the PMA pretest ($n = 58$), approximately 57% were in the top group on the Dapar also; but of the FIE students who were in the top group on the pretest ($n = 34$), some 88% were also in the top group on the Dapar. Of the GE students who were in the bottom group on the PMA pretest ($n = 31$), approximately 87% were in the bottom group on the Dapar also; but if the FIE students who were in the bottom group on the pretest ($n = 61$), only 54% were in the bottom group on the Dapar also.

In the third analysis the authors sought evidence on what they termed the "divergent effects hypothesis," the hypothesis that FIE effects are not only maintained but actually increase over time. The authors sought to test this hypothesis using a procedure that unfortunately is described in only one or two sentences. Apparently, however, the procedure involved identifying individuals ($n = 163$) for whom scores were available for all four test periods [pretest (PMA), first-year posttest (PMA), second-year posttest (PMA), and follow-up (Dapar)], standardizing subjects' scores on PMA and on Dapar, computing difference scores at each of the four time periods, and performing a trend analysis on these differences. (Some things about the analysis are not clear. For example, the authors imply that these difference scores were obtained from matched pairs of subjects but do not explain why the N used in the analysis is an odd number.) The result of this analysis, which the authors (Feuerstein et al., 1981) report in a single sentence, was that "The obtained linear function was confirmed by trend analysis, which yielded a highly significant ($p < .000$) linear trend and no significant quadratic trend." [The corresponding statement in the other report of this study (Rand et al., 1981) is similar.]

This study is interesting, particularly in its use of nonverbal measures of intellectual abilities, its effort to measure overt behavior in a nontest situation, and its effort to follow up subjects some 2 years after the intervention had ended. The results of the study, however, lend themselves to more than one interpretation. Examination of experimental/control-group differences show that these differences tend to be larger and more clear-cut on those measures that are most similar in content to the FIE materials used in the intervention (e.g., the PMA subtest on spatial relations, the D-48, and the Embedded Figures Test). One must ask (particularly with regard to the measures of intellectual ability) whether the study produced anything more than mastery of near-transfer or "practice effects" (cf. Anastasi, 1981; Messick & Jungeblut, 1981), that is, whether the real effect of the intervention was simply to improve subjects' ability to solve problems of the type found on tests such as those used in the study. (A similar concern is expressed by Bransford et al., 1985, and by Campione, Brown, and Ferrara, 1982). The study did include measures of behavior in a nontest situation (classroom participation scales); but these measures consisted of ratings given by individuals (the regular classroom teachers) who were aware of the experimental/control status of the students who were being rated. The measures were therefore not independent and cannot be viewed as providing evidence concerning behavioral effects of FIE. The follow-up data are consistent with the idea that FIE effects (however they are interpreted) are lasting, but the fact that pretest and posttest data were obtained with different instruments introduced at least a degree of uncertainty. There are also the more general questions of what one does about the increased probability of

> This study is interesting, particularly in its use of nonverbal behavior in a nontest situation, and its effort to follow up subjects some 2 years after the intervention had ended.

Type-I error when multiple *F* tests are performed (we counted over 100 in the present study), and whether observed experimental/control-group differences, even where statistically reliable, are large enough to warrant scientific or educational attention (cf. Bradley, 1983). There are the more general questions of how one interprets data statistically when there has been no random assignment (in the case of many of the measures used, no pretest either) and how one deals with the absence of data on experimental attrition and on the psychometric properties, in the subject population, of the measures used. These latter questions, however, could be asked of most of the studies discussed in this review. Finally, there is the question of how one should interpret the study's failure to find statistically significant effects on measures that one would have expected to show such effects (e.g., the majority of the PMA subtests and the three self-concept measures). In the case of the self-concept measures, for example, the authors have elsewhere said (Feuerstein & Jensen, 1980) that one of the program's subgoals "consists in changing drastically the student's perception of himself or herself from a passive recipient of information to an active producer, creator, and generator of new information. This is probably the central goal of our program . . ." (p. 429).

> ... the reports of these studies are striking and suggest the possibility ... that FIE is capable of producing some lasting improvement in the ability of some students to do well on at least some measures of intellectual ability.

What then can be said about the results of these two (initial and follow-up) studies? Taken together, the reports of these studies are striking and suggest the possibility (at least with culturally disadvantaged students) that FIE is capable of producing some lasting improvement in the ability of some students to do well on at least some measures of intellectual ability. As indicated above, however, such things as the seeming relationship between FIE-material/dependent-measure-material similarity and the magnitude or statistical significance of treatment effects, plus the absence of some effects one would have expected to find, indicate that these results can be interpreted in more than one way.

The Venezuela Studies[7]

In replication of the original Feuerstein study (Feuerstein, Rand, Hoffman, Hoffman, & Miller, 1979; Rand et al., 1979), Ruiz and Castaneda (1983) administered FIE to a sample of Venezuelan children, ages 10-14, over the 2-year period 1980-82. From the population of public and private schools in the city of Guayana the investigators randomly selected 12 schools—six considered middle class ("high SES") and six considered low ("low SES")—and in each group randomly assigned the schools to experimental and control conditions. Some of the schools had more than one class at the desired (fifth grade) level, and in each of the four (FIE/control x low-/ high-SES) cells there were three schools/four classes. Instructors for the eight FIE classes (one instructor for each class) were given special training; and over the following 2 years these instructors devoted one hour each day, 5 days a week, to FIE, making a total of about 275 hours (11 FIE instruments). Except for this daily one hour of FIE, experimental and control classes were exposed to the same (standard) fifth-grade (and, later, sixth-grade) curriculum.

Subjects were pretested and (2 years later) posttested on (a) the Cattell-2 intelligence test (in the subject population, reliability estimates for the total test range from .82 to .87); (b) the BARA test (a combined language and math achievement test that in the subject population has reliability estimates of .70 and .80 for the language and math subtests, and .85 for the total); (c) a three-factor (personal, social, intellectual) self-concept inventory (overall reliability estimated for the subject population is .91); and (d) a three-factor (adaptiveness to work demands, self-sufficiency, and interpersonal conduct) classroom-participation scale (a combined adaptation of the two classroom participation scales that were used in the Israel study) filled out on the students by their teachers and by visiting supervisors (total test reliability estimate in the subject population is .91). In addition, the authors constructed an index of socioeconomic status (SES) and, based on responses to the items making up the index, subjects were classified as high or low in SES. At the end of the 2-year period the investigators, separately within each SES category, selected pairs of students, one from an experimental class and one from a control class, who were similar in age, sex, SES, and pretest score on the

Cattell-2 test. The results of this pairing was that there were 170 pairs in the high-SES group and 148 pairs in the low-SES group, making 636 subjects altogether. Data were analyzed by analysis of covariance, with Cattell-2 pretest scores (and age) being used to adjust dependent-measure scores on the Cattell-2 pretest scores (and age) being used to adjust dependent-measure scores on the Cattell-2 and BARA tests, with self-concept pretest scores being used to adjust dependent-measure scores on the self-concept inventory, and with classroom-participation pretest scores being used to adjust dependent-measures scores on the classroom-participation scales. The covariance analyses indicated that FIE subjects scored significantly higher than controls on the Cattell-2, the BARA, and the classroom-participation measures. FIE subjects also scored higher than controls on the combined three-factor self-concept measure; but no one of these self-concept factors, by itself, showed a significant treatment or interaction effect. In the case of the BARA test there was an interaction indicating that the treatment effect was clearer in the high-SES than in the low-SES group, with the simple effect for the low-SES group not being significant. And on each of the three classroom-participation factors there was an interaction indicating that the treatment effect was clearer in the low-SES than in the high-SES condition, but here the simple effect was significant in both SES groups.

In 1983 and again in 1984, one and two years after the end of the intervention, the investigators collected follow-up data on those of their original 636 subjects who were still available (Ruiz, 1985a). These subjects (234 in 1983 and 180 in 1984) were given the Cattell-2 test, the Lorge-Thorndike test of general intelligence (nonverbal, level 4), and the D-48 (described as a nonverbal test of ability to conceptualize and apply systematic reasoning to new problems). As indicated above, the Cattell-2 is a nonverbal test of general intelligence and is generally viewed as having satisfactory reliability estimates. The Lorge Thorndike, level 4, consists of three subtests: figure classification, number series, and figure analogies. Reliability estimates in the subject population range from .77 to .92, and its correlation with other intelligence tests ranges from .79 to .81. The D-48 has reliability estimates ranging from .85 to .91.

In 1984, the investigators selected from those former subjects still available (separately within each SES group) pairs of subjects, one who had been in one of the experimental classes and one who had been in one of the control classes, who were similar in age, sex, and score on Cattell-2B (total $N = 114$). These 114 (57 pairs) were the subjects who provided data for the three analyses that made up the second-year follow-up study.

First analysis. A covariance analysis was performed on the second-year follow-up scores on the Lorge-Thorndike and the D-48, with Cattell-2 pretest score (and age) used as a covariate. The results indicated significant treatment effects on the Cattell-2 and the Lorge-Thorndike but not on the D-48; and although there was a main effect of SES on all three variables, there were no treatment x SES interactions.

Second analysis. Following the general procedure used by Feuerstein (Feuerstein et al., 1981; Rand et al, 1981), the investigators classified their 57 (matched) pairs as high or low on the Cattell-2 pretest (using the mean as the cutting point) and, within each group, classified individual subjects as high or low on the Lorge-Thorndike follow-up measure (again using the mean as the cutting point). As in the Israel follow-up study (Feuerstein et al., 1981; Rand et al., 1981), a chi square analysis of the cell frequencies indicated that significantly more of the experimentals than the controls were in the top half of the follow-up distribution, and this was the case both for those who were high on pretest scores and for those who were low. Of the control subjects who were in the top group on the pretest ($n = 25$), 44% were in the top group on the follow-up measures also; but of the FIE subjects who were in the top group on the pretest ($n = 25$), 80% were in the top group on the follow-up. Of the control subjects who were in the bottom group on the pretest ($n = 32$), 69% were in the bottom group on the follow-up measure also; but of the FIE subjects who were in the bottom group on the pretest ($n = 32$), 34% were in the bottom group on the follow-up.

Third analysis. To provide evidence on the divergent effects hypothesis, the authors did the following: (a) identified subjects' scores from four testing periods (Cattell-2A pretest, Cattell-2B posttest, Lorge-Thorndike first-year follow-up, and Lorge-Thorndike second-year follow-up); (b) converted to z-

scores the raw scores obtained on each of these tests; (c) computed an FIE-minus-control difference score for each of the matched pairs at each of the four test periods; and (d) performed a trend analysis. The authors report the results of this analysis (the relevant descriptive statistics are not presented) by saying that the linear component is statistically significant ("$p < .000$") but the quadratic component is not.

In 1983 FIE was administered to a sample of post-secondary-school students who were enrolled in remedial math and languages courses at the Guayana Technical Institute and who had an average IQ of about 85 (Ruiz, 1985b). These students ($n = 86$) were randomly assigned to experimental (FIE) and control (non-FIE) classes (one class in each case), with the experimental group receiving an hour of FIE each day during the 17-week semester (about 85 hours total). FIE was taught by three specially trained instructors (not the regular classroom teachers) who had taken part in an earlier study (Ruiz & Castaneda, 1983). These instructors rotated teaching the FIE classes, each instructor being used every third day. Nine of the 14 FIE instruments were used, the nine being grouped into blocks of three, and each day the instructor used a page from each of the instruments in a given block. The blocks were rotated throughout the semester, the sequence being blocks 1, 2, 3, 1, and so forth. The time not devoted to FIE teaching was spent in regular remedial classes. Subjects were pretested and posttested on the Cattell-2 test of general intelligence, and posttest scores were subjected to an analysis of covariance, with pretest scores serving as the covariate. Experimental subjects scored significantly higher than controls.

The Venezuela studies are similar in many aspects to those conducted in Israel (Feuerstein, Rand, Hoffman, Hoffman & Miller, 1979; Feuerstein et al., 1981; Rand et al., 1979; Rand et al., 1981). There are, however, some important differences. First, the study was conducted in a different country with a different culture and traditions. Second, although the basic replication was conducted with students approximately the same age as the students who got the FIE intervention in the Israel studies (i.e., approximately ages 12-15), one of the Venezuela studies was conducted with post-secondary-school students and thus provides some evidence about possible effects in a somewhat older group. Third, with respect to the basic replication, the subjects used in the Israel studies came from a culturally disadvantaged population whereas the subjects used in the Venezuela studies (or, rather, the schools attended by these subjects) were selected randomly from the total set of schools in the city. The results of the Venezuela studies are generally consistent with those found earlier in the Israel studies. FIE-control differences were again found on a nonverbal (though different) measure of general intelligence, and, on two of the three follow-up measures of intelligence, group differences were observable some 2 years after the end of the intervention. And, as before, the authors report that a trend analysis shows differences that are not simply maintained over the 4-year period, but actually get larger. The Venezuela study found a fairly clear effect on the achievement test whereas the Israel study did not, but there are some possibly important differences between the tests used in the two studies. The Israel study used what might be referred to as an "omnibus" achievement test (general knowledge, Bible, geometry, reading, arithmetic, etc.) where the Venezuela study used a test consisting of only two (math and language) subjects. Finally, the Venezuelan adaptation of the classroom participation scale used in the Israel study found clear and consistent effects favoring the FIE group. Again, however, the measures consisted of ratings given by individuals (the regular classroom teacher plus, in this study, another member of the project staff) who were aware of the experimental/control status of the students who were being rated. According to the first author of the report (personal communication, April 19, 1985), the rating procedure was supplemented by the use of videotape, but it is unfortunately not clear just how this videotaping was used or what role it played in the measurement process. Taken as a whole, the results of the Venezuela studies (like the results of the Israel studies) are striking and suggest the possibility that FIE can produce lasting improvement in some students' ability to do

> **FIE-control differences were again found on a nonverbal (though different) measure of general intelligence, and, on two of the three follow-up measures of intelligence, group differences were observable some 2 years after the end of the intervention.**

well on at least some nonverbal measures of intelligence. As indicated above, however, these results can be interpreted in more than one way.

Studies from the Nashville Center

A programmatic effort consisting mainly of several one-year studies (plus a pilot study and several studies investigating the locus of cognitive change, which we have not discussed here) was carried out by a group of individuals associated with the John. F. Kennedy Center of Vanderbilt University. According to the investigators, several of these (one-year) studies were intended to be simply the first year of a 2-year study. The investigators write:

> Unfortunately for us, the Nashville public school system has been undergoing some upheaval, and it has been extremely difficult to continue classes intact for the second year of IE; therefore, we have repeated the first year with a succession of different groups and have very few data on the two-year program. (Haywood et al., 1982)

Note also that these investigators conducted a number of smaller studies (cf. Arbitman-Smith et al., 1984; Haywood et al., 1982) seeking to assess FIE recipients' mastery of the materials and procedures they had been taught, as well as their ability to apply these principles to everyday problems and tasks. In one study (Haywood et al., 1982, pp. 17-18), for example, educable mentally retarded (EMR) students were given either no FIE ($n = 10$), 10 hours of FIE ($n = 10$), or 67 hours of FIE ($n = 10$), and then given a behavioral measure of task persistence. Examination of the resulting data indicated that the 67-hour group persisted longer and worked more efficiently than the 10-hour group, which in turn persisted longer and worked more efficiently than the no-FIE group, and that the set of differences was statistically significant. Studies like these are valuable, although interpretation is difficult because of the absence of information about how the three groups were formed and whether the overall trend and/or the individual contrasts are significant.

Data were collected in classes of various sorts in Nashville, Louisville, and Phoenix, although in most cases data from two or more studies are presented in a single report. The reports of these studies (Arbitman-Smith & Haywood, 1980; Arbitman-Smith et al., 1984; Haywood & Arbitman-Smith, 1981; Haywood et al., 1982) vary in their completeness, and none provides all the information needed for full understanding. It is not always clear in particular studies, for example, how many of the FIE instruments were used, how many subjects were involved, which dependent variables were measured, how large an effect a given difference represents, or what the effects were (if any) of experimental attrition. Also, although "type of disability" was usually included in the design as an independent variable, data are not provided on the statistical reliability of treatment x type-of-disability interactions. Essentially, however, the studies were carried out on students, ages 11-15, whose mean educational achievement was 2-7 years below what would be expected for students of their age. The design appears in the main to have been similar to the one used in the original Israel study, that is, an untreated control group design with pretest and posttest.[8]

FIE instructors at the three sites were all given about the same amount of training (80-plus hours before the start of the school year as well as follow-up supervision and consultation). In certain respects, however, the studies conducted in Phoenix were different from those conducted in Nashville and in Louisville. In the first place, in Phoenix the FIE classes were taught by regular classroom teachers who during the rest of the day taught the students in other classes, also, whereas in Nashville the practice was to use "itinerant" FIE teachers, who in most cases had the students only for FIE. (It is not entirely clear which of these practices was followed in the Louisville studies.) In the second place, at the Nashville schools, the investigators said they were unable to get much more than 50 hours of FIE, "while in the other sites, especially in Phoenix, a minimum of 80 hours—and often many more—has been the rule" (Haywood et al., 1982, p. 21). In the third place, the subjects in Phoenix, most of whom where children of Mexican-American migrant farm workers, "most closely resembled the Israeli immigrant population on which Instrumental Enrichment was developed and originally tested" (Haywood & Arbitman-Smith, 1981, p. 132). In the fourth place, there was apparently a difference in the way students at the two (sets of)

locations were assigned to FIE and non-FIE groups. At the
Phoenix site, "administrative policy was to assume that FIE
would be an effective remedial treatment and therefore to
assign lowest-achieving students to IE, with the result that the
initial scores on criterion instruments always favored the
comparison groups" (Haywood et al., 1982, p. 11). Because of
this fact, at least some of the post-treatment differences at this
site could be attributed to differential experimental regression.
Since these differences were thought by the investigators to have
been responsible for the differences between the results
obtained in Phoenix and the results obtained in Nashville and
Louisville (Haywood et al., 1982), the data collected at the two
(sets of) locations will be discussed separately.

Data collected in Phoenix. The students who took part in
this study ($N = 70$ during the first year) were, as indicated
above, mostly the children of migrant farm workers; during the
first year those in the experimental group received more than 80
hours of FIE from teachers who taught them in other classes
also. On the two measures administered, the Lorge-Thorndike
Nonverbal IQ and the Ravens Matrices, FIE students consistently showed greater gains than the control students with
whom they were compared; with one exception (gains on the
Lorge-Thorndike in the tutored controls) the difference was
statistically significant. During the following year (the N was
now down to 36) examination of the data showed that the
previously-observed differences between FIE and controls were
still in evidence.

Data collected in Nashville and Louisville. As part of the
study that collected data in Phoenix, data were also collected in
Nashville ($N = 47$) and Louisville ($N = 98$). This study found no
consistent effects on either the Lorge-Thorndike or the
Reasoning subtest of the PMA (the two tests of general
intelligence that were used), or on any of several other measures
that were administered. In a second Nashville study (N not
specified) reliable effects were not found on PMA but were
found on Ravens Matrices and four of the five subtests of the
Woodcock-Johnson Psycho-Educational Battery (the fifth being
Perceptual Speed). The authors comment that the failure to
find significant effects on this last subtest is not surprising since
FIE students are explicitly taught to "stop and think." Actually,
one could predict either way here and perhaps different ways in

different situations. One could certainly hypothesize that this "stopping to think" would result in a student's spending more time on the test as a whole, but one could also hypothesize the opposite, namely, that the student would arrive at satisfying answers to the questions more quickly and, as a result, have to spend less time on the test as a whole. Another consideration here is that FIE emphasizes adaptability; one would presumably predict that, if FIE is effective, experimental students would respond more appropriately to the time demands (or the absence of such demands) than the controls. In any event, 2 years later when the N was down to an unspecified number, follow-up measures found no experimental/control-group differences.

Conclusions. Although these studies appear to have been well-conceived and well-designed, one cannot, because of the great variability in outcomes and the lack of information needed for full interpretation, be very confident in drawing conclusions about the studies. One is inclined, however, to agree with the investigators that the differing procedures used at Nashville and Louisville, versus those used at Phoenix, were instrumental in producing the differing patterns of results at the two (sets of) locations. What these patterns suggest is that FIE can improve performance on standard nonverbal IQ-type measures: (a) when it is used by teachers who are also teaching the students some other subject matter and are thus able to apply the relevant principles ("bridge") to some subject matter that has its own identity, and (b) when students get a significant degree of exposure (perhaps 80 hours or more in a given year). Neither of these conditions was found in the Nashville studies, and at least one of them was absent in the Louisville studies; it is therefore not surprising that at these sites FIE effects were generally inconsistent or nonexistent. Both of the conditions, however, were found at the Phoenix site, where results consistently favored the FIE group.

Other Nashville Studies

J. N. Hall (1982) set up three groups consisting of students age 12 and older who were enrolled in a special education program in the Nashville/Davidson County Public Schools. One group (3 classes, total $n = 33$) was given FIE; a second group (6 classes, total $n = 55$) was given an intervention called "social learning curriculum" (SLC), and a third group (6 classes, total $n = 55$) was given its usual program and considered a comparison group for the other two. Regular class instructors were given FIE training (amount of time not specified) in a workshop that met before and during the intervention, which continued for the full school year. FIE students, going through a total of four FIE instruments, received FIE instruction one period a day each day, making about 4 hours a week altogether. Data were analyzed by analysis of covariance, with pretest scores on the various dependent variables being used as covariates. FIE students showed significantly greater gains (i.e., greater reduction in the number of errors) than the comparison students on the Matching Familiar Figures Test and on the general information subtest of the Peabody Individual Achievement Test, but there were no effects on the Ravens Progressive Matrices, the Test of Social Inference, a nonstandardized "test of social knowledge," and the Piers-Harris Children's Self-Concept Scale. The author comments that the absence (as well as the presence) of effects in this study is difficult to interpret because of the occurrence of several "threats to validity," for example, the low statistical power of the tests that were used, the fact that none of the criterion measures had been standardized on groups similar to the (EMR) students she was using, and the non-uniformity of treatment implementation.

McRainey (1983), who studied not thinking skills but social outcomes, arranged to have the University School of Nashville devote one of its enrichment classes ($n = 17$) to FIE and to use an enrichment class in dramatic arts ($n = 19$) as a comparison group. Pretest scores on the Ravens indicated that the two groups were not significantly different on that measure. There were approximately 30 40-minute class sessions and, altogether, the FIE group received about 20 hours on four of the FIE instruments. At both the beginning and the end of the course, students' social behavior was rated (pretest $r = .89$) by the FIE and dramatic arts teachers, as well as by other teachers who taught the students in other courses. When judged by their experimental or control group teacher, students in the former group showed significantly more improvement than students in the latter group; but when judged by their other teachers the two groups did not differ significantly. In other words, where experimental subjects were rated by the teacher who had provided the experimental treatment (as contrasted with controls, who had had no particular involvement in the FIE program), improvement ratings for the experimentals were higher than those of the controls; but when both experimental and control students were rated by teachers who had had no particular involvement in the program, these differences were not found. A second measure was a classroom environment scale consisting of 90 true/false statements (information about the scale's psycho-metric properties was not provided) to be responded to by the students. Pretest-posttest comparisons on this scale showed no experimental effects.

When judged by their experimental or control group teacher, students in the former group showed signficantly more improvement than students in the latter group; but when judged by their other teachers, the two groups did not differ significantly.

What can be said about the results of these other Nashville studies? In one case (J. N. Hall, 1982) the results are mixed; but as the author notes these results are difficult to interpret. Also, the number of FIE instruments used was only four and the adequacy of the instructor training period is difficult to assess. In the other case (McRainey, 1983) the author was studying not thinking skills but "social outcomes," and in that study—possibly because of the relatively small amount of exposure to FIE (20 hours and 4 FIE instruments)—there were no easily interpretable effects.

Studies from Toronto

In a study conducted with 150 ninth-grade students at a "city-core, multi-ethnic" school in Toronto, Graham (1981) assigned classes in remedial-English ($n = 2$) and common-English ($n = 4$) to FIE and control conditions, with FIE classes ($n = 3$) getting 3 hours a week of FIE and 2 hours of remedial or common English for the duration of the school year. Control classes ($n = 3$) received remedial or common English 5 days a week. (Graham, 1981, says that the school administration assigned students to the various English classes, presumably within class type, but does not say how these classes were then designated as experimental and control.) During the course of the year the experimental subjects were exposed to six FIE instruments. Each teacher taught only one (FIE or control) class and the author began, appropriately, by testing the data for between-teacher and between-class effects. Based on the results of this testing, the author decided that some of the dependent measures (those that had shown such effects) could not be used. The remaining data, which the author analyzed with some misgivings, were examined by means of an analysis-of-covariance design, with pretest scores used as covariates. The results of this analysis showed FIE students scoring reliably higher than controls on the remaining measure (Lorge-Thorndike, test 3), with five times as many FIE students as controls reaching the ceiling for this test.

In a second study, Yitzhak (1981) administered FIE to learning-disabled students, ages 14-16, at each of two vocational high schools, with other learning-disabled students at these schools serving as controls. The FIE students, who were given FIE by their regular classroom teachers, were exposed during the year to four instruments (number of FIE hours not indicated). The total N for the two schools was initially 66, but by the end of the year the number had dropped to 51. FIE effects, which were measured on Piaget-type conservation tasks using multivariate and univariate analyses of covariance, were not significant.

Narrol, Silverman, and Waksman (1982) administered FIE to five classes of low-performing vocational high school students, with four other classes at these schools serving as controls. The total N was 102, with one of the control classes serving as a comparison for two of the experimental classes. Experimental classes received one hour of FIE each day 5 days a week for the school year, and during the year they were exposed to four FIE instruments. Data were obtained, using an analysis-of-covariance design, on Lorge-Thorndike (level 3), PMA (letter series), the Piers & Harris self-concept scale, a locus-of-control measure, and a measure of school morale. The design consists essentially of a set of five nonequivalent pretest-posttest control-group designs (rather than, as in several of the other studies, a single design), with approximately 40 subjects in each design.

On the Lorge-Thorndike all differences favored the FIE group, and in three of the comparisons the difference was statistically significant. On the PMA (letter series) all differences again favored the FIE group, and four of these comparisons were statistically significant. On the self-concept measure, and on the locus-of-control measure, none of the differences was statistically significant. On the school morale measure two of the five differences were statistically significant, and both of these differences favored the FIE group.

> Several studies, including a pilot (Martin, 1984a), have been carried out using hearing-impaired students at the Model Secondary School for the Deaf.

What can be said regarding the Toronto studies? Generalizations are difficult, in part because not all the information about dosage is provided in each study. One notes, however, that both of the studies that reported fairly clear experimental effects (Graham, 1981); Narrol et al., 1982) seem to have provided more than 80 hours of FIE (in one case, perhaps up to 150), and one of them used six of the 14 available instruments.

Other Studies

Several studies, including a pilot (Martin, 1984a), have been carried out using hearing-impaired students at the Model Secondary School for the Deaf (MSSD). One of these was a 2-year (1982-84) study, the first year of which is reported in Jonas and Martin (1985). In that study, FIE was given each day, 2-3 days a week during the school year to 50 MSSD students in Math and English classes; a similar number of students in these kinds of classes served as controls. Four of the FIE instruments were used. By the end of the year, 41 students remained in the experimental group and 47 remained in the comparison group; for each of the experimental subjects the investigators identified a comparison group member who could be matched on sex, age, and level of class placement (remedial, regular, or advanced). These 82 students (41 matched pairs) were the ones who provided first-year data for that experiment. Dependent measures included Ravens Progressive Matrices; diagramming and letter-set tests from the Kit of Factor Referenced Cognitive Tests (KFRCT); three problem statements requiring written solutions; and the reading-comprehension, math-concepts, and math-computations subtests from the Stanford Achievement

Test for Hearing Impaired (SAT-HI). At the end of the year, FIE gains on the Ravens were significantly greater than the corresponding gains in the comparison group. Data for the SAT-HI, however, were not available at the time of the initial report. The investigators have recently reported additional data from the study. In this more recent report (Jonas & Martin, 1984) the investigators report that FIE effects on Ravens scores continue to be observed at the end of the second year, by which time a total of eight FIE instruments have been used, and that the (2-year) data on SAT-HI indicate significant effects on these measures also. With respect to the KFRCT, no FIE effects were found; with respect to the three problem statements (average inter-rater $r = .82$), effects were found for one but not the other two.[9]

McDaniel (1983) examined FIE effects in a sample of 70 students in self-contained EMR classes in an urban school system who were mainly male, low SES, and black, and who ranged in age from 10 to 15. (Seventy is the number of students who were available for the full period. The author does not mention attrition, but one assumes that the original n was greater than this.) Thirty-three of these students were in classes exposed to 25 hours of FIE, and in these classes students were trained on the FIE Numerical Progression instrument (20 hours) and on variations of the Ravens Matrices (5 hours). The remaining 37 students were in other classes that were used for comparison. FIE teachers were given FIE training in two 2-hour workshops. Pretest-posttest comparisons indicated that FIE students showed significantly more improvement on the Ravens Matrices and on the mathematics subsection of the Stanford Achievement Test than did the comparison group, but no greater improvement than the comparison group on the Columbia Test of Mental Maturity. The data suggest that these EMR students were capable of learning the kinds of things they were taught (at least, when they are taught with FIE procedures), but because of the similarity of instructional and testing materials the data provide little evidence about the efficacy of FIE as a method of teaching thinking skills.

Brainin (1982) studied FIE effects with 49 underachieving sixth-grade youngsters in Westchester County in New York. Students had been randomly assigned to four small-core classes that had been set up for students who were reading at more than 2 years below grade level. The FIE group consisted of two classes (total $n = 27$), as did the comparison group ($n = 22$). In the experimental classes FIE was given for 30 minutes to an hour, 2-3 days a week, for about 59 hours (four instruments) total for the year. These teachers, the FIE students' regular teachers in these classes, received about 50 hours of training and consultation. Experimental effects were found on a criterion-referenced test developed by the investigator (internal consistency = .76), indicating that the experimental subjects had learned the special material they had been taught. With respect to the primary dependent variables, pretest-posttest comparisons found no evidence of an experimental effect on the Thorndike-Hagen Cognitive Abilities Test or the Devereaux Elementary School Behavior Rating Scale, but did find evidence of an effect on the Total Reading Score of the Comprehensive Test of Basic Skills.

Genasci (1984) examined FIE effects in two samples: (a) 88 high-achieving seventh and eighth graders (46 experimental and 42 comparison) at four regular high schools; and (b) 38 students, ages 15-18 (29 experimental and 9 comparison), from learning-center classrooms in 10 "alternative" high schools. Students at the regular high schools had suffered 18% attrition (21% in the experimental group and 16% in the control group), whereas students at the alternative high schools had suffered 63% attrition (66% in the experimental group and 59% in the control group). The (high-achieving) students at the regular high schools were given FIE 2-3 days a week by their regular math and computer science teacher (about 22 hours total) with the other 2-3 days each week being devoted to the regular (math, algebra, and computer science) course subject matter. Students at the alternative high schools were also given FIE 2-3 days a week (about 19 hours total), but for these students, FIE was given by someone other than their regular teacher, that is, an "itinerant" teacher who came to the school just for the FIE instruction. In each group, five FIE instruments were used. For the (high-achieving) students from the regular high school there were no effects on a measure of academic self-confidence, and there was no effect on the total score of the Primary Mental Abilities (PMA) test. On the PMA verbal subtest, however, significantly more improvement was shown by the FIE than by the comparison students. For the alternative high school students there were no effects at all.

Muttart (1984) administered FIE (three instruments) to seventh- and eighth-grade students in remedial programs over a period of nine months, with FIE being given 2-3 hours per week. The author does not say how experimental and control groups were constituted except to say that the original N was 22 and that the final ns were 9 (experimental) and 8 (control). The two groups were compared by t test on measures of intelligence (PMA total), academic achievement (composite score on Canadian Test of Basic Skills), and self-concept (Brookover Self-Concept of Ability Scale, St. John Academic Self-Concept Scale, Achievement Self-Esteem, and Lipsett Self-Concept Scale). Significant differences favoring the FIE group were found on the achievement measure and no one of the four self-concept measures.

What can be said about these five "other" studies? It should be noted first that one of the studies was conducted with a population (hearing-impaired) not used in previous studies. In that study, which used the regular teachers, administered FIE for 2 years, and used eight instruments, the original finding with respect to nonverbal measures was replicated. Second, two of the studies (one involving high-achieving and the other involving underachieving students) produced mixed effects. In both these studies the number of hours and the number of instruments were relatively small, but in each of the studies the students were given FIE by individuals who taught them in other classes also and who were able to use FIE principles during these other class sessions. The remaining studies, which provided relatively small dosages of FIE and used special rather than regular teachers, found no effects.

DISCUSSION

This paper has reviewed FIE studies conducted in Israel, Venezuela, Canada, and the United States. Many of these studies failed to find clear FIE effects and most, for one reason or another (e.g., weakness of the experimental intervention, conflicting outcomes on different measures, inadequacies of experimental control, insufficiencies in the information provided), are difficult to interpret. Within the total set of studies, however, there is a subset that produced data that are striking and suggest that FIE may indeed be having an effect even though it is not clear (as discussed further below) just what this effect means. What we have done in this concluding section is (a) state several generalizations and conclusions about FIE effects that, in spite of the various insufficiencies, seem reasonable and appropriate; (b) identify some questions for programmatic FIE research on FIE; and (c) indicate some of the things that would make future FIE studies more readily interpretable.

Some Generalizations and Conclusions about FIE Effects

1.   Statistically significant FIE/comparison group differences have been observed in a number of populations: in at least four countries (Canada, Israel, United States, and Venezuela), in middle and low social class groups, in groups considered normal as well as groups considered culturally or educationally disadvantaged, and in groups classified as hearing impaired.

2.   The effects most commonly reported in these studies have been effects on certain standard nonverbal measures of intelligence (tests such as PMA, Lorge-Thorndike, Cattell, and Ravens that are largely measures of skill in processing figural and spatial information). Effects on other types of measures (e.g., self-esteem, impulsivity, classroom behavior, academic achievement, course content) have been absent, inconsistent, or difficult to interpret.

3.   The effects that have been reported have been observed almost entirely with individuals who were in elementary or secondary school (and in the 12-18 age range) at the time they were exposed to FIE. A few studies have used college or college-age subjects, but, with one exception that we know about (Ruiz, 1985b), the intervention used in the studies has been too weak to provide a satisfactory test. This exception, however, since it showed the predicted experimental/comparison group differences, suggests that FIE may be able to produce effects with individuals who are beyond adolescence.

4.   Studies showing experimental/comparison group differences have had a number of things in common: at least a week of training for FIE instructors; generally 80 hours or more of student exposure to FIE over a 1- or 2-year period; and FIE

taught in conjunction with some other subject matter of interest and importance to the student. Sometimes this latter was accomplished by having the instructor designate, say, 2 hours each week for course subject matter instruction and 3 days for FIE (usually with a different instructor teaching the FIE); and sometimes it was accomplished by selecting teachers who had their students most or all of the school day and having these teachers devote, say, one period each day to FIE.

Some Questions for Future Research
The first question is whether interpretable FIE effects can be reliably demonstrated in a population similar to the one in which they were originally studied, that is, in a population of culturally and educationally disadvantaged adolescents. By "interpretable FIE effects" we mean effects that, by consensus, would be said to confirm the hypotheses advanced by FIE theorists. Such effects would go beyond the standard intelligence test scores that have shown most of the FIE effects to date and include supporting data of at least three kinds. One would be data that go beyond near-transfer effects (effects on measures that are similar to the experimental materials but systematically different in certain ways, e.g., showing that one can discriminate differences after having been taught to discriminate similarities) to far-transfer effects (effects on measures of capabilities and behaviors different from those taught in the FIE course, e.g., ability to formulate and carry out a plan of action). A second kind (though it could be viewed as an instance of the first kind) would be data on ability to learn when placed in one or more standard learning situations. Ability to learn is an important part of Feuerstein's system, and failure to be able to show improvement in this ability would cast serious doubt on the validity of FIE. A third kind would be data on snowballing (the increasing magnitude of FIE effects over time). This is perhaps the central concept of Feuerstein's theory, and here again it is essential for the theory to demonstrate it unambiguously. As indicated above, there are data consistent with this concept, but the results need to be replicated with additional controls, with more appropriate measures, and with pretest and follow-up measures drawn from the same population of measures. If these effects can be demonstrated—if it can be shown that FIE is effective in

producing the kinds of effects Feuerstein and his colleagues say it can produce—then a number of interesting question such as the following arise.

1. Is FIE effectiveness related to age and, if so, what is the nature and direction of the relationship? And is there a single relationship, or is there a whole family of relationships depending on the level of some other factor, for example, initial level of intellectual functioning?

2. To what extent can FIE effects be observed in other populations, for example, the mentally retarded or above-average intellectual ability? It has been suggested that FIE can help mentally retarded individuals if the program is slowed down sufficiently, with more hours being devoted to fewer instruments, but this has yet to be demonstrated.

Ability to learn is an important part of Feuerstein's system, and failure to be able to show improvement in this ability would cast serious doubt on the validity of FIE.

3. Why have measures of self-esteem failed (for the most part) to show FIE effects? As noted earlier, self-esteem is considered an important construct in FIE theory.

4. How much FIE instruction on how many instruments is needed to produce the effects intended by FIE theorists? As noted earlier, Feuerstein and others have suggested that up to 300 hours over a period of 3 years may be needed, but it has also been suggested that a shorter period may be sufficient, depending on the students' initial level of functioning. A somewhat different suggestion has been that what is important is not that a certain number of hours be devoted to FIE instruction but that all 14 of the (increasingly complex) instruments be gone through. Campione, Brown, and Ferrara (1982) suggest that "…the actual materials themselves may have less to do with the success of the program than the training procedures" (p. 449). And Haywood et al. (1982) say "…it is possible that *what* works is a general mediational teaching style rather than mainly the curriculum and its paper-and-pencil exercises themselves" (p. 14). In any event, one would presumably hypothesize that the amount of time required would vary with the students' initial level of functioning.

5. How much training and support is needed to prepare teachers to provide effective FIE instruction? Are there selection

factors that need to be taken into account, or can almost any teacher be trained in this way?

6.   How does "bridging" take place? Do regular teachers who are trained in FIE teach their other (non-FIE) classes differently than before? If so, what is it they do differently and are there indirect effects of FIE on the (non-FIE) students enrolled in these classes?

7.   What is the best way to measure FIE effects? The studies reviewed here used a total of 43 different measuring instruments (not counting separately such things as PMA subtests): 9 intelligence tests, 10 achievement/aptitude tests, 8 measures of self-esteem, 8 other personality/cognitive style measures, and 8 other measures of various types (including 3 behavior rating scales). Clearly there is a need both to specify the effects that need measuring and to construct a set of instruments and procedures that, by common agreement, measure these effects.

8.   How large an effect is it reasonable to look for? The answer presumably depends on such things as who the subjects are, dosage, and, particularly, when the effect is measured. Given the central importance for FIE theory of divergent (snowballing) effects, it is essential that the answer to this question be based on data that provide evidence regarding such effects.

Things that Would Make FIE Studies More Readily Interpretable

As is apparent from the review and as noted above, most of the studies examined here are difficult to interpret. The reasons for this difficulty have sometimes to do with the study itself (e.g., its design or implementation), sometimes with the sufficiency of information provided about the study (e.g., FIE dosage or method of assigning experimental units to FIE and non-FIE conditions), and sometimes with both. What follows is a list of things (some of them perhaps obvious) that, if followed, should eliminate most of these difficulties and increase the probability of finding an FIE effect—if there is an effect there to be found.

1.   *Articulating the goals of the research, the questions the research is intended to answer.* What this does is provide a base for examining the dependent measures that have been selected

and deciding whether, with these measures, the questions are likely to be answered.

2.   *Selecting a subject population similar to the one (culturally and educationally disadvantaged) in which FIE theory was developed.* It may be the case that FIE will be found to work with other populations (e.g., mentally retarded), but this remains to be seen.

3.   *Selecting dependent variables that adequately reflect the goals of the program and that, according to FIE theory, can be expected to show intervention effects.* Depending on what goals were set, appropriate candidates might be thinking skill, cognitive style, impulsivity, self-esteem, practical problem-solving, and ability to communicate, although not necessarily all of these in the same study.

4.   *Constructing/selecting measures that are capable of providing information about the specified variables, and saying how they relate to each other and to the test of FIE.* In most of the cases examined in this review, the report gives no indication as to whether one of the dependent measures is any more or less important than the others for testing the efficacy of FIE. Therefore it is difficult in these cases to say whether the particular study's results provide support.

5.   *Determining the administrative feasibility of the study and the trade-offs involved.* Conducting an interpretable FIE study is extremely difficult, and one could decide that in a particular situation it would not be possible to do the kinds of things that would tend to insure interpretability. In these cases, conducting the study appears to be a waste of time.

6.   *Providing the maximum possible dosage of FIE* (maximum number of hours and instruments; see earlier discussion).

7.   *Providing the recommended amount of training for FIE instructors before the start of the first year and each succeeding year* (see earlier discussion).

8.   *Providing the recommended amount of support for the FIE instructors during the intervention* (see earlier discussion).

9.   *Randomly assigning experimental units* (e.g., individuals, classes) to experimental and control conditions, and providing information regarding the procedure used in accomplishing this.

10. *Selecting a suitable set of teachers* (preferably pairs of teachers who are competent in the same subject matter area, e.g., math, English, history), *and randomly assigning them* (preferably within pairs) *to experimental and control conditions.* And having a large number of experimental and control teachers reduces the likelihood that any FIE effects (or absence of such effects) will be traceable to the special capabilities of a particular FIE or control teacher.

11. *Providing statistics on changes in group composition* (gains and losses) *in the experimental and control groups over time and showing what effect (if any) these changes have on the interpretation of the results.*

12. *Structuring things in a way that maximizes the possibility for bridging.* For example, after teachers are assigned (randomly) to experimental and control groups, arranging for these teachers to teach an additional class (in their subject matter area) assures that whatever it is that the (FIE or control) teacher does will have a chance to be done in another (subject matter) class as well. It is desirable also, to assure that control-group students are not enrolled in subject-matter classes taught by FIE teachers since being in such classes increases the likelihood of unintended second-order effects of the FIE teacher.

13. *Formulating design and procedures for following up the experimental and control subjects after the intervention has ended so that data can be obtained on the Feuerstein's snowballing hypothesis.*

14. *Providing descriptive statistics for the effects investigated; and, if classes were used as experimental units, providing information about degrees of freedom and choice of error term.*

15. *Providing information about the implementation's completeness.* Data are needed on the nature and extent of the intervention that is provided (How many hours of FIE were given and which pages of which instruments were used?) and on the nature and extent of the intervention that was "received" (as indicated by the magnitude of mastery and near-transfer effects). Data are needed also on the nature and extent of instructor training (number of hours, procedure, spacing), on the extent to which instructors were able to apply what they had learned, and the nature and extent of the support provided to the instructors while the study was going on.

16. *Controlling and/or providing information concerning naturally-occurring sources of experimental error* (e.g., pre-training differences between instructors assigned to experimental and control groups. For a discussion, see Lindquist, 1953, pp. 8-11.)

REFERENCES

Anastasi, A. (1981). Coaching, test sophistication, and developed abilities. *American Psychologist, 36,* 1086–1093.

Arbitman-Smith, R., & Haywood, H. C. (1980). Cognitive education for learning-disabled adolescents. *Journal of Abnormal Child Psychology, 8,* 51–64.

Arbitman-Smith, R., Haywood, H. C., & Bransford, J. D. (1984). Assessing cognitive change. In C. M. McCauley, R. Sperber, & P. Brooks (Eds.), *Learning and cognition in the mentally retarded* (pp. 443-471). Hillsdale, NJ: Lawrence Erlbaum.

Beasley, F. (1984). *An evaluation of Feuerstein's model for the remediation of adolescents' cognitive deficits.* Unpublished doctoral dissertation, University of London.

Bradley, T. B. (1983). Remediation of cognitive deficits: A critical appraisal of the Feuerstein model. *Journal of Mental Deficiency Research, 27,* 79–92.

Brainin, S. S. (1982). The effects of instrumental enrichment on the reasoning abilities, reading achievement, and task orientation of sixth grade underachievers (Doctoral dissertation, Columbia University Teachers College, 1983). *University Microfilms International,* AAD82-157-19.

Bransford, J. D., Arbitman-Smith, R., Stein, B. S., & Vye, N. J. (1985). Improving thinking and learning skills: An analysis of three approaches. In J. W. Segal, S. F. Chipman, & R. Glaser (Eds.), *Thinking and learning skills: Relating instruction to basic research: Vol. 1* (pp. 133-206). Hillsdale, NJ: Lawrence Erlbaum.

Bransford, J. D., & Stein, B. S. (1984). *The IDEAL problem solver: A guide for improving thinking, learning, and creativity.* New York: W. H. Freeman.

Campione, J. C., Brown, A. L., & Ferrara, R. A. (1982). Mental retardation and intelligence. In R. J. Sternberg (Ed.), *Handbook of human intelligence* (pp. 392-490). New York: Cambridge University Press.

Chance, P. (1982, October). The remedial thinker. *Psychology Today,* pp. 62–73.

Cook, T. D., & Campbell, D. T. (1979). *Quasi-experimentation: Design and analysis issues for field settings.* Boston, MA: Houghton Mifflin.

Cordes, C. (1984, May). Reuven Feuerstein makes every child count. *APA Monitor,* pp. 18, 20.

Covington, M. V., Crutchfield, R. S., Davies, L., & Olton, R. M., Jr. (1974). *The productive thinking program: A course in learning to think.* Columbus, OH: Charles E. Merrill.

De Bono, E. (1975). *CoRT thinking.* Blandford, Dorset, England: Direct Education Services.

Detterman, D. K., & Sternberg, R. J. (1982). *How and how much can intelligence be increased?* Norwood, NJ: Ablex.

Feuerstein, R., & Hoffman, M. B. (1985). The importance of mediated learning for the child. *Human Intelligence International Newsletter, 6*(2), pp. 1–2.

Feuerstein, R., & Jensen, M. R. (1980, May). Instrumental enrichment: Theoretical basis, goals, and instruments. *The Educational Forum,* 401–423.

Feuerstein, R., Miller, R., Hoffman, M. B., Rand, Y., Mintzker, Y., & Jensen, M. R. (1981). Cognitive modifability in adolescence: Cognitive structure and the effects of intervention. *Journal of Special Education, 15,* 269–287.

Feuerstein, R., Rand, Y., & Hoffman, M. (1979). *The dynamic assessment of retarded performers: The learning potential assessment device, theory, instruments, and techniques.* Baltimore, MD: University Park Press.

Feuerstein, R., Rand, Y., Hoffman, M., Hoffman, M., & Miller, R. (1979). Cognitive modifiability in retarded adolescents: Effects of instrumental enrichment. *American Journal of Mental Deficiency, 83,* 539–550.

Feuerstein, R., Rand, Y., & Hoffman, M. B., & Miller, R. (1980). *Instrumental enrichment: An intervention program for cognitive modifiability.* Baltimore, MD: University Park Press.

Furth, H. G. (1970). *Piaget for teachers.* Englewood Cliffs, NJ: Prentice Hall.

Furth, H. G., & Wachs, H. (1975). *Thinking goes to school.* New York: Oxford.

Genasci, H. K. (1984). The effects of instrumental enrichment on aptitudes and affective measures of adolescent studies in selected classroom settings (Doctoral disseration, University of Oregon, 1983). *University of Microfilms International,* AAD84-03728.

Glaser, R. (1982). Instructional psychology: Past, present, and future. *American Psychologist, 37,* 292-305.

Glaser, R. (1984). Education and thinking: The role of knowledge. *American Psychologist, 39,* 93–104.

Goldstein, K. M., & Blackman, S. (1978). *Cognitive style.* New York: Wiley.

Graham, E. E. (1981). Feuersteins's instrumental enrichment used to change cognitive and verbal behavior in a city-core, multi-ethnic Toronto secondary school (Doctoral dissertation, University of Toronto, 1981). *Dissertation Abstracts International, 43*/02-a, 428.

Hall, E. (1982, January). Schooling in a nasty climate. *Psychology Today,* pp. 57–63.

Hall, J. N. (1982). Evaluation and comparison: Social learning curriculum and instrumental enrichment (Doctoral dissertation, George Peabody College for Teachers of Vanderbilt University, 1981). *University Microfilms International*, AAD82-08453.

Hayes, J. R. (1981). *The complete problem solver*. Philadelphia, PA: Franklin Institute Press.

Haywood, H. C., & Arbitman-Smith, R. (1981). Modification of cognitive functions in slow-learning adolescents. In P. Mittler (Ed.), *Frontiers of knowledge in mental retardation: Vol. 1. Social, educational, and behavioral aspects* (pp. 129–140). Baltimore, MD: University Park Press.

Haywood, H. C., Arbitman-Smith, R., Bransford, J. D., Delclos, V. R., Towery, J. R., Hannel, I. L., & Hannel, M. V. (1982, August). *Cognitive education with adolescents: Evaluation of instrumental enrichment*. Paper presented at the sixth annual meeting of the International Association for the Scientific Study of Mental Deficiency, Toronto, Canada.

Hobbs, N. (1980, April). Feuerstein's instrumental enrichment: Teaching intelligence to adolescents. *Educational Leadership*, pp. 566–568.

Jackson, Y. V. (1984). Identification of potential giftedness in disadvantaged students. (Doctoral dissertation, Columbia University Teachers College, 1983). *University Microfilms International*, 8403266.

Jonas, B. S., & Martin, D. S. (1984). *Summary analysis of instrumental enrichment effects at the Model Secondary School for the Deaf (MSSD). A summary report for the period 1982–84*. Unpublished manuscript.

Jonas, B. S., & Martin, D. S. (1985). Cognitive improvement of hearing impaired high school students through instruction in instrumental enrichment. In D. S. Martin (Ed.), *Cognition, education, and deafness: Directions for research and instruction* (pp. 172–175). Washington, DC: Gallaudet College Press.

Kagan, J. (1965). Impulsive and reflective children: Significance of cognitive tempo. In J. Krumboltz (Ed.), *Learning and the education process* (pp. 133–161). Chicago: Rand McNally.

Kersh, M. E., & Gehrke, N. J. (1984, April). *The process of teacher change through instrumental enrichment training and implementation*. Paper presented at the annual meeting of the American Educational Research Association, New Orleans.

Kieta, M., Pfohl, W., & Redfield, D. (1982, March). *Use of Feuerstein's instrumental enrichment to promote cognitive change in underprepared college students: A pilot study*. Paper presented at the annual meeting of the Southeastern Psychological Association, New Orleans.

Lindquist, E. F. (1953). *Design and analysis of experiments in psychology and education*. Boston, MA: Houghton Mifflin.

Link, F. (1980). Instrumental enrichment: The classroom perspective. *Educational Forum*, pp. 425–428.

Lipman, M., Sharp, A. M., & Oscanyan, F. S. (1980). *Philosophy in the classroom* (2nd ed.). Philadelphia, PA: Temple University Press.

Lochhead, J., & Clement, J. (Eds.). (1979). *Cognitive process instruction.* Philadelphia, PA: Franklin Institute Press.

Martin, D. S. (1984a). Cognitive modification for the hearing-impaired adolescent: The promise. *Exceptional Children, 51,* 235–242.

Martin, D. S. (1984b, November). Infusing cognitive strategies into teacher preparation programs. *Educational Leadership,* pp. 68–72.

Martin, D. S. (1985). Enhancing cognitive performance in the hearing-impaired college student: A pilot study. In D. S. Martin (Ed.), *Cognition, education, and deafness: Directions for research and instruction* (pp. 176–179). Washington, DC: Gallaudet College Press.

McDaniel, A. (1983). Learning potential assessment in educable mentally retarded students. (Doctoral dissertation, Georgia State University, College of Education, 1982). *University Microfilms International,* AAD83-04815.

McRainey, L. (1983). Social outcomes of a cognitive education program (Doctoral dissertation, George Peabody College for Teachers of Vanderbilt University, 1982). *University Microfilms International,* AAD83-13846.

Messerer, J., Hunt, E., Meyers, G., & Lerner, J. (1984). Feuerstein's instrumental enrichment: A new approach for activating potential in learning disabled youth. *Journal of Learning Disabilities, 17,* 322–325.

Messick, S., & Jungeblut, A. (1981). Time and method in coaching for the SAT. *Psychological Bulletin, 89,* 191–216.

Muttart, K. (1984). Assessmen of effects of instrumental enrichment cognitive training. *Special education in Canada, 58,* 106–108.

Narrol, H., Silverman, H., & Waksman, M. (1982). Developing cognitive potential in vocational high school students. *Journal of Educational Research, 76,* 107–112.

Nickerson, R. (1984, September). Kinds of thinking taught in current programs. *Educational Leadership,* pp. 26–36.

Nickerson, R. S., Perkins, D. N., & Smith, E. E. (1985). *The teaching of thinking.* Hillside, NJ: Lawrence Erlbaum.

Nisbett, R., & Ross, L. (1980). *Human inference: Strategies and shortcomings of social judgment.* Englewood Cliffs, NJ: Lawrence Erlbaum.

Passow, H. (1980, May). Instrumental enrichment: Redeveloping cognitive structure. *The Educational Forum,* pp. 393–400.

Peleg, R., & Adler, C. (1977). Compensatory education in Israel: Conceptions, attitudes, and trends. *American Psychologist, 32,* 945–958.

Piaget, J. (1954). *The construction of reality in the child.* New York: Basic Books.

Rand, Y., Mintzker, Y., Miller, R., Hoffman, M. B., & Friedlander, Y. (1981). The instrumental enrichment program: Immediate and long-term effects. In P. Mittler (Ed.), *Frontiers of knowledge in mental retardation,*

Volume 1: Social, educational, and behavioral aspects (pp. 141–152). Baltimore, MD: University Park Press.

Rand, Y., Tannenbaum, A. J., & Feuerstein, R. (1979). Effects of instrumental enrichment on the psychoeducational development of low-functioning adolescents. *Journal of Educational Psychology, 71*, 751–763.

Redfield, D. (1984, April). *Application of instrumental enrichment to college students.* Paper presented at the annual meeting of the American Educational Research Association, New Orleans.

Redfield, D. L., Kieta, M. A., Pfohl, W. F., & O'Connor, J. (1983, March). *Feuerstein's instrumental enrichment applied to underprepared college students.* Paper presented at the annual meeting of the Southeastern Psychological Association, Atlanta, GA.

Royer, C., & Swift, C. (1984, August). *Feuerstein's "instrumental enrichment": An analogy for teaching writing.* Paper presented at the Harvard Conference on Thinking, Cambridge, MA.

Ruiz, C. J. (1985a). *Modificabilidad cognoscitiva y irreversibilidad: Un estudio sobre el efecto a mediano plazo del programa enriquecimiento instrumental* (Publicacion No. 4). [Cognitive modifiability and irreversibility: A study of the midterm effect of the instrumental enrichment program (Publication No. 4)]. Ciudad de Guayana, Venezuela: Universidad de Guayana.

Ruiz, C. J. (1985b). *Effects of Feuerstein Instrumental Enrichment Program on pre-college students.* Unpublished manuscript.

Ruiz, C. J., Castaneda, E. (1983). *Efectos del programa enriqueicimiento sobre los factores cognoscitivas y no-cognoscitivas in sujetos de diferentes estratos socioeconomicos* [Effects of the instrumental enrichment program on cognitive and non-cognitive factors in subjects of different socioeconomic strata]. Ciudad Guayana, Venezuela: Universidad de Guayana.

Russ-Eft, D. F., McLaughlin, D. N., Oxford-Carpenter, R. L., Harman, J., Simutis, Z., & Baker, G. L. (1984). *Formative education of the Feuerstein Instrumental Enrichment Program in the U.S. Army Basic Skills Education Program (BSEP II)* (Tech. Rep. 650). Alexandria, VA: U.S. Army Research Institute for the Behavioral and Social Sciences.

Sternberg, R. J. (1983, February). Criteria for intellectual skills training. *Educational Researcher*, pp. 6–26.

Sternberg, R. J. (1985). Instrumental and compontential approaches to the nature and training of intelligence. In S. Chipman, J. Segal, & N. R. Glaser (Eds.), *Thinking and learning skills: Current research and open questions* (Vol. 2, pp. 216–243). Hillsdale, NJ: Lawrence Erlbaum.

Tannenbaum, A. J., & Levine, S. (1968). *Classroom participation scale.* Unpublished manuscript, Haddassah-Wizo-Canada Research Institute, Jerusalem.

Twohig, P. T., Rachford, D. R., Savell, J. M., & Rigby, C. K. (1985). *Implementation of a cognitive skills training program in ROTC: Leadership*

Enrichment Program (LMTA Working Paper 85-9). Alexandria, VA: U.S. Army Research Institute for Behavioral and Social Sciences.

Vye, N. J., & Bransford, J. D. (1981, October). Programs for teaching thinking. *Educational Leadership*, pp. 26–28.

Vygotsky, L. (1962). *Thought and language.* Cambridge, MA: MIT Press.

Waksman, M., Silverman, H., Messner, J. (1982). *Instrumental enrichment: Assessment of the effects of a cognitive training procedure on a group of gifted students.* Unpublished manuscript.

Waksman, M., Silverman, H., & Messner, J. (1984). Cognitive training for gifted children. *Human Intelligence International Newsletter, 5*(3), 2–3.

Walsh, E. (1984, August 20). Education's 3Rs become four: Schools put stress on reasoning. *Washington Post*, pp. A-1, A-24.

Whimbey, A., & Lochhead, J. (1980). *Problem solving and comprehension: A short course in analytic reasoning* (2nd ed.). Philadelphia, PA: Franklin Institute Press.

Yitzhak, V. (1981). The effect of Feuerstein's instrumental enrichment program on the cognitive reasoning of retarded performers as measured by Piaget's conservation tasks (Doctoral dissertation, University of Toronto, 1981). *Dissertation Abstracts International, 42*/10A, 4407.

Ziegler, E., & Berman, W. (1983). Discerning the future of early childhood education. *American Psychologist, 38*, 894–906.

NOTES:

1. At the present time the distinction is largely academic since Feuerstein's materials seem to be the only ones that have been used.

2. According to Frances Link (personal communication, September 8, 1984), whose organization (Curriculum Development Associates) provides training and materials for FIE instructors, FIE is currently being used in some 500-800 school districts in 40 states in the U.S., in five colleges, and in 15 local education authorities in the United Kingdom. Reuven Feuerstein (cited in Cordes, 1984), whose organization (Hadassah-Wizo Canada Research Institute) also provides FIE training and materials, says that about 30,000 of Israel's 500,000 students are enrolled in programs involving FIE.

3. The intervention used in the study by Jackson (1984), which reports a reanalysis of data obtained from the Atlanta public school system, is the only one we have found that used all 14 of the available instruments.

4. These two articles report the same study. The main difference between them is that one of the articles (Feuerstein, Rand, Hoffman, & Miller, 1979) includes data from posttest-only as well as from the pretest-posttest measures, whereas the other article (Rand et al., 1979) includes only the latter. This study, including the posttest-only data, is also reported in Feuerstein et al., 1980, Chapter 10.

5. This study, like the previous one, was reported twice.

6. One of the reports of this study (Rand et al., 1981) presents data from three other measures that were administered by the Army; the other report (Feuerstein et al., 1981) does not. We have chosen not to discuss these other data on the grounds that (a) their relevance is not entirely clear, and (b) the measures used in collecting these data do not seem to have been entirely objective.

7. Some of the information presented here was provided by Ruiz in personal communications, April 19, 1985 and May 28, 1985.

8. In designs of this type a main effect of treatment appears as a 2-way (treatment x time-of-testing) interaction, whereas in designs of the type used in the Israel studies it appears simply as a main effect. As noted above, however, many of the Nashville studies included a subject variable (type of disability) in addition to the treatment and time of testing. At the Nashville site the experiment was conducted with four experimental and control subgroups (educable mentally retarded, learning disabled, varying exceptionalities, and behavior disordered); at the Phoenix site it was conducted with one experimental and two control groups (control-tutored and control-nontutored). At one of the Nashville schools, students were assigned to FIE and control groups by means of a systematic procedure (see Arbitman-Smith & Haywood, 1980, p. 58), although in most cases this was apparently not the case.

9. According to J10onas (personal communication, January 11, 1985), the problem statement on which significant effects were found may have been more interesting to the students than the two on which significant effects were not found. Jonas said that he had not yet analyzed the relevant data but it was his recollection that (a) on the average, students had used more words in responding to this problem than to the other two problems; and (b) in comparison to the other two problems, this particular problem, number 3 in the list of statements presented, was less often omitted by those who failed to respond to all the problems.

Author's note: The authors are grateful to the following persons who read and commented on an earlier version of this paper: Michael Begab, Sema Brainin, John Bransford, Rueven Feuerstein, M. A. Fischl, Kay Genasci, Joan Harman, William Haythorn, Carl Haywood, Frances Link, David Martin, Wilbert McKeachie, Harry Passow, Ya'acov Rand, Carlos Ruiz, Robert Sternberg, Harry Silverman, Abraham Tannenbaum, and Robert Vecchiotti. The views, opinions, and findings contained in this paper are those of the authors and should not be construed as an official Department of the Army position, policy, or decision unless so designated by other, official documentation.

Project Highlights: Cognitive Education Project

by Robert Mulcahy and Associates, University of Alberta

R ATIONALE
Over the past decade, there has been a significant increase in interest and desire from teachers, school districts, colleges, and universities to teach thinking skills. This interest has been associated with the emergence of various cognitive education programs aimed at enhancing students' cognitive and metacognitive skills in the hope that they might become more independent learners and more efficient problem solvers.

Although cognitive education programs have been growing in number and popularity, many questions concerning their effectiveness remain. Part of the reason is the lack of long-term evaluation of these programs. Associated with this lack of comprehensive evaluation is the question of selecting from alternative approaches to teach thinking. That is, linking this evaluation issue to instruction, the central question becomes *how to teach learning/thinking*. Educators are faced with choosing between an in-content or out-of-content instructional approach.

Although cognitive education programs have been growing in number and popularity, many questions concerning their effectiveness remain.

OBJECTIVES

The Cognitive Education Project was a cooperative venture involving: 1) Alberta Education; 2) the Department of Educational Psychology, the University of Alberta; and 3) various school jurisdictions in north-central Alberta. It was established with the general purpose of undertaking a long-term evaluation of two cognitive education programs in relation to traditional instruction in elementary and junior high classrooms. For the out-of-content approach, Feuerstein's *Instrumental Enrichment* (IE) was selected because it is one of the most comprehensive and field-tested learning and thinking programs available to date. The *Strategies Program for Effective Learning/Thinking* (SPELT) was chosen as an in-content instructional approach. It integrates the features of several prominent cognitive theorists and intervention procedures, and it emphasizes the teaching of learning/thinking strategies directly within content across the curriculum.

The effectiveness of cognitive education—represented by the IE and SPELT programs—was compared with the effects of traditional instruction at two initial grade levels (grades 4 and 7) for three diagnostic groups (gifted, learning disabled and average achievers). Specifically, the objectives of the project were fourfold:

1. to assess the relative effectiveness of the two programs in terms of their impact on students' affect and motivation, academic achievement, cognitive ability, and learning/thinking and problem-solving strategies;

2. to examine the differential effects of the programs on gifted, normal achieving, and learning disabled students;

3. to ascertain the feasibility of implementing learning/ thinking strategies instructional programs on a large scale as part of the regular curriculum of schools; and

4. to identify appropriate methods for providing the level and quality of teacher training necessary for implementation.

THE TWO SELECTED PROGRAMS
The common goal of the two programs is to help students learn 'how to learn' and thus become independent, organized, active, and purposeful thinkers and problem solvers. The critical factor for distinguishing between the two is the nature of integration of the program into the curriculum. IE is considered a *detached* program because it is first taught without using curriculum content and later integrated into the curriculum. On the other hand, SPELT is described as an *embedded* program because it is taught directly using curriculum content.

Instrumental Enrichment
Feuerstein's Instrumental Enrichment (IE) (Feuerstein, Rand, Hoffman, & Miller, 1980) was selected to represent the out-of-content approach to instruction. This program, originally designed for culturally disadvantaged children and youth, is currently being used with a broader population of children in upper elementary, junior, and senior high schools. A distinguishing feature of IE is its emphasis on the importance of mediation for strategy development. In IE, social interaction is important because it is believed that it is not the content, but the *means of interacting,* that is internalized by the child.

> In IE, social interaction is important because it is believed that it is not the content, but the *means of interacting,* that is internalized by the child.

The Feuerstein program utilizes pencil-and-paper tasks with related intensive teacher-student discussion. It consists of 15 'instruments' or dimensions. The program is intended to be content-free. That is, the contents of any particular exercise are merely a vehicle, or an instrument, to achieve the overall goals of the program. The major goal of IE is to enhance the cognitive modifiability (that is, learning potential) of the individual.

The IE program can be integrated into the regular school curriculum, but is taught in a decontextualized form first. Typically, IE instruction extends over a two- to three-year period, with a minimum of three sessions per week devoted to work on the instruments. An IE lesson normally begins with a ten-minute introduction, followed by individual work, class discussion and summary. The teacher ensures that adequate mediational experiences are provided to students especially in the introductory and discussion stages. The program is characterized by students discovering a pattern in the instruments through mediation; determining the underlying principle, then "bridging" this principle to other examples. It is this dynamic involvement of the teacher in a dialogue with the student, along with the change in orientation from product to process, that depicts this program.

Strategies Program for Effective Learning/Thinking
The Strategies Program for Effective Learning/Thinking (SPELT) (Mulcahy, Marfo, & Peat, 1984) was selected as the in-content program in the study. Initially aimed at children in the upper elementary and junior high school grades, it has since been extended to high school and college populations. SPELT aims to foster strategic learning and thinking. The teacher plays the role of a mediator between the learner and the external world, structuring the learning environment and providing opportunities necessary to establish and improve strategic behavior in learning, thinking, and problem-solving situations. A general teaching orientation is embedded within SPELT whereby the teacher's goal in all planning and instruction is to actively involve the student in the learning process (Peat, Mulcahy, & Darko-Yeboah, 1989).

SPELT, however, differs from IE in its instructional context. While IE has been designed as a structured package to be taught independently of existing curriculum content, the SPELT approach holds that the teaching of learning/thinking strategies should take place within content and not as an independent or isolated curricular activity. With regular school curriculum as a vehicle, SPELT through inservice demonstrates how the teacher can use specific strategies to activate and regulate students' learning activities.

SPELT uses a three-phase instructional perspective. It progresses from the first phase—direct teaching of strategies in content areas—to the second phase—teaching for strategy transfer—and finally, to the third phase where students can themselves generate new strategies to acquire, analyze, and apply information and ideas. The active involvement of the students in the learning process is maintained as a goal throughout the three phases of SPELT instruction. For both Phases II and III, the teacher engages in Socratic Dialogue—an interactive relationship between the teacher and students where the teacher leads the students through questioning to discover relationships for themselves. Thus, mediational teaching is also a feature of the SPELT program.

METHODOLOGY
Research Design
The study was a three-year longitudinal evaluation implemented in two phases (Phase 1: 1984-87; and Phase 2: 1985-88). It utilized a repeated measures factorial design involving:

- the three types of instructional programs (IE, SPELT, and Control);
- three categories of students (gifted, average, and learning disabled); and
- two initial grade levels (grades 4 and 7).

The complete study involved four data points (repeated measures): pre-test in the fall of the initial year, and two post-tests in succeeding May/June periods corresponding to the end of grades 4, 5, 7, and 8, and a maintenance post-test at the end of grades 6 and 9.

Program Implementation
Teachers assigned to the control condition (traditional instruction) were told to teach as usual, whereas teachers assigned to the two cognitive education procedures received inservice training from project staff prior to giving strategy instruction. Students in the control condition received traditional instruction, while students involved in the two cognitive education programs received a minimum of 120 minutes of strategy instruction per week over two school years. Strategy instruction was followed by one year of maintenance, during which all strategy instruction was withdrawn. Since IE is an out-of-content program, teachers were required to take time

out of a variety of curricular content areas to implement the program. Essentially, the IE instruction time was taken from language arts. For SPELT, teachers incorporated strategy instruction across content areas, and language arts was the major content medium.

Subject Identification
Based on intellectual, academic and behavioral characteristics, about 900 pupils comprising gifted, average, and learning disabled students were identified from the total initial population of 2,400 students in 1984-85 and 1,600 students in 1985-86.

The **gifted** students selected for this project were those who:
- obtained scores of 115 or higher on the verbal and the nonverbal and sub-scales of the Canadian Cognitive Abilities Test (CCAT),
- were rated as being above average in achievement in reading and at/or above grade level in math on the Canadian Achievement Test (CAT),
- were rated as being above the mean (of the total study population) on all three of the Renzulli and Hartman Scales for the Rating of Behavioral Characteristics of Superior Students (SRBCSS) categories (motivation, learning and creativity characteristics).

The **average-achieving** students in this study were those who:
- obtained scores within one standard deviation of the mean on both the verbal and nonverbal sub-scales of the CCAT (85-115),
- obtained achievement scores on the reading and math sub-scales of the CAT within approximately one standard deviation of the mean.

The **learning disabled** students in this study were those who:
- obtained scores within one standard deviation of the mean on both the verbal and nonverbal sub-scales of the CCAT (85-115),

- obtained achievement scores of approximately one standard deviation or more below the mean on the reading sub-scale of the CAT.

Reading was chosen as the major academic measure because it is one of the most important skills necessary for school success. Furthermore, the majority of learning disabled children experience learning difficulties in this area. Consequently, it was the critical achievement measure used in the identification of all three diagnostic groups (gifted, average and learning disabled).

Assessment of Program Effects
The instruments used in this study can be grouped into four categories: (1) cognitive ability; (2) academic achievement; (3) affective perceptions; and (4) cognitive strategies.

1. To assess general **intellectual/cognitive ability**, the Canadian Cognitive Abilities Test (CCAT) was administered. This test measures verbal, quantitative and non-verbal reasoning abilities.

2. For **academic achievement**, the Canadian Achievement Test (CAT) was used. This test consists of two separate batteries measuring skills in reading (vocabulary, comprehension) and mathematics (computation, concepts, application).

3. To assess **affective perceptions**, several measures were employed:

    Perceived competence: Harter's Perceived Competence Scale was used to measure students' self-perceptions in four areas (cognitive, social, physical and general).

    Self-concept: Coopersmith's Self Esteem Inventories were employed to assess evaluative attitudes toward the self in social, academic, family and personal areas of experience.

    Locus of control: Crandall's Intellectual Achievement Responsibility Questionnaire (IARQ) was administered to examine students' beliefs regarding responsibility for outcomes in academic achievement situations.

4.   To measure **cognitive strategies**, several tests were selected or developed:

Reading awareness: Paris' Reading Awareness Questionnaire was used to examine students' awareness of the evaluation, planning, and regulation skills involved in reading.

Reading strategies: A cloze task was developed to evaluate students' reading comprehension abilities and strategies. It is a procedure in which words are systematically omitted and students are required to fill in the blanks with the appropriate words.

Comprehension monitoring: An error detection task was designed to assess students' comprehension monitoring skills. This task requires students to detect anomalous information in the passages; their awareness of faulty comprehension is taken as a measure of their comprehension monitoring.

Perceived problem-solving ability: Heppner and Petersen's Problem-Solving Inventory (PSI) was adopted to examine the underlying dimensions of students' perceptions of their real-life, personal problem-solving process.

Problem solving strategies: A problem-solving task was developed to assess students' problem-solving strategies in mathematics. This task requires students to think aloud (verbalize their thoughts) as they try to solve the given math problems.

To test the effects of the experimental programs, most of the above measures were implemented in both the pre-test and post-test phases. Measures of cognitive strategies, however, were not available at the pre-test point and were thus administered at the post-test point only.

Assessment of Participants' Perceptions
In addition to the above criterion measures, participants' perceptions about their involvement in the Cognitive Education Project were also assessed by survey questionnaires.

Teachers: Annual assessment of perceptions of the project included support and consultation provided by the team, test administration concerns, usefulness of test data provided, pupil behavioral change, inservice effectiveness, appropriateness of experimental program to variation in grade, class size, and time allotted for strategy instruction. A follow-up teacher questionnaire was administered after the completion of the study.

Principals: Perceptions of both the implementation of the experimental programs and participation in the Cognitive Education Project were assessed of all principals on an annual basis. A follow-up survey was also administered to principals of experimental condition schools after the completion of the project to determine their perceptions regarding their involvement in the study.

Parents: A questionnaire was sent to all subjects' parents. Parents were asked if they recognized any positive changes in their child in the following nine behaviors: attention to homework, time spent on task, ability to accept criticism, willingness to tackle more difficult tasks, questioning, alternative points of view, self-confidence, originality in thinking, and vocabulary.

Summary of Methodology
The study involved the evaluation of two learning/thinking strategy teaching programs in comparison to traditional classroom instruction in elementary and junior high schools in north-central Alberta. Teachers received inservice training and then taught the programs for a period of two years. Strategy instruction was followed by one year of maintenance, during which all strategy instruction was withheld. Nine hundred pupils comprising gifted, average, and learning disabled students were initially identified to be followed. Change with respect to cognitive ability, reading and math achievement, affect, perceived competence and cognitive strategies in reading and math was evaluated over the course of the three years. As well, the perceptions of teachers, administrators and parents about the two experimental programs were assessed.

RESULTS

Student Change

The results appear very promising, particularly for learning disabled students and, to a somewhat lesser extent, gifted students (see Table 1). The most pronounced effects were observed for the grade 4 learning disabled students, most notably in reading comprehension and related strategies. There was also evidence that the average and gifted students benefited, but to a lesser degree. Generally, SPELT instruction tended to produce more changes as compared to IE and Control. This finding was not unexpected since the SPELT instruction, in large part, involves teaching cognitive strategies directly within content areas.

> The results appear very promising, particularly for learning disabled students and, to a somewhat lesser extent, gifted students.

The lack of consistent maintenance of behavioral change, which was sometimes observed for IE students, may be due to insufficient time allotted for IE instruction. Maintenance of the program might well be achieved if IE instruction could have been continued for a longer period of time.

This study is a highly conservative one, as in most cases only one or two teachers in a school, at one grade and subject level, taught either the IE or SPELT program. If all teachers at each grade level were engaged in the teaching of cognitive education procedures, quicker and more comprehensive effects would likely have emerged.

Participants' Perceptions

The perceptions of teachers, parents, and administrators regarding the two cognitive education programs are extremely encouraging. The vast majority of experimental teachers reported that they would continue to use the instructional procedures from the two programs. Indeed when a significant number was surveyed again in November 1988, two years after involvement in the project, over 85% of the teachers reported they were continuing to use aspects of the programs in their teaching. This was coupled with the fact that all teachers indicated they would still recommend the programs to their colleagues.

With respect to the inservice training for the two experimental programs, the vast majority of the teachers indicated that inservice training was sufficient to allow them to implement the programs adequately. There was some indication from a number of teachers that more "in-school support" would have enhanced implementation of the programs. A feeling of isolation (being the only teacher in the school involved), was voiced on occasion by some teachers. The administrators and other staff were not familiar with the programs. Nevertheless, teachers were able to learn and implement the programs with some degree of facility. The need to have all staff become familiar and involved from the beginning of the program was evident.

The teachers in both experimental programs indicated the desirability for additional follow-up inservice sessions over the years. This could be handled to a considerable extent through peer coaching and staff meetings devoted to discussion of teaching procedures, and generalization over content areas and grades.

Parents' responses, although limited to the second and third years, also indicated positive changes in their youngsters, in a number of important behavioral areas such as self-confidence, task persistence, accepting alternative points of view, originality of thinking, and questioning.

Administrators' perceptions of the two experimental programs were also generally very positive. Some concern was evident with respect to the high cost of IE materials as well as the practice of teaching IE in isolation from the rest of the curriculum. However, on follow-up questionnaires, one and one-half to two years after their involvement in the initial implementation, over half of the 24 principals said they would consider adopting the experimental programs. Many of these principals stated they would also recommend the cognitive education programs to other schools.

TABLE 1
Summary of the Results

| | | Program Effect | | |
| | | Learning | | |
	Grade	Disabled	Average	Gifted
Cognitive Ability				
	4	No	No	No
	7	No	No	No
Academic Achievement				
Math Computation	4	No	No	No
	7	Yes (1)	No	Yes (1,2)
Math Concepts and Application	4	Yes (1,2)	No	No
	7	Yes (1)	No	(Yes (1,2)
Reading Vocabulary	4	No	No	No
	7	No	No	No
Reading Comprehension	4	Yes (2)	No	No
	7	Trends (2)	No	No
Affective Perceptions				
Perceived Competence	4	No	No	No
	7	No	No	No
Self Concept	4	No	No	No
	7	No	No	No
Locus of Control	4	Yes (1,2)	Yes (2)	No
	7	No	No	No
Cognitive Stratgies				
Reading Strategies Awareness	4	Yes (1,2)	No	Trend
	7	No	No	Yes (1,2)
Reading Cloze Performance	4	Yes (2)	No	Yes (1,2)
	7	Yes (2)	Yes (2)	Yes (1,2)
Comprehension Monitoring	4	Yes (2)	No	Yes (1,2)
	7	Yes (1,2)	No	Yes (1,2)
Math Problem Solving Strategies	4	Yes (2)	No	Yes (1,2)
	7	Yes (1,2)	No	Yes (1)
Perceived Problem Solving Ability	4	No	No	No
	7	No	No	No

1=IE
2=SPELT
3=CONTROL

IMPLICATIONS
Cognitive Education as a Part of School Curriculum
The results observed with respect to pupil change, coupled with the perceptions of parents, teachers and administrators, suggest that the teaching of learning/thinking strategies should be made an integral part of the school curriculum.

The question of whether the cognitive education programs are more appropriate at different grade levels or for different diagnostic groups could not be answered definitively. However, instruction at the lower grades was associated with better gains than instruction at the higher grades. The results clearly indicate that both programs have a greater effect on students at the grade 4 level. The teachers involved in the experimental conditions also indicated general appropriateness of both programs for grade 4 students. Both programs appear to be most effective for grades 4 and 7 learning disabled students and to a lesser extent for gifted students. It is somewhat puzzling that there appeared to be less impact on average students as compared to learning disabled or gifted students. This may be due to the fact that learning disabled students generally lack a systematic strategic approach to tasks and thus benefit more quickly when provided with a systematic approach. Average students may already have a somewhat effective approach in place, and thus fail to benefit significantly from the programs at the outset. Gifted students have the intellectual ability to perceive the usefulness of the strategies and then to use and extend them immediately. Many of the teachers commented that they found the higher ability students to "take off" with the strategies in extending and applying them.

> **It is somewhat puzzling that there appeared to be less impact on average students as compared to learning disabled or gifted students.**

The results have clear implications for the mainstreaming of students with learning difficulties, as well as gifted students. The impact of the teaching of cognitive strategies on the learning disabled students, particularly at grade 4, suggests that if the teaching approaches are used systematically throughout the elementary school, it may prevent some students from developing severe learning problems, and keep them in the mainstream.

Assessment of Cognitive Strategies
The two cognitive education programs affected the cognitive strategies utilized by students after instruction as well as increased their degree of metacognitive reading awareness. The

comprehension monitoring skills of students after two years of instruction in the two cognitive education programs were observed to be generally better than their control counterparts, and so was their performance on a cloze reading task. Both these tasks require students to use context to fill in missing words and to determine the comprehensibility of the text.

The assessment of cognitive strategies was addressed to some extent by the project. However, it may be that more pervasive strategic change could have been identified if more appropriate criterion measures of cognitive strategies were available. Further research must address the development of these instruments for researcher as well as practitioner use. The math problem solving strategy approach, the Metacognitive Reading Strategy Awareness Inventory, and to some extent, the Perceived Problem Solving Inventory, used in this study appear to hold some promise both from face validity and/or from results reported here and elsewhere.

RECOMMENDATIONS
Alberta Education
It is recommended that Alberta Education:

1. make the teaching of cognitive education procedures an integral part of the Alberta school curriculum for elementary and junior high students and that this become policy;
2. develop and make available appropriate resource materials for teachers to use in the teaching of cognitive education procedures;
3. develop and make available to teachers and school administrators cognitive strategy assessment instruments in differing content areas as well as affective domains;
4. make available to all its field consultants training opportunities in theory, research, and application issues relating to cognitive education procedures.

School Jurisdictions
5. It is recommended that inservice training be made available for teaching and evaluating learning/ thinking strategies in classrooms.

Universities

6.   It is recommended that teacher training programs in Alberta provide compulsory training in the principles and practice of cognitive education for all preservice teachers.

CONCLUDING REMARKS

Education has tended to easily grab on to new instructional approaches, the most recent one being learning/thinking strategy teaching or in more popular terms "metacognitive instruction". This type of instruction, regardless of which particular program is used, attempts to teach students to plan, implement, monitor and evaluate specific strategic approaches to tasks. The recent literature, including this study, suggests that this type of instruction has the potential to make enduring positive changes with respect to student learning and problem solving. It is likely that no one particular, added-on program, at one instructional level, will provide the adequate emphasis needed. In fact, some experts in the field suggest that it may not be *what* you teach (in terms of particular strategies or materials used) but *how* you teach it that is most critical to positive student change. Many teachers in the study reported here would support this view.

> ... some experts in the field suggest that it may not be *what* you teach (in terms of particular strategies or materials used) but *how* you teach it that is most critical to positive student change.

The results of this study are very encouraging. There are potential benefits to students and teachers of implementing cognitive education procedures in mainstream elementary and junior high school classrooms. The study reported here suggests that a number of positive changes in student behaviors do occur for different types of learners. The approaches examined in this study, however, are only two out of a wide variety available and these two might best be viewed as initial attempts at teaching learning/thinking which do hold some promise. Further development and evaluation is still necessary.

Despite the problems and unanswered questions we need to pursue metacognitive instruction in our classrooms. There is clearly the need to provide for a comprehensive integrated approach to the teaching of cognitive strategies across all levels of education beginning at kindergarten through to post-secondary. The most appropriate ways of doing this to enhance learning/thinking have yet to be determined. However, we do now know enough to begin to make a start.

REFERENCES

Feuerstein, R., Rand, Y., Hoffman, M., & Miller, R. (1980). *Instrumental Enrichment: An intervention program for cognitive modifiability.* Baltimore: University Park Press.

Mulcahy, R., Marfo, K., & Peat, D. (1984). *SPELT: A strategies program for effective learning and thinking. Research edition* (available from the Cognitive Education Project, Department of Educational Psychology, University of Alberta).

Peat, D., Mulcahy, R., & Darko-Yeboah, J. (1989). SPELT (Strategies program for effective learning/thinking). A description and analysis of instructional procedures. *Instructional Science*, 18, 95-118.

For Further Information

Further information can be obtained from:

Dr. Robert Mulcahy
Dept. of Educational Psychology
Faculty of Education
University of Alberta
Edmonton, Alberta T6G 2G5
Telephone: (403) 492-5211
Facsimile: (403) 492-1318

Dr. Nelly McEwen
Policy and Planning
Alberta Education
11160 Jasper Avenue
Edmonton, Alberta T5K 0L2
Telephone: (403) 427-8217
Facsimile: (403) 422-5255

Reviving Thought Processes in Pre-adolescents. Towards a Dynamic Conception of Intelligence: Is it Possible to Learn How to Think?

by Rosine Debray

A BSTRACT
Feuerstein's theory of Mediated Learning Experience through Instrumental Enrichment (IE) leads to a revolution in the teaching of thinking. An IE two-year experiment conducted in a college with low socioeconomic status pupils shows the possibility of reviving thought processes. Preadolescents can be taught to think through special proceedings far removed from the usual school programs.

* * *

Problems surrounding the notion of intelligence are still a controversial subject in the field of psychology. To summarize, the extreme positions have been:

1. that intelligence is hereditary and determined once and for all, an idea which is defended in particular by Eysenck (1975); or, on the contrary,
2. that intelligence develops only in relation to the environment, an idea which is backed by sociologists or psychosociologists.

From International Journal of Cognitive Education & Mediated Learning, Vol. 1, No. 3, 1990. Reprinted with permission.

Both these perspectives have had their hour of glory. Today, however, a more reasonable consensus exists around an interactionist conception of intelligence where what is genetically inherited is reinforced, backed up or inhibited by the weight of environmental factors. Our notion of a given individual's intelligence, whether a child, an adolescent or an adult, often appears to be a statement of inescapable fact that seems objective because it is based on a psychological examination, particularly if it is careful and thorough (Sanglade-Andronikov & Verdier-Gibello, 1983; Debray, 1982).

> ... children learn, that is develop their intelligence, when they are captivated by a lively and stimulating interpersonal relationship.

To be able to teach children branded "disabled" how to think - that is to say, for them to learn how to use the procedures of intellectual reasoning - is in France a novel, if not revolutionary, idea. In fact, it is contrary to trends in psychiatry dating back to Esquirol as early as 1838 and continued by Binet and Simon (1907), all of whom saw mental retardation as incurable. Thus, there is a considerable cultural tradition which encourages specialists in mental retardation to accept that the intellectual capacities of children described as not very intelligent are limited. Yet the opposite can be observed when what we call "cognitive resuscitation" is applied.

Feuerstein's Theory of Mediated Learning Experience and Its Application Through Instrumental Enrichment (IE)

Professor Reuven Feuerstein's theory of Mediated Learning and its application through IE provides a method to teach, or teach again, procedures of intelligent thinking that are by definition deficient in mentally handicapped children. The causes of the deficiency are not important in this context: in Trisomic children it is genetic, whereas it is essentially environmental in those described as "culturally deprived". The problem is not to find out why but rather how we should remedy it. The following results show convincingly that a remedy does exist (for further detail see Debray, 1989). The theory of Mediated Learning stresses above all, from the author's point of view, the importance of the human mediator's role in the act of transmitting knowledge. It insists on one basic fact: children learn, that is develop their intelligence, when they are captivated by a lively and stimulating interpersonal relationship. Teachers know this only too well, as do loving parents who are concerned about the development of their child's capacity to think. Feuerstein's contribution lies in his assertion - supported by both theory and practice - that when intelligence has not developed at the right time, the disability is not therefore irreversible, because the deficiency is not fixed forever at adolescence or even adulthood. Intelligence in the sense of a capacity to learn intelligent behaviour, and hence solve problems, can thus be acquired. In our Western industrial cultures, this happens almost automatically in the first relations with the mother and father and other important contacts for the child, through educational activities, games, learning and therefore the transmission of language. When the family environment is stimulating and encouraging, the baby, and then the young child, discovers the world and learns to fend for himself thanks to his parents: they make his surroundings intelligible and let him demonstrate that he can cope.

Feuerstein, through IE, proposes a method for re-educating intelligence by teaching those who have missed out on this human mediation how to learn - this is indispensable for what we call "l'appareil psychique" (the psychological/mental apparatus) and he calls intelligence. The essential agent in re-educating intelligence is the human being, the teacher, the only person capable of giving a sense to the knowledge he is conveying to his pupils.

This study assesses the impact of IE on Supervised Education Section classes in France.

METHODS
Description of the Population
On the whole, the first-year pupils in the school come from what one could describe as a modest, if not disadvantaged, socio-cultural background. Their fathers are mainly manual workers or lower-level white collar, and nearly 10 per cent of them are unemployed. Most of their mothers are housewives and 25 per cent of them work. Families are large, with three,

four, five or more children - far above the national average, which is closer to one or two children (INSEE figures).

Lastly, the ethnic origin of the pupils is extremely varied. French pupils form the majority (44.4 per cent), but a high proportion are foreign: no less than 32 different nationalities are represented, mainly from North Africa, Portugal, Asia and sub-Saharan Africa.

These general characteristics do not mean that all the pupils in the first year of secondary school are "culturally deprived" in Feuerstein's sense, though some, usually the older ones, may well be. The age-range is wide, from 10 to 16, the majority of our pupils being between 11 and 14 years old.

Research Design

Eleven professors out of a total of 58, recruited on a voluntary basis and teaching various subjects (French, English, maths, physics, music, natural science, history and geography, fine arts and physical education) and a teacher of a nearest primary school were paired off to make up three IE sessions a week in two different classes. Ten classes in the first year of secondary school were given IE, and at the beginning of the experiment there were 227 pupils (October, 1986). But this total was found to have dropped to 91 at the end of the second year. At the end of the first year of secondary school, a percentage of 21.6% of pupils were moved to a new school which had just opened. Except for this change, the characteristics of the population remained the same in these two new groups. A test/re-test procedure was set up at the end of the experiment to try to assess the progress of the pupils receiving IE. Their results were compared with those of a control group made up of pupils from four classes in the first year of secondary education from a neighboring school who had not been given IE. There were 93 pupils at the start of the experiment and 53 at the end. The following tests were applied:

1.   PMS 38 (Progressive Matrices Standard), which aims to measure the logical and non-verbal level of intelligence;

2.   Analytic Intelligence Tests (AIT), which are intended to provide an assessment of the pupil's verbal, numerical and spatial aptitude;

3.   Drawing a picture. This was the "Dame de FAY" test: the pupil is asked to write the sentence: "a woman is going for a walk and it is raining", then to draw it.

Statistical Analysis

Comparison of the progress of the experimental group (EG) and the control group (CG) requires resolution of a major problem: the averages of the two groups are not identical to the pre-tests (AIT = 70.2 for the EG and 81 for the CG; PMS 38 = 35.5 for the EG and 42.2 for the CG). When this happens, it is difficult to compare progress, since the CG is clearly better than the EG. The reason for this no doubt lies in the fact that the experimental school takes children with greater difficulties than the neighboring schools used as the CG. This difference in levels at the start requires use of special statistical techniques.

An Analysis of Co-variance

This statistical technique transforms the starting marks (using linear regression) so as to make the two groups comparable and then assesses the significance of the two factors involved.

The analysis was carried out on 144 pupils (EG = 91, CG = 53). The results obtained from the AIT (numerical, spatial, verbal and total) and PMS 38 tests were then examined. The marks obtained from the pre-test were treated as independent variables, as were those for the two groups, experimental and control. The results from the post-tests are dependent variables.

The variations between the two groups reveal the differences in progress between the pupils given IE and those following normal schooling, without any other external influence. Table 1 provides the values of Snedecor's *F*-test for each individual activity, with their level of significance.

These variations between the two groups reveal the differences in progress between the pupils given IE and those following normal schooling, without any other external influence.

Only the Spatial AIT test reaches the 5 per cent level of significance. The overall scores on AIT and PMS 38 were significant only at slightly above the 10 per cent level. The verbal and numerical tests had by far the lowest significance levels.

Analysis by Paired Groups

This second technique does the same thing as the co-variance analysis. In this particular instance, the idea is to pair off a pupil from the EG and one from the CG with the same original marks and so construct two comparable groups by getting rid of the differences in pre-testing.

This approach has many drawbacks because of the size of the two groups and the disparity of the marks obtained. Since the control group had only 53 members, almost half the pupils in the experimental group ($N = 91$) had to be dropped in order to make the pairing. In addition, pairs could not be found for some EG pupils because they did not match the CG exactly, so that in the end, only 40 pairs remained.

Table 1 Values of Snedecor's F-Test

Activity Tested	Value of F	Significance
Numerical AIT	0.134	$p = 0.715$
Spatial AIT	3.632	$p = 0.059$
Verbal AIT	0.857	$p = 0.356$
Total AIT	2.076	$p = 0.188$
PMS 38 Total	1.750	$p = 0.188$

A second problem has been described by Bacher (1983). The pairing of two disparate groups leads to better pupils being selected from the weaker group and matched with relatively poorer members of the stronger group. This has a "differential regression effect", which pulls up the average of each of the sub-groups closer to the average of the group which it belongs, that is, the comparison of the averages of the two groups paired off will be distorted by an effect which accentuates their differences. In our case, this will make it all the more difficult to demonstrate a difference between the two groups in progress on the post-tests.

We nevertheless managed to pair off the two groups: experimental and control. There were in fact two distinct pairings: the first was carried out on the basis of the total marks obtained in PMS 38, where a difference of + or - 1 point in the pre-test scores was deemed acceptable and so 44 subjects were grouped. The second was based on the overall AIT figures. These scores are much higher and a difference of + or - 2 was tolerated in each group, hence 43 pairs could be made.

An analysis of the marks obtained in the numerical, spatial and verbal subtests did not lead to new pairings being made, that is, the pairings based on the overall marks were retained.

Results obtained in PMS 38

1.   Figure 1 shows the change in the averages for the two paired groups, as well as the pre- and post-test margins.

2.   The starting points were virtually the same (CG=40.68; EG=40.57) with almost identical dispersions (σCG = 5.77; σEG = 5.86).

But the experimental group made considerably greater progress than the control group (CG: m = 43.68 and σ = 6.67; EG: m = 46.79 and σ = 3.61) - that is +6.22 against +3 points (Student's t significant at p = 0.01).

Figure 1 Progress of scores obtained in PMS 38 in the two paired groups (44 subjects)

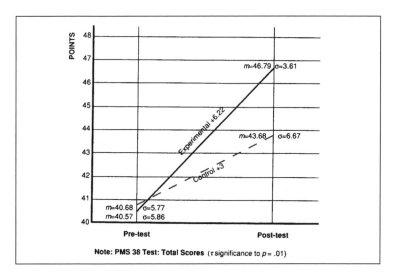

Note: PMS 38 Test: Total Scores (τ significance to p = .01)

Results obtained at the AIT (total score)
As for PMS 38, Figure 2 shows the close identity of the starting levels (CG: $m = 77.74$ and $\sigma = 16.14$; EG: $m = 77.72$ and $\sigma = 15.97$).

Once again the improvement is greater in the experimental group (CG: $m = 98.21$ and $\sigma = 14.71$; EG: $m = 102.77$ and $\sigma = 12.69$) - that is, +25.05 points as against +20.46 points (Student's t significant at $p = 0.05$).

Figure 2 Progress of scores obtained in AIT in the two paired groups (43 subjects)

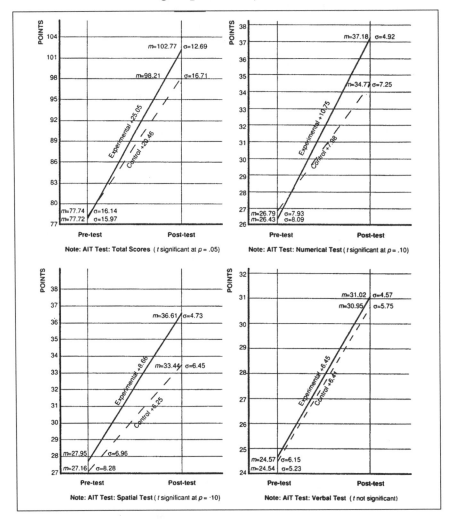

Results obtained from the numerical, spatial and verbal tests of the AIT

1.   There is very little difference between the starting levels (26.43/26.79 for the numerical tests; 27.95/27.16 for the spatial tests; 24.57/24.54 for the verbal tests, for the experimental and the control groups respectively).

2.   Although the change in the averages is more pronounced in the EG than in the CG on the two numerical and spatial subtests, the Student's t shows only a tendency ($p = 0.10$) rather than real significance.

3.   The verbal results, however, are identical in both groups and the progress is the same.

DISCUSSION OF THE RESULTS

Despite the various drawbacks of the method using the paired groups, we obtained results using this technique which are more conclusive than with the analysis of co-variance. The changes are in the same direction, with the most influential factors remaining the same.

The two statistical methods produced different results because our groups (experimental and control) were not totally comparable in level. An "IE effect" does, however, seem to exist, with greater improvement in the experimental group. This tendency can be seen in the overall results of the main tests and is most pronounced in the spatial tests. To be more precise, one should really make the comparison with a control group of identical standard.

Repeating in a structured and systematic way all the concepts and thinking activities found at each stage of IE makes it possible to refine thinking structures. Thus, even if the pupil has

... even if the pupil has benefited from generally sufficient mediations, it would seem that he has much to gain from this organised repetition centred on the act of thinking.

benefited from generally sufficient mediations, it would seem that he has much to gain from this organised repetition centred on the act of thinking. Immigrant adolescents with a disturbed past, who have experienced difficulties in adapting to a new culture, can be particularly helped by this method.

In fact, whatever one's personal views with regard to the belief that everyone should have the same chance at the start of the first year of secondary school, it is unrealistic to think that one can disregard what has taken place beforehand. The importance of the quality of first interactions with the mother on the development and construction of intelligence is there to remind us of that, just as is the first learning experience at primary school. From this perspective, the first year of secondary school constitutes an opportunity for a fresh start that can perhaps be seized by the pupil if the external conditions are favourable. This is precisely what the teachers responsible for the application of the IE experience can achieve.

INDIVIDUAL DEVELOPMENT: CASE STUDIES

In addition to the general analysis of quantitative data presented already, there is much to be learnt from following the development of a child over two consecutive years, from the first to the second year of secondary school focusing on separating out what enriches and develops intellectual capacities, including the personality as a whole, and what, on the contrary slows down or prevents the general development of the person.

The "objective" assessments (the results from the tests carried out before and after the IE treatment, the school reports from the first and second year of secondary school) combined with "subjective" ones (comments of different teachers, progress with the drawings) are valuable, even if in most cases the information about the child's past is very limited or even totally non-existent. The following vignettes illustrate, on an individual level, what the general data partially demonstrates on a group level. These vignettes sometimes provide insight into some of the other positive effects of IE interventions.

Sinbad

The IE teachers who worked with Sinbad, aged 12 years, 1 month at the start of his first year in secondary school, spoke of a great step in maturity. This boy is one of five children. His father is a worker from the Comore Islands, his mother a housewife. His first year was very poor, particularly his second term in which he seemed to become undisciplined under the influence of restless classmates. It was his participation in IE sessions which gradually distanced him from them and allowed him to get back to work. His second year was good and he passed into his third year with encouragement from the staff. He is a pupil who has become both responsible and mature. Sinbad is very ambitious since he wants to become a doctor, which his results in the test as well as his progress in the past 18 months should not prevent him from doing.

Willai

Willai, who is 14 years, 2 months old, joined the IE programme during her second year in secondary school. The teachers responsible for the sessions said that it was an advantage for her, since it made her integration into the class all the easier. Willai, who came from South-East Asia, had been living in France for only four years and had not been doing well at school. Serious speech difficulties made her participation almost non-existent, but she gradually opened up, followed the sessions extremely well and finished the school year with acceptable results which were good enough for her to pass into the third year.

Xao

Aged 15 years, 6 months in her first year of secondary school, Xao resembles Willai in many ways. Her father is a Cambodian labourer and her mother a housewife looking after her three children. At the beginning of the second year, Xao was described as lacking self-confidence, being extremely reserved, even very uncommunicative, and never smiling. She had difficulties in French, spelling and grammar, but was hardworking and good at mathematics and English. It was the IE sessions that taught her to relax and smile, much to the teacher's relief. She never participated much in the oral sessions but kept improving in the written ones. At the end of the second term of the second year, because of her age (nearly 17) she was guided towards a vocational lycée, but her progress meant that she was finally admitted into the third year. She made it perfectly clear to her IE teacher that she wanted to continue with the programme and complete the last three instruments which had as yet not been seen.

Lionel

Things are quite different in Lionel's case, since at the age of 12 years, 1 month at the start of his first year, he was bad at all subjects and his teachers said that he was not interested in school. His results in the tests were poor at the beginning of IE (he was below average for his age in PMS 38).

The IE sessions were the only classes where Lionel really joined in, and his French teacher who was carrying out the programme noted with some surprise that "there, he could find the right words to talk about things", and she and her colleagues came to think more highly of him because of these contributions. She added that the French lessons had not allowed her to discover the "richness of his personality."

Lionel himself recognises that IE has taught him to express himself. His school results, though still only mediocre, were good enough for him to pass into the third year. The post-tests reveal an improvement (in PMS 38 his score rose from 29 to 39 points).

CONCLUSION

The extreme variation in individual situations as they can appear in the first year of secondary school is only partially illustrated in the five cases which we have just briefly looked at. In our low socio-economic status school, the pupils could hardly be more heterogeneous: in one of the classes the ages ranged from 10 to 16 at the beginning of the first year!

> ... it seems that one of the best solutions to prevent teachers from becoming understandably discouraged when faced with an almost impossible task is to involve them in motivating pedagogic projects.

In such circumstances, it seems that one of the best solutions to prevent teachers from becoming understandably discouraged when faced with an almost impossible task is to involve them in motivating pedagogic projects. The Principal of the school achieved this remarkably well, not only with the introduction of IE but also with other educational projects, such as teaching using computers or giving individual attention in physical education and sport.

The teachers who used the IE programme felt that their general pedagogic approach had been radically modified. The "IE frame of mind" transformed their way of teaching their own subjects, since it threw light on what is involved in thinking and intelligence. The "cognitive modifiability" described by Feuerstein clearly also affects the teachers, perhaps affects them above all. In addition, their attitude to the children themselves was altered: they no longer judge pupils simply on the basis of their success or failure in their subject, but are more concerned about a pupils' overall mental processes in some specific activity.

The nature of the IE sessions themselves has made the teachers sensitive to the fact that pupils who are considered shy or "not very bright" can come alive and show signs of intelligence when they are placed in a situation far removed from the usual school routine. That in itself is a very "reviving" realisation for the teachers, since it is in complete contrast to the depressing feeling that there is nothing to be done and that despite all their efforts, school results do not improve. But there is more: if the teacher feels more hopeful, the pupils will almost certainly follow suit, in a similar way to mother/baby interactions in the first stages of life (Debray, 1987). The many studies of the role of teachers' expectations all point to the decisive influence on a vulnerable pupil of whether he feels that his teacher believes he can succeed. The more a pupil has doubts about himself - which is often the case for older pupils who have experienced a number of failures in the past - the more this factor will determine the final outcome. We have seen that the IE programme gives both teachers and pupils this kind of heightened awareness, and that the subsequent school career can thus be radically changed. The cases of Xao and Lionel each showed this in their different ways.

In order to adapt to the first year of secondary school, the pupil must be capable of organising his work within the weekly schedule. This ability to organise one's timetable in advance takes a long time to master, and children from privileged backgrounds receive considerable help from their families. For children who come from so-called underprivileged environments there is no such assistance. The child has, in addition to the handicap of having to cope on his own, the burden of overtaking his parents intellectually. Clinical psychologists and psychiatrists know only too well the strength of the subconscious failure mechanisms which are triggered off in order to minimise such "transgressions" (Malandin, 1988). The best way of preventing this from happening is through a teacher in whom the pupil can place his trust and who will open up the world of learning. This is precisely what the IE teacher can achieve through Mediated Learning. Learning systematically how to organise one's time can help the pupil to avoid the traps of the failure mechanisms.

In this context, the IE experience can provide an efficient way of giving new opportunities - if not equal chances - to children who come from underprivileged families, and thus significantly increase the number of pupils able to stay on at school. In addition, it helps children from difference cultural backgrounds to integrate. This aspect, underlined by Feuerstein and his team, is confirmed by our own research (e.g., the examples of Sinbad from the Comore Islands, and Willai and Xao from South-East Asia). Interestingly, when such pupils are given a fresh start, it is their results in mathematics, physics and even English which improve first of all. This shows that intelligent pupils find it easier to deal with abstract logical reasoning through the language of mathematics than through a language. Indeed, the most insuperable cultural differences relate to the manipulation of the various nuances and subtleties of a language, because how well someone finds the words to express himself is taken as an indication of the quality of his intellectual potential.

> ... Mediated Learning as it is provided during the IE sessions by a well-trained teacher offers a wide range of stimuli: verbal, graphic, abstract, concrete, linked to daily life and to all branches of knowledge.

Thus, Mediated Learning as it is provided during the IE sessions by a well-trained teacher offers a wide range of stimuli: verbal, graphic, abstract, concrete, linked to daily life and to all branches of knowledge. Each member of the group will latch onto whatever suits his particular needs of the moment.

This notion of a stimulating external environment deserves our attention. *A priori*, this is what any teacher will be seeking to achieve, since he knows from experience, that lessons are better assimilated if they are taught in an atmosphere where the pleasure of learning and the desire to know more are the overriding factors. It is precisely this long-forgotten, perhaps unknown feeling that IE arouses when the pupil realises that he can achieve something which he did not think he was capable of. This renewed self-confidence, fragile at first, will allow him to take the risks - often costly in terms of self-image - required for subsequent intelligent action. For this to occur, however, the person must be confronted with difficult and stimulating problems that he can solve. In France, both adolescents and adults who are assumed to be not very intelligent have no chance whatsoever of achieving this, since the mere recognition of an intellectual deficiency often leads to a dramatic fall in the expectation of success, as well as a similar reduction in stimulation from the external environment.

The SES classes (Specialised Education Section) of this school have benefited from the very first IE programme in France. Given the positive effects observed on both the pupils and the teachers, the extension to first and second-year secondary school classes seems highly desirable.

CORRESPONDENCE

Professor Rosine Debray, Institut de Psychologie, Université de Paris-V René Déscartes, Centre Henir Piéron, 28 Rue Serpente, Paris 72005, France

REFERENCES

Debray, R. (1987). *Bébés-Mères en revolte, traitements psychanalytiques conjoints des déséquilibres psycho-somatiques précoces.* Paris, le Centurion, coll. Paidos p. 207.

Debray, R. (1989). *Apprendre à penser, une issue à l'échec scolarie et professionnel,* Paris, Eshel ed., p. 261.

Debray, R., & Douet, B. (1989). La "réanimation cognitive" à la préadolescence. *Psychologie Française, 34*(4), 285-292.

Douet, B. (1988). Expérimentation du Programme de'Enrichissement Instrumental auprès de'élèves en grande difficulté scolaire". *Bulletin de Psychologie, no. 388, vol. XLII.*

Malandin, C. (1989). Scolarité et développement de la personalité. *Publications de l'université de Rouen, 153,* p. 186.

Combining Instrumental Enrichment and Creativity/ Socioemotional Development for Disadvantaged Gifted Adolescents in Soweto: Part 1

by Mervyn Skuy, Mandia Mentis, Isaac Nkwe, Angela Arnott & Joyce Hickson

A

BSTRACT

Provision of enrichment for disadvantaged gifted children has particular relevance in South Africa. Here, sociopolitical conditions have conduced to a wide-spread deprivation of mediated learning experience (MLE). Feuerstein's Instrumental Enrichment programme (IE), as a vehicle for providing MLE, is a viable programme option for enrichment programmes. However, while evidence suggests the value of IE for improving the intellectual functioning of disadvantaged students, no tested effects on self-concept or creative thinking have been demonstrated, and reported effects on scholastic performance have been variable. This study, accordingly, involves the design and implementation of a programme of socioemotional development and creativity to complement the IE programme. In addition, a component of explicit bridging into scholastic and everyday life areas was added to IE. A description is provided here of the design and implementation of the adapted IE and the Creativity and Socioemotional Development (CASE) Programmes, as well as specially-devised measures used to assess students' performance in each. The programmes were implemented over two years with 200 adolescents from seventh

From International Journal of Cognitive Education & Mediated Learning, Vol. 1, No. 1, 1990. Reprinted with permission.

to eleventh grade in the Soweto Gifted Child Programme. This was done within the framework of a rigorously controlled experiment, the outcome of which will be reported in a sequel to this article.

INTRODUCTION

Passow (1972) asserted that disadvantaged children represent a nation's largest neglected source of talent. This is particularly true in South Africa, where people other than white have been the victims of an unjust government policy which has meant deprivation of equal opportunities. While there remains in this country a need for radical societal change, and for the redistribution of education resources, certain modifications have occurred within the current sociopolitical dispensation. Among them have been the recognition of the need to tap potential and to discover and enhance giftedness and talent among the black majority. Accordingly, several extra-mural enrichment programmes have been established in South Africa from 1982 to cater specifically for gifted black children. However, these programmes have not systematically documented the effects on the intellectual and/or emotional functioning of the participants.

The need to identify and foster giftedness among the disadvantaged has been widely documented (e.g., Baldwin, 1987; Richert, 1987; Torrance, 1986). The corresponding multiplicity of programme options needed to develop their potential creativity, critical thinking and motivation has also been recognised. In addition, the loss of self-esteem characterising black disadvantaged children as a result of racism, and the undermining of their cultural mores coupled with the restricted access to the dominant culture, are phenomena which have been particularly prevalent in South Africa. In terms of Feuerstein's (1979, 1980) theory, such children would experience a deprivation of mediated learning experience (MLE), and would experience intensive and extensive cognitive deficits.

Instrumental Enrichment (IE, Feuerstein, 1980), as a vehicle developed for the transmission of appropriate and optimal MLE, could thus provide the basis for a programme that serves the needs of South African children in a gifted programme. In order to increase IE's likelihood of success and expand its areas of effectiveness, however, certain modifications and complementary dimensions are needed. In particular, while reviews of IE consistently conclude that it holds considerable promise for improving the functioning of disadvantaged students (Adams, 1989; Savell, Twohig & Rachford 1986; Sternberg, 1984), no tested effects of self-concept have been demonstrated. IE has also been seen as more suitable for promoting convergent rather than divergent or creative thinking abilities (Sternberg, 1984). Yet, it can be argued that both creativity and self-esteem are important to Feuerstein's theory in that the construct of MLE includes inter alia mediation of challenge, novelty and risk-taking, as well as competence. Moreover, Feuerstein's theory of structural cognitive modifiability involves the development of autonomous thinking and learning.

It is in the area of intellectual abilities that the best results for IE have been achieved (Savell et al., 1986; Sternberg & Bhana, 1986). A possible explanation for this finding is that IE deals most explicitly with cognitive skills, while not specifically addressing itself to creativity or self-concept. Moreover, the lack of explicit academic bridging activities may militate against transfer of the thinking skills in the school curriculum. Bhana and Sternberg (1986) acknowledge transfer effects to school work in some cases, but deny the generality of transfer, in part because, "the extent of transfer attained will be so much a function of how well teachers are able to conduct the required bridging" (page 63). Similarly, Savell et al. (1986) state that IE taught in conjunction with some other subject matter of interest and importance to the student (that is where IE is integrated into the curriculum) is more likely to be effective in improving general school achievement. Savell et al. (1986) further point out that it is thus useful to have the IE instructor as the instructor for other coursework too. However, it is not enough to leave the bridging to the teacher concerned; one must provide explicit directions and bridging examples between the IE and the subject content.

Because of the documented lack of specific bridging examples provided for IE teachers, and the concomitant limita-

> ... IE deals most explicitly with cognitive skills, while not specifically addressing itself to creativity or self-concept.

tions in transfer of IE gains, an explicit programme of bridging was incorporated into the IE programme of the present study. In addition, because of the deficiencies in the practical implementation and outcome of IE in relation to the affective (e.g., self-concept) and creativity dimensions of functioning, a programme was developed here to explicitly extend the principles of MLE into these areas. The effectiveness of this in combination with the IE programme, in enhancing the cognitive, affective and academic functioning of disadvantaged adolescents in a gifted programme, was investigated in a rigorously controlled study. Part 1 of the study, which is presented here, describes the implementation of the IE programme, as well as the development of the socioemotional development/creativity dimension. Part 2, which will follow in a subsequent article, will document the results of the study.

DEVELOPMENT OF INTERVENTION PROGRAMMES WITHIN THE SOWETO GIFTED CHILD PROGRAMME (SGCP)

Introduction of IE and the IE/CASE Programme

At the beginning of 1988/89, a two-year experimental programme was introduced into the Soweto Gifted Child Group (SGCP). This involved the random division of seventh to eleventh grade students (n=200) into three groups; one group received a combination of Instrumental Enrichment and the conventional academic enrichment programme; a second group received a combination of IE, and a programme specially designed for this project entitled The Creativity and Socioemotional Development (CASE) programme, and the academic enrichment programme; a third (Control) group received only the academic programme. The experiment was conducted over two years on the 52 Saturday mornings on which the Gifted Programme was held.

Tutors working within the SGCP were randomly assigned to the IE, IE/CASE, or Control programmes. Those tutors participating in the experimental programmes were exposed to an intensive nine-day workshop on IE, and received weekly supervision for the duration of the two-year programme. Beyond this, the tutors working within the IE plus CASE intervention group also received training and supervision on the CASE from experienced trainers. Control group tutors attended seminars and received supervision on issues related to conventional teaching from experienced personnel.

Implementation of the IE Programme within the SGCP
Seven of the IE instruments were used over the period (i.e., Organisation of Dots, Comparisons, Orientation in Space, Analytic Perception, Categorisation, Family Relations, and Illustrations). Work on the actual pages of the IE Instruments was interspersed with direct and explicit bridging to the academic subjects, as well as to everyday life situations.

This can be exemplified with reference to the Analytic Perception Instrument. Among the strategies employed here include "disembedding" (locating and identifying simple elements embedded in a complex whole), "closure" (synthesising parts into a meaningful whole) and "perspectivism" (uniting discreet parts into a new whole). Once practised on the pages, "embedding" was bridged into the English subject content in the form of identifying parts of speech, using prefixes as an aid to vocabulary building, and analysing essay-writing into its component parts. In biology, "disembedding" was discussed in terms of analysing the vital systems of the body, e.g., the circulation and digestive system, and using models to show the inter-connections of the parts of the organs of the body. In maths, "disembedding" was bridged to discuss fractions as parts of numbers.

> Work on the actual pages of the IE Instruments was interspersed with direct and explicit briding to the academic subjects, as well as to everyday life situations.

Similarly, "closure" was bridged to maths in discussing the synthesis of all the parts in solving story sums, algebraic and geometric problems. In biology, breaking foods into their nutrients was related to "closure" through designing menus for a balanced diet. Synthesis of atoms into molecules and compounds and how changing the parts results in the different wholes, was discussed in science.

Again, "perspectivism" was used to mediate creativity (e.g., in designing tangrams), to promote self-awareness (e.g., seeing the whole self in terms of the different parts others see us as) and to develop a community and ecological consciousness (e.g., in a life skills game students took the role of ministers of different portfolios of a fantasy land and functioned as individual parts in interacting, co-operating and making laws for the good of the whole land).

Concurrent with the bridging activities, another aspect of the IE programme implemented was the identification and remediation of cognitive dysfunctions, and the provisions to scholars of the tools for metacognition. To achieve this, Feuerstein's (1979) list of criteria for mediation and his list of Cognitive Functions were adapted and modified. The tutors were able to monitor their own mediation by using an MLE rating scale both in lesson preparation and in critical evaluation and feedback of their teaching session. Secondly, Feuerstein's Cognitive Functions list was used for diagnosing the student's performance. A first version of the Cognitive Rating Scale involved the placing of Feuerstein's criteria of input, elaboration and output on a continuum from cognitive function to dysfunction, and was used by the tutors in rating each individual student over time. A second scale simplified the cognitive functions for use by the students to evaluate their own thinking skills. These scales were administered continually so that the scholars could monitor their own progress, and thus engage in metacognition.

At group supervision sessions, each tutor presented an oral and written feedback of the previous IE session. The oral presentation served as a springboard for discussion and sharing of ideas. The written report consisted of an outline and an evaluation of a lesson procedure as well as a self-evaluation of the mediation strategies used within the session. Tutors presented and explained their bridging examples, which were evaluated in a workshop. Discussion then involved the development of strategies for presenting further IE pages and/or improving skills as mediators.

Design of a Measure for the IE Programme
A test was designed to assess four levels of competence associated with exposure to the IE programme, as follows:

Level 1: To sample competence on the actual instrument pages, a moderately difficult page from each of two instruments (namely, Analytic Perception and Categorisation) was chosen.

Level 2: To test students' metacognitive insights, they were asked to explain the strategies they used to solve the test items.

Level 3: The ability to label and explain the cognitive operations used in solving test items was examined.

Level 4: The students' ability to bridge the skills learnt from each of the instrument pages both to everyday life and academic situations was tested. Students were given programs to solve in each of these areas, using skills relevant to these Instruments.

Thus, the IE test involved a progression from concrete execution of a task through a systematic explanation of the process involved in problem-solving to the labelling and discussion of the cognitive sill, and finally to the application of these processes and skills in relevant everyday life and academic areas.

> **The creativity aspect of the programme stimulated the assertion of individuality, enrichment of the imagination, and the expression of ideas through various modalities.**

Design and Implementation of the Creativity and Socioemo- tional Development (CASE) Programme within the SGCP

Objectives: The CASE Programme complemented and extended the IE programme by applying principles compatible with MLE to the emotional development and creativity enhancement of the students. For example, metacognition - or awareness of one's thinking processes - was extended into "meta-emotion", or the self-awareness of emotions. Generally CASE aimed at facilitating self-awareness, awareness of others and the environment, improved interpersonal communication, self-mastery, and a positive self-concept. The creativity aspect of the programme stimulated the assertion of individuality, enrichment of the imagination, and the expression of ideas through various modalities. Unique approaches to problem-solving and conflict situations were incorporated.

The approach of the programme was based on the work of Rogers (1961, 1969) and Gordon (1970), and various handbooks were used as resource materials (e.g., Canfield & Wells, 1976; Clark, 1983; Howe & Howe, 1975; Ringness, 1975). The programme was developed over the duration of the project, through an interaction between the tutors and their supervisors at their weekly meetings. This in turn was guided by an ongoing consideration of student attitudes, needs and situations. Based upon this initial implementation of the CASE Programme within the present project, a set of guidelines and activities useful for this population will be drawn up. However, to some extent, the nature and underlying theoretical orientation of the programme will always necessitate spontaneity and individuality of implementation.

> Tutors served as role models by modelling good communication skills and by displaying openness and acceptance towards students' ideas and feelings.

At their meetings, tutors had the opportunity to express their feelings regarding the programme and to discuss the success of their activities or interactions. As for the IE Programme, a weekly written report was also furnished. Both tutors (one of whom was black and the other white) reported the validity and the feasibility of applying the principles and exercises to South African students, and did not report problems related to the fact that the programmes were based on American models, and thus potentially culture-bound. Tutors did, however, emphasise the importance of drawing on the students' own experiences and world views.

Activities: Tutors served as role models by modelling good communication skills and by displaying openness and acceptance towards students' ideas and feelings. Thus a permissive and non-threatening environment was created, in which students were encouraged to experience personal and interpersonal growth, and to express their individuality. Tutors focused the students' attention on their own emotional experiences as well as those of others, and encouraged them to label their own feelings and to clarify their communication. Thus, they taught the students a vocabulary with which to express and share their feelings. Throughout the implementation of the programme, tutors used the spontaneous interaction that occurred to facilitate socioemotional development.

A range of activities were used to enhance self-knowledge, self-awareness, self-esteem and interpersonal communication and to foster creativity. These can be exemplified as follows: A

Name Game was used as an ice-breaker to integrate new members into the class; *Collages* were compiled to promote self-awareness and self-esteem; a *Trust Game* was used to promote the building of trust and the development of confidence in others, and to encourage risk-taking among the pupils; a *Students' Inventory* was compiled, where children were encouraged to make a list of qualities they liked most about themselves, and to share their list with other group members.

This exercise was designed to encourage students to think positively about themselves and to encourage self-disclosure. *Feature Films* were used as a springboard for discussion on interpersonal situations: in the *Strokes* Exercise, students were asked to make comments on one another in order to facilitate easier sharing of positive and negative feedback and to enable them to be more readily in touch with their feelings about themselves and others in their environment.

Activities were also designed to enhance creativity. Students were encouraged to develop independence in thinking and problem-solving by the use of simulated situations. Fluency and diversity in thinking were encouraged by requesting students to generate numerous alternative methods of solving a particular problem. Unique strategies and unusual responses to familiar situations were modelled and elicited. An example of a creative task was one in which the student had to think of a novel and efficient device for weighing an elephant. The students were given free rein as to what materials they used and they presented their solutions pictorially and/or verbally in a sharing exercise. This activity is an example of how one task could be used to target both creative expression and effective experience, inasmuch as students were asked to reflect upon their feelings as they searched for a solution to their problem situation.

Design of Measure for Aspects of the CASE Programme

A test of two equivalent parts, each consisting of 20 items, was developed to assess the extent to which pupils had learnt the socioemotional skills which were the focus of classroom activities and interactions. In Part 1, the pupils were asked to choose the appropriate response from five alternatives. An example of Part 1 is presented below:

1.   Your teacher has taught you elements of a plan you would follow in your work and now asks you to repeat them. You have found them difficult to understand. What should you do?

    (i)   You do not respond when he asks you.

    (ii) You quickly to try to find the answer in your notes.

    (iii) You ask you friend to help you by giving the answer to the teacher.

    (iv) You admit to him/her that you did not quite understand the elements of the plan, and ask him to repeat this. (Appropriate Answer)

    (v)   You tell the whole class that you did not understand what the teacher was saying because Japie was making disturbing noises next to you.

In Part 2, the appropriate options of Part 1 are recast and the pupil is required to say if he/she agrees or disagrees with the suggested responses in a given situation. If there is disagreement, the correct response is required of the pupil. Part 2 is exemplified below by presenting the counterpart to the example given for Part 1.

1.   After your teacher has worked hard to get you to understand a science experiment you still do not understand it and cannot tell him how you go about the experiment. A good response is: *To admit that you found the experiment difficult to understand and ask him please to repeat the lesson.* Agree/Disagree. If you disagree, give the appropriate response.

This measure assessed the extent to which students had acquired an understanding of appropriate interpersonal attitudes and communication styles. Measures of the creativity component were incorporated into the pre-post battery, and are described in Part 2 of the study.

CONCLUSION

This article serves to give an abbreviated description of the development of intervention programmes within the Soweto Gifted Child Programme (SGCP). Fuller details will be supplied by the senior author on request. The specially-designed measures of the IE and CASE Programmes will hopefully enable us to assess the effectiveness with which each of the respective programes was implemented. In Part 2 of the article, the design of the experiment is described and results given on the IE and CASE tests as well as on pre-post measures utilised within the controlled experiment. The measures were employed to determine the extent to which the respective intervention conditions (i.e., IE and IE plus CASE) had an effect on various dimensions of functioning. These include cognitive abilities, creativity, scholastic aptitude and performance, self-concept and social skills.

CORRESPONDENCE

Professor Mervyn Skuy, Division of Specialised Education, University of Witwatersrand, 1 Jan Smuts Avenue, Johannesburg 2050, South Africa

REFERENCES

Adams, M. J. (1989). Thinking skills curricula: Their promise and progress. *Educational Psychologist, 24*, 35-37.

Baldwin, A.Y. (1987) I'm black, but look at me, I'm also gifted. *Gifted Child Quarterly, 31*, 180-185.

Canfield, A., & Wells, A.C. (1976). *100 ways to enhance self-concept in the classroom: A handbook for teachers and parents.* Englewood Cliffs, NJ: Prentice-Hall.

Clark, B. (1983). *Growing up gifted: Developing the potential of children at home and at school.* (2nd ed.), Columbus, OH: Merrill.

Feuerstein, R. (1979). *The dynamic assessment of retarded performers.* Baltimore: University Park Press.

Feuerstein, R. (1980). *Instrumental Enrichment.* Glenview, IL: Scott, Foresman.

Gordon, T. (1974). *Teacher effectiveness training.* New York: Peter H. Wyden.

Howe, L.W., & Howe, M.M. (1975). *Personalizing education.* New York: Hart Publishing.

Passow, A.H. (1972). The gifted and the disadvantaged. *The National Elementary Principal, 51*, 24-31.

Richert, E.S. (1987). Rampant problems and promising practices in the identification of disadvantaged gifted students. *Gifted Child Quarterly, 31*, 149-154.

Ringness, T.A. (1975). *The affective domain in education.* Boston: Little, Brown.

Rogers, C.R. (1961). *On becoming a person.* Boston: Houghton Mifflin.

Rogers, C.R. (1969). *Freedom to learn.* Columbus, OH: Merrill.

Savell, J.M., Twohig, P.T., & Rachford, D.L. (1986). Empirical status of Feuerstein's Instrumental Enrichment techniques as a method of teaching thinking skills. *Review of Educational Research, 56*(4), 381-409.

Sternberg, R.J. (1984). How can we teach intelligence? *Educational Leadership, 42,* 38-49.

Sternberg, R.J., & Bhana, K. (1986). Synthesis of research on the effectiveness of intellectual skills programme: Snake oil remedies or miracle cures? *Educational Leadership, 44,* 60-67.

Torrance, P. (1968). Finding hidden talents among disadvantaged children. *Gifted Child Quarterly, 12,* 131-157.

Combining Instrumental Enrichment and Creativity/ Socioemotional Development for Disadvantaged Gifted Adolescents in Soweto: Part 2

by Mervyn Skuy, Mandia Mentis, Angela Arnott & Isaac Nkwe

A BSTRACT
Extensions to the Instrumental Enrichment (IE) programme described in Part 1 of this article included a component of explicit bridging, and a dimension relating to creativity and socioemotional functioning (the CASE programme). Part 2 presents the experiment which compares IE, IE/CASE, and a control (academic enrichment) group. Seventh and eighth grade students (n = 120) in the Soweto Gifted Child programme were randomly allocated to one of the three groups. Intervention was conducted on 52 Saturdays over two years. The groups were compared on process variables, specially-designed measures of IE and CASE, and outcome measures of cognitive ability, creativity, self-concept and social skills. The results showed a consistent trend in favour of the experimental groups (IE and IE/CASE). In many instances, (including cognitive, creativity and process measures) these findings were significant. The IE/CASE group was superior in its provision of mediated learning experience, and other relevant aspects of teacher-student interaction. It was concluded that an IE programme which affords explicit bridging into the curriculum, and is supplemented by a programme of socioemotional development, may be most pervasively effective in enhancing the functioning of disadvantaged South African adolescents.

From International Journal of Cognitive Education & Mediated Learning, Vol. 1, No. 2, 1990. Reprinted with permission.

INTRODUCTION

In Part 1 of this article (Skuy, Mentis, Nkwe, Arnott & Hickson, 1990b), the rationale for and a description of extensions to the Instrumental Enrichment (IE) programme (Feuerstein, 1980), were provided. Briefly, it was suggested that sociopolitical conditions in South Africa have conduced to a widespread deprivation of mediated learning experience (MLE), which could be alleviated inter alia by the implementation of the IE programme. It was also argued that, while reviews of IE have consistently attested to its promise for improving the functioning of disadvantaged students, the programme has certain limitations. Two extensions proposed to counteract these were as follows: first, the addition to the IE of a component of explicit bridging into scholastic and everyday areas; secondly, a specific dimension relating to creative thinking and socioemotional functioning. These would complement the programme and thus relate to areas which are apparently not explicitly catered for in the IE programme.

The Creativity and Socioemotional Development (CASE) programme was designed to complement and extend IE by applying principles compatible with MLE, emotional development and creativity enhancement. This combination was considered to be particularly important for South African children, who suffer from a widespread loss of self-esteem as a result of racism, the undermining of their cultural mores, and their restricted access to the dominant culture. In South Africa, even children who are identified as gifted and who are, on this basis, selected for extramural enrichment in for example the Soweto Gifted Child Programme (SGCP), suffer from extensive cognitive deficits, (compare Skuy, Gaydon, Hoffenberg, & Fridjohn, 1990a). This is postulated to be the result of a deprivation of MLE, brought about by the country's socio- political and educational systems. It was thus considered that the extended Instrumental Enrichment programme might be valuable for such children.

Accordingly, this study aimed to assess the effectiveness of incorporating the extended IE programme into the SGCP. Specifically, it aimed to compare a combined IE/CASE programme and a regular IE programme, both of which would promote explicit bridging of IE principles into the curriculum. It also aimed to compare each of these groups with a Control group undergoing the conventional academic enrichment programme of the SGCP. It was intended to compare the three groups on the following: 1. several process variables (including the amount of MLE provided, the level of teacher questioning, and the quality and extent of teacher-pupil interaction); 2. specially-designed measures of competence achieved on the IE and CASE programmes; 3. outcome measures of cognitive ability, creativity, self-concept, and social skills.

METHOD
Subjects
The sample was drawn from the Soweto Gifted Child Programme (SGCP), all participants in which had been selected from Soweto and Alexandra, two largely impoverished black ghettoes within the greater Johannesburg area. The basis for selection had been overall academic adequacy, and good performance in at least one school subject. The mode of parental occupational and educational status was manual/skilled workers and tenth grade respectively. Subjects were thus of low socioeconomic status. Slightly more than half (54%) were female. (Mean age of the sample = 13.5 years).

Of the three hundred children participating in the SGCP, the 200 who were in the seventh/eighth and ninth/tenth grade classes were originally included in the study. However, because of the limited resources (that is, IE teachers) available, the three-way comparison of IE, IE/CASE and Control was implemented in the seventh/eighth grade only. The 120 students in those grade thus comprise the subjects of this study.

Procedure
Before the start of the academic year and thus of the SGCP, subjects were randomly and equally divided into the IE, IE/CASE and Control groups, respectively. Of the six highly qualified and experienced teachers employed by the SGCP for the 7th and 8th grades, four were randomly selected for participation (with about thirty other professionals) in an intensive nine-day IE workshop. The four IE-trained teachers were then randomly and equally divided between the two experimental groups.

For each experimental condition, there were two groups (grades 6 and 7, respectively) of twenty students, one at each of the two Centres of the SGCP. Each of these groups functioned as a separate, self-contained unit for the duration of the project. This was carried out on 52 Saturdays over two years, which reflected the normal timetable of SGCP. The teachers remained with their same groups for their contract period of one academic year. In the second year of the project's duration, three of the teachers (one from each of the experimental conditions) had to be replaced by new teachers, two of whom underwent a nine-day IE workshop prior to the start of the second academic year.

The weekly programme for each of the three experimental conditions is presented in Table 1 below.

Table 1 Programme for each of the experimental conditions

	Programme		
Period	IE Group	IE>CASE Group	Control Group
1 (9:00–11:00 am)	Work on the instruments of the IE programme and bridging into academic subjects	Work on the instruments of the IE programme and bridging	Work on school' subjects
2 (11:00 am–1:00 pm)	Work on the instruments of the IE programme and bridging	Implementation of CASE	Work on school subjects
3 (2:00–3:00 pm)	Work on school subjects (English, science, maths)	Work on school subjects	Work on school subjects

As can be seen from Table 1, the difference between the two experimental groups was that, while the IE group received IE for two thirds of the time and academic enrichment (i.e., extra tuition in school subjects) for one third, the IE/CASE group received IE, the specially-devised programme of creativity and socioemotional development, and academic enrichment, in three equal parts. The CASE programme complemented and extended the IE programme by applying principles and activities compatible with MLE to the emotional development and creativity enhancement of the students. Thus, metacognition was extended into "meta-emotion" or emotional self-awareness. For both IE groups, work on the actual pages of the IE Instruments was interspersed with direct and explicit bridging to the academic subjects (i.e., English, mathematics and science), as well as to everyday life situations. The Control group was exclusively concerned with the provision of additional input into scholastic subjects, (see Skuy et al., 1990, for a detailed description of the programmes).

Measures

Four categories of measures were included: 1. specially-designed tests administered after intervention, to assess the effectiveness with which the respective programmes (IE and CASE) were implemented; 2. analysis of a systematic sampling of videotaped lessons, to assess certain process variables; 3. measures of intellectual functioning, creativity and socioemotional functioning, conducted before and after intervention, to determine differences among the groups as a function of intervention, and 4. a Student Feedback Questionnaire, administered after the intervention to ascertain students' attitudes to their respective programmes. A description of each set of measures is presented below.

(1) *Specially-Designed Measures of the Intervention Programmes.* These are described in detail in Part 1 of this study (Skuy, et al., 1990b). For the IE and CASE programmes respectively, the measures comprise items which reflected the purposes, principles and activities of the programme. The IE test comprised two sections; one which required students to complete exercises from two of the IE Instruments (namely, Analytic Perception and Categorisation), and to label the cognitive operation and describe the strategies used to solve the problem; that is, to provide metacognitive insights into the way in which they had completed the exercises. The second section provided examples requiring bridging of the cognitive concepts to scholastic and everyday life areas. The *CASE test* also comprised two sections, reflecting two approaches to the assessment of the stu-

dents' ability to communicate construc- tively, empathically, and effectively.

(2) *Process Measures.* In order to measure teacher-student interaction, several scales were used as a basis for analysing videotaped material taken from the classroom. On a given day, in the first and second periods, each teacher in the two experimental groups was videotaped. For the purpose of analysis, each videotaped lesson was viewed in segments of five-minutes. Two raters independently viewed and rated each session and, where differences occurred, consulted and reached consensus. Three separate analyses of the videotapes were undertaken, involving the rating of the teachers on the following three scales: *Flanders' Interactive Analysis Categories* (FLAC; Flanders, 1970) is a ten-category system which assessed the amount of time the teacher talks, students talk or there is silence or confusion. The objective is to record the frequency of each interaction within a given period of time. The FLAC categorises various dimensions of the interactional process and, in particular, affective aspects of classroom behaviour. *The Orme Scale* (Orme, 1977) assesses the cognitive level of teachers' questions. It distinguishes between lower-level cognitive probes - where the teacher requests basic factual information or asks the student to rephrase or clarify his/her first answer - and higher level probes, where the teacher's questions require the student to predict, relate ideas, justify, critically analyse, evaluate, extrapolate and summarise. The modified version of the Orme Scale used by Silverman and Waxman (1988) was used here. The *Questionnaire on Mediated Learning Activities in the Classroom* (Egozi; reproduced in Sharron, 1987) served as the basis on which teachers were rated on the extent to which they implemented the various parameters constituting Feuerstein's (1979) construct of MLE. Using this scale to operationally define each of these parameters, ratings were made of the extent to which a teacher satisfied the criteria of MLE in her interaction with the pupil. These parameters included mediation of intentionality and reciprocity, transcendence, meaning, feelings of compe-

> In order to measure teacher-student interaction, several scales were used as a basis for analysing videotaped material taken from the classroom.

tence, sharing behaviour, indviduation, goal-seeking and achieving behaviour, challenge, and self-change. An eleventh category was included (i.e., "non-MLE") to assess activity contradictory to mediated learning.

For each of the Scales, the frequency of each response was recorded and subsequently averaged out so as to give an average number of interactions per five-minute period.

(3) *Pre-post Measures of Cognitive and Socioemotional Functioning and Creativity.* The *Similarities* test applied here was comprised of the combined Similarities subtests of the respective Verbal Scales of the Wechsler Intelligence Scale for Children (WISC-R) and the Weschsler Adult Intelligence Scale (WAIS-R). They measure verbal reasoning, conceptual ability and abstraction. The *Organiser* (Feuerstein, Rand, Haywood, Hoffman & Jensen, 1983) is a verbal test with a numerical component which assesses hypothetical or inferential thinking, the use of strategies for hypothesis testing, the gathering and application of logical evidence, and summative behaviour. The Similarities and Organiser were chosen as tests of cognitive functioning on the basis of their previously-demonstrated reliability, validity, and usefulness with South African adolescents (Skuy & Shmukler, 1987; Skuy, et al., 1990a). Rand & Kaniel (1987) report reliability coefficients of .8 and .9 for the Learning Potential Assessment Device (LPAD), of which the Organiser is part.

The two creativity measures used were taken from the Torrance tests of creative thinking (Torrance, 1974). They present unstructured stimuli which are devised to tap the subject's creative talent. The *Unusual Uses* test is a verbal measure where respondents are required to elicit as many new, different and exciting ideas surrounding a "newspaper" as a basic material in play or construction. *Circles* is a non-verbal test which required the students to use circles, which are pre-drawn on the protocol, to make as many new, different and exciting things as possible. Both tests were scored on criteria of Fluency, Flexibility and Originality of thought.

Two measures of self-concept were used here: first, the *Coopersmith (1967) Self-Esteem Inventory* designed to measure evaluative attitudes towards self in social, academic, family and personal areas of experience. This study used the School Short Form which provides a correlation with the original Form of

.86. Internal consistency has been estimated between .81 and .92 for different age groups, while acceptable levels of construct, concurrent and predictive validity have been documented (Coopersmith, 1967). In addition to this verbal, self-report questionnaire, a non-verbal, projective technique - that is, the *Draw-a-Person Test* (DAP) - was administered as a self-concept measure. The DAP is considered to reflect the drawer's perception of him/herself and his/her body image and self-concept. The DAP was scored in terms of four criteria drawn from a review of literature on the salient indicators on self-concept (Kamano, 1960; Koppitz, 1968; Machover, 1949; Ogden, 1978). The four items consisted of *size of drawing, fantasy/reality-based figure, profile versus frontal view,* and *placement on the page.* These dimensions were rated on a five-point scale, with a score of 1 representing the most deviant response, and a score of 5 reflecting a response that has consensually been regarded as reflective of adjustment/good self-concept (Rosenbaum, 1989).

To assess social behaviour, a *Social Skills Questionnaire* (Spence, 1985) was used. It involved a rating by the teachers of their students' skills in interacting with adults and peers (e.g., handling of aggression; ease of communication, etc.). The Questionnaire involves 24 items, each with a five point rating scale. There are no validity or reliability data on this scale, which is used clinically, as the basis for a structured programme of social skills training.

(4)   *Student Feedback Questionnaire.* In order to elicit feedback from students themselves regarding their attitudes to their respective programmes of intervention (IE, IE/CASE and Control), a rating scale was devised. This covered issues concerning attitudes towards group membership, extent of enjoyment and perceived learning afforded by the group, social relationships within the group, and programme content. Items required students to respond on a five point rating scale, ranging from Strongly Agree to Strongly Disagree. There was also an open-ended section for comments.

RESULTS

Overall Results on the Pre-Post Measures

To determine whether there were any significant differences among the experimental conditions on the pre-post measures following intervention, several multiple analyses of variance (MANCOVAs) were conducted on different groupings among the measures. For all the measures taken together, Wilks' criterion yielded no significant difference. This was also true for measures subsumed under the heading of socioemotional functioning (namely, the Coopersmith Self-Esteem Inventory, the DAP, and the Social Skills Questionnaire). On the other hand, Wilks' criterion for the combined verbal measures (Similarities and the Unusual Uses creativity test) demonstrated a highly significant difference among the three experimental conditions; F $(4,120) = 5.32$; p. $<.001$. Using a least squares mean test, the difference was shown to lie between the two experimental groups on the one hand (IE and IE/CASE) and the Control on the other.

Although the MANCOVA did not yield an overall significant difference among the groups on the pre-post measures, the overall trend on all the categories of measures was a consistent one, in that the experimental groups were invariably favoured over the Control group.

Results on the Individual Pre-Post Measures

To determine whether there were significant differences among the IE, IE/CASE and Control groups on any of the individual pre-post measures, separate analyses of co-variance (ANCOVAs) were conducted on their respective results. Where significant differences among the groups were found, a least squares mean test was conducted to determine between which groups the significance lay. Table 2 presents the mean differences on each measure for each of the groups, and indicates on which of the measures significant differences were found.

As Table 2 (see next page) shows, the Similarities test significantly differentiated both experimental groups from the Control group, with a tendency for the IE/CASE group to do better than the IE group. There was also a significant difference found for the Unusual Uses verbal creativity test, in this case

Table 2 Mean changes and significant differences between the IE, IE/CASE and Control groups on the outcome measures

Measure	IE	Mean Change		F	Least Squares Mean	
		IE/CASE	Control			
Cognitive						
Similarities	3.4	4.8	2.2	8.80***	IE/CASE>Control	***
					IE>Control	*
Organiser	3.8	2.9	1.8			
Creativity						
Circles						
Total test	9.8	8.7	5.8			
Fluency	2.8	3.1	2.1			
Flexibility	5.0	3.9	2.4	2.86#	IE>Control	*
Originality	2.0	1.7	1.2			
Unusual Uses						
Total test	13.8	12.1	9.9	3.57*	IE>Control	*
Fluency	5.2	6.7	2.1			
Flexibility	4.9	3.3	2.4	5.78**	IE>Control	*
					IE/CASE>Control	*
Originality	3.7	3.1	1.2	3.36*	IE>Control	*
Socioemotional						
Draw-a-person	-.06	0.7	-0.6	2.81#	IE/CASE>Control	*
Coopersmith	1.6	5.2	1.1			
Social skills	1.9	3.4	1.7			

Key: df 2,117   #p = .07   *p < .05   **p < .01   ***p < .001

Table 3 Means and significant differences between the IE, IE/CASE and Control groups on certain items of the process measures

Measure	IE	Means	Control	F	Bonferroni (Dunn) t Test
		IE/CASE			
FIAC					
Praises pupils	3.3	6.7	0.6	8.30*	IE/CASE>Control
					IE/CASE>IE
Accepts/uses ideas	0.7	2.6	1.1	3.45*	IE/CASE>IE
Asks questions	10.8	21.6	6.7	4.28*	IE/CASE>Control
Orme Scale					
Prompt/hint/rephrase	1.9	5.0	1.0	4.42*	IE/CASE>IE
					IE/CASE>Control
Critical awareness	1.6	1.6	0.1	3.52*	IE/CASE>Control
					IE>Control
Summary	0.0	0.9	0.0	6.01**	IE/CASE>IE
					IE/CASE>Control
Frequency of interaction	61.9	97.3	46.7	4.59**	IE/CASE>Control
QML					
ML activity	61.1	105.6	47.0	24.4***	IE/CASE>IE
					IE/CASE>Control
					IE>Control
Non-ML activity	2.9	0.4	14.6	22.5***	IE/CASE>IE
					IE/CASE>Control
					IE>Control

Key: df 2,117   *p < .05   **p < .01   ***p < .001

FIAC = Flanders Interaction Analysis Categories
QML = Questionnaire on Mediated Learning (ML)

between the IE and Control groups, with the IE/CASE group tending to be higher than the Control. This was true also for the Originality dimension of the Unusual Uses test, while for the Flexibility dimension, both the IE and IE/CASE groups performed significantly better than the Control group. As Table 2 also indicates, the difference among the groups tended towards significance ($p = .07$) on both the Circles (non-verbal) creativity test and the Draw-a-Person Self-Concept Measure.

Findings for IE and CASE Tests

The mean scores obtained for the IE and IE/CASE groups were 52.8 and 51.3, respectively, while the Control group received a mean of 39. The analysis of variance (ANOVA) yielded a highly significant difference among the three groups ($F = 15$; $p < .0001$), which the Bonferroni (Dunn) t-test demonstrated to lie between IE and CASE on the one hand, and the Control on the other. As would be expected, the degree of metacognition and bridging skills demonstrated on this test by the groups receiving IE was significantly superior to the group not exposed to this intervention. For the CASE test, the difference among the groups shown by the ANOVA also reflected significance (Means: IE/CASE = 12, IE = 11, C = 10.6, $F = 3.08$; $p < .05$). In this instance, the results of the IE/CASE group were shown by the Bonferroni test to be significantly better than the Control group. Thus, and again as expected, the IE/CASE group performed more effectively on a measure of interpersonal skills than the other two groups.

> As would be expected, the degree of metacognition and bridging skills demonstrated on this test by the groups receiving IE was significantly superior to the group not exposed to this intervention.

Results on the Process Measures

Table 3 presents results pertaining to the analysis of the videotaped teacher-pupil intervention. Results for the MLE Scale, frequency of interaction, as well as for items significantly discriminating among the groups on the *Flanders Interaction Analysis Categories* (FIAC) and the Orme Scale are presented.

As Table 3 indicates, the ANOVA conducted on the results of the three groups on the MLE Scale yielded a highly significant difference among the three experimental conditions both in the amount of MLE and of non-MLE activity. In both instances, the Bonferroni (Dunn) *t*-test showed the IE/CASE groups' results to be significantly better than those of the IE group, which in turn performed significantly better than the Control group. Three items on the FIAC yielded significant differences among the groups, in each case significantly favouring IE/CASE. Two of these items related to acceptance and use of pupil's ideas, and praise and encouragement of pupils, respectively. The third item indicated that, in the IE/CASE group, the teacher was significantly more inclined to ask questions.

On the Orme Scale, the IE/CASE group produced a significantly better result on both a lower-order probe (questions calling for expansion of student response) and on two higher-order questions (namely, those calling for critical awareness on the part of the students, and those requiring students to summarise discussion points). Finally, an assessment of the average number of teacher-student interactions of any kind produced during a session yielded a significant difference among the groups, with the IE/CASE group displaying a significantly greater frequency of interaction than the Control group.

Results on the Student Feedback Questionnaire

Comparison of the mean ratings by students on the Pupil Feedback Questionnaire indicated that the IE/CASE group tended to rate their programme more positively ($x = 32.29$), followed by the IE groups ($x = 31.07$) and then the Control group ($x = 27.28$). An ANOVA yielded a significant difference among the groups ($F = 3.15$; p $<.05$), while the Bonferroni test indicated that the difference lay between the IE/CASE and Control groups. The open-ended section indicated that most students of the IE/CASE and IE groups were motivated to report (positively) on their experience, while only about half the Control group commented, many of them negatively. The IE/CASE students were particularly forthcoming in their comments, and 85% of these were unreservedly positive. Several negative comments which did emerge from both the IE and IE/CASE groups related to students' concern that they were receiving less academic input than the Control group. They nevertheless favoured their respective groups over the Control group.

DISCUSSION

The importance of identifying the essential variables involved in the successful implementation of IE has been stressed by Burden (1990). Clearly, as Burden points out, the most important of these would be the quality of mediation provided by the teacher. In this study, the videotapes taken of the teachers implementing their respective programmes afforded an opportunity to determine the extent to which they had applied the criteria of MLE, and at the same time afforded an assessment of their functioning in terms of other process variables, including level of questioning, and quality and quantity of teacher-pupil interaction. The results on those process variables reflected a consistently superior performance for the IE/CASE group in relation to the Control group. Thus, the quality, level and quantity of interaction along these dimensions was highest for IE/CASE and, in the case of quality of MLE, the IE group was significantly superior to the Control.

These findings suggest that the key variables underlying the IE programme were in fact present, and were particularly well-implemented when IE was combined with the CASE programme. This suggests that an emphasis on interpersonal communication skills, a concern with "meta-emotion" or with greater awareness of one's feelings and attitudes, and participation in activities designed to improve social skills, are facilitative of an optimal level of interaction, and thus enhance implementation of the IE programme. For, the significantly high level of interaction evidenced in the IE/CASE group as compared with the Control groups suggests that the IE/CASE teachers were more interpersonally-oriented, and used the IE in a more dynamic,

> ... concern with "meta-emotion" or with greater awareness of one's feelings and attitudes, and participation in activities designed to improve social skills, are facilitative of an optimal level of interaction, and thus enhance implementation of the IE programme.

interpersonal fashion than the IE group, which may have become too bogged down on the tasks and materials themselves.

Thus, while the children in the IE/CASE programme had only half as much IE as their IE group counterparts, the IE/CASE group nevertheless performed almost as well as the IE group on the test specially-designed to assess the effectiveness with which the IE programme had been implemented. On that test, there was a clear indication that the IE has been effectively implemented in both groups, insofar as subjects displayed enhanced metacognition (awareness of strategies and operations) and ability to bridge principles learned into everyday life and academic areas. On the other hand, the significantly better result of the IE/CASE group on the CASE test suggests that students in that programme learnt the principles of interpersonal communication which they had been taught.

It is noteworthy that, on a cognitive measure, that is, the combined Similarities subtests of the WISC-R and WAIS-R, the IE and the IE/CASE programmes achieved significantly better results than the Control group after intervention. Here again it is interesting that the affective component afforded by the CASE programme exerted a facilitative effect, together with the IE programme, in improving conceptual ability. The positive findings for both IE groups are particularly salutary in that most of the significant positive results in the cognitive area previously reported in studies of IE have been obtained on standard *non-verbal* measures of intelligence: that is, largely on measures of skill in processing figural or spatial information, (Savell, Twohig, and Rachford, 1986). Similarly, in their review of the studies of IE, Sternberg and Bhana (1986) concluded that greatest gains were likely to be in the areas of abstract reasoning and spatial visualisation rather than in the area of verbal skills. The positive effects achieved here with the extended IE programme in the verbal conceptual area is of particular relevance in South Africa - where language and verbal conceptual abilities are major difficulties for disadvantaged communities. The results tie up with those found in a previous study using the Similarities subtests in the Soweto Gifted Child Programme (SGCP; Skuy, et al., 1990a). In that study, the Similarities subtest emerged as a significant predictor of performance in the

SGCP, suggesting the importance of verbal conceptual skills in determining success in an academic enrichment programme.

Further evidence for the effectiveness of the IE programme in improving verbal abilities was provided by the verbal creativity measure. The encouragement of autonomous thinking, as well as of a broad application of concepts and expansion of ideas (bridging) could explain the enhanced performance in the flexibility and originality dimensions of creative thinking. In this regard, the IE group produced better results than the IE/CASE group, pointing up the opportunities that the IE programme *per se* offers for promoting creativity. It should be remembered that the IE group had twice as much opportunity to engage in creativity as the IE/CASE group by virtue of the former's more extended exposure to the IE programme itself. In any case, while the CASE programme was originally intended to focus explicitly on creativity as well as socioemotional development, it tended in practice to underplay the creativity dimension. A future study should include a "creativity process measure" which would assess the degree to which tutors actually implemented IE creatively.

Although the important dimension of motivation was not tapped here, the Student Feedback Questionnaire, both in its quantitative and qualitative aspects, gave some indication of the relative attitudes of students in the experimental and control groups. Of the three groups, the students in the IE/CASE group were most positive about the experience, and significantly more so than the Control group. However, concerns of students undergoing IE that their scholastic success might be compromised by reduced academic input, will have to be more effectively addressed.

With regard to the measures of socioemotional functioning, no significant differences among the groups was found, but there was a consistent tendency for the IE/CASE group to perform better than the IE group, which in turn consistently tended to perform better than the Control group. For the Draw-a-Person test, the result favouring the IE/CASE group approached significance. This is positive in light of the widely-documented stability of tested self-concept. It is also an interesting finding in relation to the novel approach to testing developed here (Rosenbaum, 1989) and suggests that this bears further investigation.

Generally, the findings suggest that the explicit inclusion within the IE programme of a component of socioemotional development can improve the effectiveness with which tutors implement IE - both in terms of the quality of MLE and the sustained level of interaction. The results also suggest that, while the IE programme without the explicit focus on interpersonal interaction can have a positive influence on cognitive functioning, the effects may be at least as good, and possibly more pervasive and holistic, when the affective dimension of functioning is explicitly addressed too. Further, the opportunities for bridging of the IE concepts into the academic curriculum were shown to exert a facilitative effect on the students' ability to carry out such bridging. It appears that the extensive bridging activity may also be associated with enhanced creative thinking, in that both require an expansion and an extension of concepts and ideas. Thus IE can enhance creative thinking.

> ... the explicit inclusion within the IE programme of a component of socioemotional development can improve the effectiveness with which tutors implement IE.

The viability of the IE programme and of the dimension of socioemotional development for disadvantaged South African adolescents was demonstrated. The acid test, which still lies ahead, requires an evaluation of the long-term effectiveness of the programme, as measured against such objective criteria as school success and social adjustment. A study of this nature is in progress.

CORRESPONDENCE
Professor Mervyn Skuy, Division of Specialised Education, University of the Witwatersrand, P.O. Wits 2050, Johannesburg, South Africa

REFERENCES

Burden, R.L. (1990). Whither research on Instrumental Enrichment? Some suggestions for future action. *International Journal of Cognitive Education and Mediated Learning, 1*(1) 83-86.

Coopersmith, S. (1967). *The antecedents of self-esteem.* San Francisco: W.H. Freeman.

Feuerstein, R. (1979). *The dynamic assessment of retarded performers.* Baltimore: University Park Press.

Feuerstein, R. (1980). *Instrumental Enrichment.* Glenview, IL: Scott Foresman.

Feuerstein, R., Rand, Y., Haywood, C., Hoffman, M.B., Jensen, M.R. (1983). *Learning Potential Assessment Device.* Unpublished manual, Hadassah-Wizo Institute, Jerusalem.

Flanders, N.A. (1970). *Analysing Teaching Behaviour.* New York: Addison-Wesley.

Kamano, D.K. (1960). An investigation on the meaning of human figure drawing. *Journal of Clinical Psychology, 16,* 429-430.

Koppitz, E.M. (1968). *Psychological evaluation of children's human figure drawings.* New York: Grune & Stratton.

Machover, K. (1949). *Personality projection in the drawing of the human figure.* Springfield, Illinois: Charles C. Thomas.

Ogden, D. (1978). *Psychodiagnostics and personality assessment: A handbook.* (2nd Ed.) California: Western Psychological Services.

Orme, M. (1977). Teaching strategies and consultation skills: probing techniques. In Miezitisis & M. Orme, (Eds.), *Innovation in School Psychology. Toronto: The Ontario Institute for Studies in Education.*

Read, Y., & Kaniel, S. (1987). Group administration of the Learning Potential Assessment Device. In C.S. Lidz (Ed.), *Dynamic assessment* (pp. 196-214). New York: Guilford Press.

Rosenbaum, L.A. (1989). Enhancement of self-concept in gifted disadvantaged children. Unpublished M.Ed. thesis. University of the Witwatersrand, South Africa.

Savell, J.M., Twohig, P.T., & Rachford, D.L. (1986). Empirical status of Feuerstein's Instrumental Enrichment techniques as a method of teaching thinking skills. *Review of Educational Research, 56* (4), 381-409.

Sharron, H. (1987). *Changing children's minds: Feuerstein's revolution in the teaching of intelligence.* London: Souvenir Press.

Silverman, H., & Waksman, M. (1988). Feuerstein's Instrumental Enrichment: elicitation of cognitive interaction in the classroom. *Canadian Journal of Special Education,* 4(2), 133-150.

Skuy, M.S., Gaydon, V., Hoffenberg, S., & Fridjohn. (1990a). Predictors of performance of disadvantaged adolescents in a gifted program. *Gifted Child Quarterly, 34*(3), 97-101.

Skuy, M.S., Mentis, M., Nkwe, P.I., Arnott, A., & Hickson, J. (1990b). Combining Instrumental Enrichment and creativity/socioemotional development for disadvantaged gifted adolescents in Soweto: Part 1. *International Journal of Cognitive Education & Mediated Learning, 1*(1), 25-31.

Skuy, M., & Shmukler, D. (1987). Effectiveness of the Learning Potential Assessment Device with Indian and "Coloured" adolescents in South Africa. *International Journal of Special Education, 2,* 131-149.

Spence, S. (1985). *Social skills training with children and adolescents.* Windsor, England: NFER-Nelson Publishing Co.

Torrance, E.P. (1974). *Torrance tests of creativity thinking: Technical-norms manual.* Lexington, MA: Personnel Press.

Sternberg, R.J., & Bhana, K. (1986). Synthesis of research on the effectiveness of intellectual skills programs: Snake oil remedies or miracle cures? *Educational Leadership, 44,* 60-67.

A Systems Approach to the Application of Feuerstein's Instrumental Enrichment

Why doesn't Instrumental Enrichment always result in gains in academic achievements? Why do Instrumental Enrichment students often experience difficulties finding and bridging examples with subject matter? Why are there so many students who believe that Instrumental Enrichment consists of thinking, and academic work is about memorizing facts and chasing right answers? This section attempts to answer these questions by explaining that the thinking paradigm ought not be limited to Instrumental Enrichment classes. Articles in this section argue that the answers to these questions directly relate to the way education is structured and delivered. Departmentalized curricula and different teaching styles; teachers' low expectations regarding cognitive modifiability; and certain social environments in schools are detractors of learning and the formation of reflective thought.

Research indicates that learning and thinking abilities greatly depend upon the development of a well-integrated cognitive system and that such a development is facilitated by rich and contextually diverse learning experiences. These findings suggest that if education is to develop cognitive abilities it must be consistent and coherent. The goal of enhancing cognitive abilities cannot be limited to the Instrumental Enrichment teacher in the Instrumental Enrichment classroom, but rather it should drive the entire curriculum. Instrumental Enrichment can help facilitate educational reform and support its institutionalization, but ought to be followed by the remainder of education. It is neither designed, nor should be expected to "save" the existing education paradigm.

In the first part of this section Presseisen, Smey-Richman, and Beyer present the desired relationship between (restructured) schools and the cognitive paradigm. Schools must be responsive to the development of all children's thinking and learning abilities. Curriculum, instruction, and assessment must be integrated in schools around concerns for students' ability to manage information and tasks, manage self development, and be cooperative learners. These three elements must be concerned with mediated learning and the processes, rather than products of knowing and problem solving.

In the latter part of this section, Williams and Kopp show that such restructuring is possible. They tell how the Taunton School officials used Instrumental Enrichment and LPAD to change the school system and how this change improved outcomes. They describe how accountability was built into the system and how cognitive modification "earned" priority and was institutionalized as a goal. The pair discusses how resistance, budget, scheduling, and other difficulties were overcome in favor of meaningful system developments. The authors tell about increased cooperation between educational service providers, enhanced expectations on the part of educators and psychologists, enhanced student self-esteem, improved student academic performance, and increased student attendance. Taunton is now an excellent source for learning about educational system reforms for other schools and college students.

Cognitive Development Through Radical Change: Restructuring Classroom Environments for Students At Risk

by Barbara Z. Presseisen, Barbara Smey-Richman, and Francine S. Beyer

The prevalent perception is that the student must adjust to the teachers and the school, while the latter remain fixed and unchanging. It is important to develop the reverse and opposite approach which focuses on the need of the system for structural modifiability and maximum flexibility. Responsibility for the student's failure always lies with the educational system rather than with the child.—S. Kaniel & R. Feuerstein (1989)

For nearly a decade, American education has been engaged in a major examination of how to reform itself. Report upon report has detailed the need, if not the alternative paradigms, for extensive revamping of the goals, means, and outcomes of preparing graduates for a new world and a new century (Adler, 1982; Goodlad, 1984; Sizer, 1984). What was previously "school reform" or "educational improvement" has become a demand to "restructure" the entire system—not merely tinker with but radically redesign current, less-than-viable models.

At the same time, government officials, business leaders, and various educational researchers have contributed views of the specific problems they believe need to be addressed in this

From J. N. Mangieri & C. C. Block (Eds.). (1993). *Creating Powerful Thinking in Teachers and Students: Diverse Perspectives.* Fort Worth, TX: Harcourt, Brace & Jovanovich.

extraordinary effort (Carnevale, 1991; Conley, 1991; McDonnell, 1989; Schlechty, 1990). They are eager to suggest solutions they believe show promise for needed school change. In terms of educational activity, a great deal of this energy has been expended since the publication of **A Nation at Risk** (National Commission, 1983). Now the time is ripe to see how well focused this era of educational reform has become. Does it make a difference to teachers and students in the classroom? Does it serve the neediest as well as the most accomplished students in America's schools? Is there a national consensus as to how the nation's schools should change, and **why**?

THE PROBLEM OF RADICAL CHANGE

Although restructuring education means different things according to different perspectives, the larger dimensions of current demands for change are fairly well agreed upon. "Dynamic and unanticipated global changes of a profound sort are shaping the world," says one report (Council of Chief State School Officers, 1991, p. 1), and with these changes come necessary shifts in political, economic, and social structures. The first aspect of restructuring suggests education must keep up with the global workplace and help American institutions prepare **all** employees for the higher-level skills required in an increasingly technological, computerized world (Secretary's Commission, 1991). Over the long haul, and into the twenty-first century, some say America must attend to the many complex transitions in its post-industrial economy or its workers may be forced to accept the alternative of lower wages and lesser work (Commission on the Skills of the American Workforce, 1990). On the heels of Russia's disintegration and with the realities of Japanese competition, America's reform educators seek a new paradigm for the nation's schools that will enable the nation to retain, or regain, its world-wide competitiveness.

A different understanding of learning is a second aspect that marks the vision of a restructured school, and with it a keener insight into the development of human potential (Dickinson, 1991; Feuerstein, 1990). The more traditional outcomes of America's schools in the 20th century—academic success for some and marginal failure for many—are now held in grave doubt and are considered inherently unequal (Darling-Hammond, 1990). Many reformers maintain that workers at all levels must develop the abilities to learn more easily and adapt flexibly to new circumstances. Whether college-bound or workplace directed, every citizen will need to be able to read complex materials, understand them, and apply multiple skills of literacy and numeracy to tasks associated with such materials (Brown, 1991a; Zuboff, 1988). Today, the "one-literacy schoolhouse," where knowledge is merely collected in a narrow, cumulative frame-work and then tested by traditional psychometric means, is as outmoded as a communication system dominated by print or a government insensitive to the influence of mass media.

Underlying this new appreciation for learning is an assumption regarding the importance of the learner's **active participation** in restructured schooling, as though the end of the century has somehow returned to John Dewey's (1964) initial vision of education and democracy (Glickman, 1991; Presseisen, 1991). The role of individual development and the significance of authentic student achievement in building intellectual competence are restructuring issues underscored in this context (Newmann, 1991). Being educated today requires that what is studied at school must mean something to the learner and change his/her perspective about the topic under examination; it calls for a particular knowledge base that is intellectually dealt with and, ultimately, reconceived. The relatively short time spent at school—compared to other activities in which students are engaged, like television viewing—must reach far beyond:

> . . .the basic decoding and encoding, even beyond basic factual knowledge, to encompass understanding how different people know what they know, communicate, think, and attack problems. Always implicit—and explicit—is the assumption that one cannot acquire such an understanding without **practicing** [emphasis added] the requisite kinds of thinking, communicating, and problem solving. (Brown, 1991b, p. 142)

In one sense, restructured schooling means the very definition of school is being reformulated. In terms of learning experience, school occupies a unique juncture between initial rearing in the home and community and ultimate performance in the world of work. In the dynamic framework of change and the growing sophistication of the global marketplace, schools are emerging as special locales for creating and refining learner competencies. To be effective, educational institutions are now also required to become human resource development centers, not mere sorters of ability. In particular, schools must address the learning needs of every student, even those historically most poorly served.

In this new view of education, there is an assumption that schooling must be involved in the enhancement of every student's learning potential. The primary focus of this chapter addresses the concerns of both Hodgkinson (1985, 1991) and Hilliard (1991); that is, how can school environments be restructured to address the key requisites of **cognitive development** of every youngster in America, including those most at risk of school failure? As the recent riots in Los Angeles indicate—in terms of the changing demographics and severe deprivations affecting the school populations of America's major cities—if we have the will to educate all our children then we must address this question. The historic concerns related to changing American schooling and the research underlying them are the focus of the following section, after which the essential elements of a restructured classroom environment are examined indepth. The chapter then presents implications of this examination for at-risk students and their learning. The final section summarizes the findings of the study and projects needed future research and development.

HISTORIC CONCERNS AND RESTRUCTURING

Ideas about reforming America's schools are rooted in various historic issues that influence changes in many social institutions. Four areas of concern are relevant to the focus of this study: an understanding of the roots of the cognitive revolution, the impetus of the current teaching thinking movement, the nature of restructured classroom environments for learning, and the needs of a burgeoning, at-risk student population in our nation's public schools. It is proposed that research and analyses of these topics form a basis for understanding the needed alterations in American schooling.

The Roots of the Cognitive Revolution

To understand the various viewpoints of restructured schooling, one needs to appreciate the impact of the so-called "cognitive revolution" that occurred during the second half of the
twentieth century . . . (Baars, 1986; Gardner, 1985). Cognition
is a branch of psychology that gradually has become a discrete
science on its own. As an interdisciplinary approach, it offers
new ways of examining mind and mental processes in humans,
other animals, and even machines. Studies of intelligence (natural and artificial), memory, brain research, and creativity in
many contents are only a part of the emergent literature on cognition (Diamond, 1988; Gardner, 1985;
Penrose, 1989). "The word 'cognitive' may
suggest that this field deals not with the
whole mind but only with knowledge, including perception, reasoning, language,
and even learning," says Boden (1990, p. 9).
But cognitive scientists also seek to explain
purpose, emotion, and even consciousness.
In cognitive neuroscience, the special connections between mind and brain are pur-

> For a long time,
> developmental psy-
> chologists were the
> lone voices interested
> in the importance
> of cognition for
> schooling.

sued as related parts of an integrated, intelligent system (Miller,
1989). It is not surprising that schools—as generators of
thoughtful learners—would find much to explore in the field of
cognitive science. But such a relationship has not always been in
fashion and, currently, many schools remain unaware of this
content and its implications for curriculum, instruction, and assessment.

For a long time, developmental psychologists were the lone
voices interested in the importance of cognition for schooling.
With them, some early childhood specialists and special educators stood opposed to an educational psychology—particularly
as practiced in the United States—marked by static behaviorism
and mechanistic theory (Baars, 1986; Elkind, 1979). The focus
on the developing learner, the explicit instruction of thinking
and metacognition, and the critical importance of learners' dispositions and attitudes, as well as the emphasis on the social
context of intellectual change, have all been outcomes of the
new hegemony of cognition in the world of teaching and learn-

ing (Collins, Brown & Holum, 1991). At the same time, however, teacher preparation and program evaluation research resisted these new modes (Beyer, 1988; Detterman & Sternberg, 1982; Dillon & Sternberg, 1986; Resnick & Klopfer, 1989; Sternberg, 1982). Today, educational research is rediscovering the works of Vygotsky (Kozulin, 1990; Lipman, 1991; Moll, 1992; Wertsch, 1985) and Feuerstein (Jones & Pierce, 1992; Lidz, 1987; Presseisen & Kozulin, 1992; Sharron, 1987). It is confronted by a rich literature on cognition which maintains that thinking and comprehension actually can be taught to all children (Bransford & Vye, 1989; Haller, Child & Walberg, 1988). Thus, says Costa (1991), if restructured schools are inherently places of cognitive development, they must—by definition—also be organized as institutions that are "homes for the mind."

Restructured schools, in this view, are places in which teachers strive to be cognitively creative in their instruction, where, as lifelong learners themselves, they seek to refine their professional ability to enhance every student's autonomy and ability to think, and where they constantly seek to create conditions for optimal student achievement. This is the heart of the new cognitive paradigm in education. It is a model that stresses the explicit need to teach students thinking—albeit in particular contents—and to focus on intellectual concerns as the central purpose of schooling.

The Teaching Thinking Movement

The teaching of "thinking" to all students in school is relatively a new concept in education, although the general goal of thoughtfulness has long been a hallmark in liberal education (Paul, 1987; Resnick, 1987a). Essentially, the current movement developed to counter the "back to basics" view as an inadequate goal for youngsters who will work most of their adult lives in the 21st century. Teaching thinking first and foremost involves cognitive outcomes; it seeks to make learners more successful in their academic achievement by helping **all** students to improve their intellectual ability. The movement also seeks student autonomy and independence of thought as an ultimate aim (Kamii, 1984).

Advocates of teaching thinking have proposed the instruction of various specific cognitive operations or skills (Beyer,

1988; Marzano et al., 1988), and the advancement of subjective dispositions (Ennis, 1991). Comprehensive listings of these processes vary according to specific objectives, such as a goal for critical thinking expertise, or creative design outcomes, or problem-solving strategies. Whatever the specific objective, several key assumptions are usually operative in all teaching thinking efforts: (1) the student needs to be actively involved in **using** the particular skills, so that his/her adaptation and control over the processes increase; (2) intervention or instruction planned for the learner should be tailored to meet his/her distinctive needs, should involve social interaction as well as personal reflection (especially as facilitated by a more knowledgeable mediator), and should aim to develop the mental potential of the learner as far as possible (Feuerstein, 1990); and (3) knowledge areas within the curriculum should be integrated with the thinking operations as quickly as possible, and be applied in varying contexts and settings (Collins, Brown & Holum, 1991; Nickerson, 1986).

Teaching thinking is associated with multiple literacies and generally focuses on higher-level content, even for young children

Teaching thinking is associated with multiple literacies and generally focuses on higher-level content, even for young children (Brown, 1991b; Eisner, 1982). The mere coverage of subject matter, the heart of the old paradigm of schooling, has been replaced as a goal for all learners by deeper understanding of disciplinary constructs, more sophisticated problem-solving strategies, and an awareness of alternate approaches to characterizing particular subject matters. The current thinking movement seeks to make students adept at building connections among similar constructs and, ultimately, aims at operational, if not systematic, transfer among similarly-patterned knowledge areas (Perkins & Salomon, 1988; Sternberg, 1990a). Domain-specific knowledge combined with higher ability in science, for example, is projected to help students develop both a conceptual and a practical understanding of scientific reasoning and inquiry that goes far beyond the memorization of discrete facts or even carefully-assembled, but rote-learned, "experiments" (Adey, 1990).

There are a variety of approaches to implementing teaching thinking in the school's curriculum (Presseisen, 1992). In one sense, every academic area has sought to make its subject more thoughtful and students more strategic. These applications have benefitted a great deal from specific thinking programs that have been developed by researchers seeking particular objectives, such as teaching philosophy and reasoning (Lipman, Sharp & Oscanyan, 1980), remediating particular cognitive dysfunctions (Feuerstein, 1980), and developing critical thinking ability (Pogrow, 1992; Winocur, 1986). The impact of these programs has been the subject of various research-based examinations (Chance, 1986; Sternberg & Bhana, 1986). Although these efforts have been found to be generally effective, more objective and extensive research is still needed. Training for these programs and various support efforts to aid their implementation are currently being conducted across the United States, as well as around the world (Presseisen, 1992).

It must be remembered that teaching thinking is a revolution in process. Although keenly intertwined with the movement to reform educational practice, and talked about extensively in educational research literature, there is no guarantee that it is a revolution that will succeed. Much depends on whether schools are successfully restructured, and what is focused upon in that transformation.

Restructured Environments for Learning

Although there is no concise, commonly held definition of restructuring, nor a single model that can be universally applied, there is general agreement on what counts as school restructuring and what does not (Harvey & Crandall, 1988; Smey-Richman, 1991). Since restructuring advocates believe that schools in their current form are performing about as well as possible, restructuring is not aimed at adding more of the same or making significant improvement to the current structure (Goodlad, 1984; Schlechty, 1989). Rather, restructuring involves altering a school's pattern of rules, roles, and relationships—both within one building and among the several schools in a district—in order to produce substantially different results from those currently obtained (Corbett, 1990; Schlechty, 1989; Sparks, 1991; Wilson, 1971). The shared belief that the current system must be dramatically rethought and redesigned to be more effective underlies all discussions about school restructuring. Herein lie the ties to both the cognitive revolution and the goal to teach intellectual skills.

The attractiveness of restructuring as a theme for educational reform may stem from its ability to "accommodate a variety of conceptions of what is problematical about American education, as well as a variety of solutions" (Elmore, 1991, p. 4). Since opinions vary, a number of schemes for categorizing restructuring activities have been proposed (Council of Chief State School Officers, 1989; David, 1987; Elmore, 1988; McDonnell, 1989). These schemes usually include three main themes: (1) focusing on teaching academic subject matter in ways that promote understanding and problem-solving, (2) shift power toward individual schools and the people who work in them; and (3) ensuring the accountability of educators to their clients and to the broader public (Elmore, 1991). Thus, reformers have focused on four broad dimensions of restructuring: curriculum and instruction, authority and decision making, new professional roles for teachers; and accountability systems (David, 1987). A fifth dimension, collaboration with others, is also often added (Smey-Richman, 1991).

> In several restructuring schemes, curriculum, instruction, and assessment are the three central school variables examined because they focus most directly on student learning.

While for analytic purposes it is useful to treat each restructuring dimension separately, in practice reform proposals frequently address more than one dimension simultaneously. Also, regarding practice, the overarching criteria for judging the potential effectiveness of a reform effort lies in its link to student achievement and other desirable student outcomes. Choosing a single dimension as a point of departure for school restructuring has serious implications for both the process of reform and anticipated results (Elmore, 1991; McDonnell, 1989). Furthermore, changes in one dimension are not always consistent with changes in the others.

In several restructuring schemes, curriculum, instruction, and assessment are the three central school variables examined because they focus most directly on student learning (Conley, 1991). They are also the key concerns of a teacher's behavior and understanding in creating a seminal environment for intellectual change. If one were to restructure the classroom environment as the major point of teacher-student-learning interaction, what would such an experience look like? Presseisen (1992) suggests:

> The construct of a 'learning environment' is an important concept on the road to intervention. Environment is more than mere surroundings or the 'climate' of a classroom. A learning environment amply provides social opportunities for instruction, and when mutual and reciprocal, for learning. Such an environment includes provocative information, but also feelings, dispositions, and lively models of cognitive strategizing. It is a qualitative locale, a nurturing, mediating, and mind-expanding exploratorium. (p. 11)

Advocacy for restructured schools must deal initially with the three variables of curriculum, instruction, and assessment, and how these variables go together in an environmental whole. How they influence the diverse students in a given classroom then becomes the essence of education's radical change. In the new paradigm for schooling, how these variables are addressed by the teacher, both in everyday and long-term planning for learning, is the key to student intellectual development. Nowhere is this more significant than in understanding students at risk of school failure.

The Needs of At-Risk Students

Just as there is no one, commonly held definition of restructuring, there is no one, commonly held definition of our nation's "at-risk student" population. Although Comer (1988) states that in this complicated age all students are potentially at-risk, for purposes of this study the at-risk student is the low-achieving learner plagued by academic failure and, unfortunately, tempted to drop out of public school. These are the children with underdeveloped talents who, through no fault of their own, are ill-prepared for schooling, for academic endeavors, and for later life and work success. Sadly, the number of youngsters for whom schools are such unhappy and unthoughtful places is steadily increasing. Hodgkinson (1991) maintains that at least one third of the nation's children are at risk of school failure, **even before they enter kindergarten!** In both urban and rural areas, many students are leaving school without diplomas, and still more find little meaning in their schooling (Beyer & Smey-Richman, 1988; Mirman, Swartz, & Barell, 1988; Report on Education Research, 1992). These problems have serious implications for the individual learner, for beleaguered educational systems, and for American society as a whole.

In many cases, at-risk students have not been presented with the same opportunities to become successful, thoughtful learners as have their higher achieving peers (Passow, 1991). Minimally challenging school programs have been compounded by discrimination—racial, cultural, class, sex and handicap—and lowered expectations. Lowered expectations, in turn, lead to an overemphasis on drill, remediation, and discipline—practices which perpetuate low self-esteem, a lack of motivation, and student alienation. More important, cognitive research has challenged the assumption of a sequence of activities from lower level "basic" skills to higher order "thinking" skills in a reductionist manner (Kozulin, 1990; Means & Knapp, 1991). Indeed, research shows just the opposite. Processes such as making inferences, constructing meaning, and problem solving are all part of a constructivist approach to learning (Fosnot, 1989; Resnick, 1987a). It is these complex cognitive abilities that are the "new basics" of the 21st century, the very outcomes which the National Assessment of Educational Progress data indicate are not currently well developed in the majority of the nation's students, and particularly, not in at-risk student populations (Educational Testing Service, 1990).

The timely reform issue is not so much to raise educational standards for "at-risk students," but to create a kind of schooling in which **all** students receive support in striving to achieve higher standards and greater expectations (National Coalition of Advocates for Students, 1991). That is the real challenge of restructuring education for the coming millennium. The new educational paradigm must be grounded in both a commitment and a researched knowledge base which demonstrates that all students have the potential to be successful, thoughtful learners (Costa, 1991; Feuerstein, 1990). America's at-risk students are no exception.

The major problem that school restructuring needs to examine is the creation of a new learning environment for all students, including student populations considered at risk of failure in elementary and secondary education. In particular, this examination must answer three key questions:

1. How can the vision of restructured schooling be interrelated with the cognitive paradigm—the movement to make schooling an intellectually developing experience?

2. How can every child, even those at-risk of academic failure, by prepared fully as thinking persons?

3. What kind of learning experiences need to be developed to serve diverse students, many of whom have been poorly served by traditional educational practices?

These are the significant queries which guide the presentation of the remainder of this chapter.

BUILDING A RESTRUCTURED CLASSROOM ENVIRONMENT

The most important task of this study is to determine, as completely as possible, the essential elements of a restructured classroom environment, for what goes on in the classroom is most influential on what students are enabled to do (Pauly, 1991). By examining pertinent literature, by seeking relevant research—especially as related to the historic concerns noted earlier—and by considering what is empowering to a youngster's cognitive development, eight elements appear to be the major characteristics of such an environment.[1] It is the authors' position that the radical change needed in a learner's experience at school involves transforming the classroom in such a way that all eight elements can operate fully and strongly influence the child's advancement.

The Essential Elements of Restructured Classroom Environments

1. The purpose of the classroom is to develop every student's mind and to enhance every learner's potential; the primary goal of a classroom restructured for learning is to increase—for every student—understanding and higher-level comprehension of the several subject matters that generally constitute elementary and secondary schooling.

2. The long-term goals of this environment are the autonomy of the learner, the development of self-regulation, and

the independence of lifelong learning. Everyday activities are to be consistently planned to reflect these objectives.

3. The learning processes emphasized in this environment involve cognition, metacognition, and conative dimensions within content epistemologies that seek both individual and group gain.

4. In this environment, all students, even those of differing abilities and diverse backgrounds, are viewed as naturally active and curious constructors of meaning who, over time, modify or seek to create conceptions of information and experience at their unique rates and in their preferred styles.

5. The teacher encourages and provides for important social interactions in this environment, thereby assuring each student a personalized, respectful, and meaningful experience in learning and cognitive development.

6. The teacher in this environment acts as a facilitator of student learning, a mediator, a coach, a mentor, and a collaborator with students and other teachers in the larger school setting.

7. The classroom is linked to life beyond its boundaries, i.e., to the school as a whole, to other educators and staff, and to the entire community, including parents and other agents.

8. The restructured classroom environment for learning integrates curriculum, instruction, and assessment in such a way as to maximize the achievement of these "essential elements" in the dynamic and practical aspects of everyday schooling.

The educational literature supporting these elements is extensive and varied. Much of the research on teaching higher-order thinking strives to realize the first element, increased thoughtfulness, as does much of the current discussion on literacy and numeracy development (Baron & Sternberg, 1987; Brown, 1991a; Hiebert, 1991). While is it acknowledged that particular contents are the appropriate domains of an education, knowing these contents and connecting them through meaningful understanding are central to the processes of learning and interpretation. The long-term goals of autonomy and lifelong learning in the second element are the outcomes for which restructured schooling must strive, countering the reductionist view of "basic skills training" and the "quick fix" mentality of programs that are trendy and superficial (Wittrock, 1987). A rich store of research information on learning and teaching within the cognitive framework is available and needs to be used by classroom practitioners in the restructured school.

Elements three and four present learning as a constructive process with building blocks that are fairly well understood and defined. In schooling, it is not sufficient to concentrate on cognitive operations alone. How metacognitive and conative dimensions interact with content knowledge are also important relationships (Presseisen, 1990). One must keep in mind that reasoning and intelligence are an individual's **developed** abilities, and that it is children's conceptual growth and mental modification **over time** that are the fundamental outcomes of schooling (Brown & Campione, 1986; Feuerstein, 1980). Beyond these outcomes, an awareness that culture and consciousness are developed through socially interactive learning may be one of the most important aspects of restructured education (Kozulin, 1990).

> In schooling, it is not sufficient to concentrate on cognitive operations alone. How metacognitive and cognitive dimensions interact with content knowledge are also important relationships.

The responsibility of the classroom teacher is underlined in elements five and six. Schooling is a very human enterprise and teachers play the key roles of diagnostician, interpreter, creator, and communicator in their mediational task (Feuerstein, 1990). Although materials and methods are significant in the restructured classroom, the ultimate goals are the experience and meaning their use has for the engaged learner (Kamii, 1984; Shulman, 1987; Wittrock, 1987). Similarly, the teacher helps link the classroom to other environments that impinge on students' lives, notably the rest of the school community and the children's experiences outside school (Comer, 1980; Wehlage, Rutter, Smith, Lesko & Fernandez, 1989). This connecting aspect is the underlying emphasis of the seventh element.

Finally, the eighth element calls for an integration of curriculum, instruction, and assessment in the restructured classroom, in order to maximize the other seven dimensions. Traditionally in education, these are rather loosely-coupled concepts.

Curriculum developers and instructional specialists sometimes integrate their efforts; however, neither of them talk frequently with assessment personnel (Valencia, 1990). The current thrusts for meaningful instruction and "authentic" assessments have heightened understanding of the need for such collaboration (Nickerson, 1989; Stiggins, Rubel & Quellmalz, 1988; Wiggins, 1989b, 1992). The following sections examine at greater length the need to integrate curriculum, instruction, and assessment in the restructured classroom environment.

Curriculum in the Restructured Classroom Environment

By tradition, curriculum is the content-oriented part of a school's program, the substantive aspect of what needs to be studied and learned (Eisner, 1982). Until recently, discrete subject matters—heavily influenced and conceived by university specialists—was the preferred curricular approach of American schooling (Tanner, 1989). But cognitive concerns in education challenge that perspective. A more dynamic conception, one in which teachers and students interact in the construction of ideas and richer meanings, has become the focus of the supportive learning environment sought for all students. The essential elements presented in this study form the underpinnings of such a curricular conception.

The curriculum of a restructured classroom needs to be organized mainly to help students develop and use ideas to understand formal knowledge systems, but, at the same time, to assist learners to formulate conceptions that are transferable to problem-solving in their everyday lives (Beyer, 1988; Presseisen, 1987; Sternberg, Okagaki & Jackson, 1990). The content of such a curriculum needs to include the skills and higher processes of cognitive functioning, but also the dispositions and awarenesses of more conative striving (Ennis, 1986; McCombs & Marzano, 1989). Affect and emotion can be key to the creative dimensions of such a cognitive-based education, and intrinsic interest and curiosity may be as motivating to meaningful learning as a teacher's absolute authority or the competitive framework of the more traditional classroom. Thus, the epistemologies of classic school subjects need to be related to both cognitive and conative aspects of the curriculum, because the concepts of a particular discipline are the "holdings bins" of students' experience in subject learning and the points of departure for learners' interests and thinking.

The curriculum of a restructured classroom needs to be organized mainly to help students develop and use ideas to understand formal knowledge systems.

The curriculum of a restructured classroom is chiefly centered on the student as a constructor of meaning and a manager of learning. There are at least four major concerns that such a curriculum needs to address:

• *Managing information* - many bits of knowledge or information are constantly present in the classroom environment; the student needs to develop skills and processes to organize these bits, and gradually to develop mental constructs that make handling these data meaningful and connected to other things that need to be known and used.

• *Managing tasks* - learning in the classroom involves activities or problems that require certain routines to complete successfully; the student needs to develop strategies for working on these tasks at school and for understanding a variety of procedures that may have differing influences over ultimate task completion.

• *Managing self* - successful learning involves awarenesses about intelligent performance by oneself and others; the student needs to develop and apply these awarenesses in a user-friendly setting to improve learning and performance.

• *Cooperation in learning* - successful learning is based on social collaboration and exchange and on the ability to communicate one's ideas; the student needs to have experience with such dynamic exchange and time to reflect on the consequences that are derived from such interaction.

Many of the ideas in current literature on restructured schooling address one or more of these concerns. A focused, practical question to ask is: What do teachers need to do with curriculum in order to help students be successful in terms of these four concerns?

Managing information. There is a great deal of information to be mastered at school. An emphasis on the cognitive development of learners highlights the point that thinking operations need to be consciously developed in relation to regular subject matters, particularly relative to the "key concepts and strategies that students must acquire to function effectively in a particular domain" (Bransford & Vye, 1989, p. 182). A curriculum needs to expose students to exemplary thinking in history, language, or science which shows both how ideas are formulated and how they are represented in that particular domain (Bruner, 1960; Oliver, 1990). But mere exposure is not sufficient. To present a list of higher-order thinking skills or to display key ideas of a particular subject is merely the first curricular act, a starting place for planning a course of study.

The problem of data in an information-rich age raises another issue of curriculum integration. Exactly how should a classroom teacher blend the thinking processes of cognition and the concepts of a knowledge domain in a student's course of study?

At a second level of curricular understanding, knowledge needs to be integrated in various ways in the instructional program (Martinello & Cook, 1992). Expert teachers understand the challenge of such a problem. Leinhardt (1990) suggests these teachers use their "craft expertise" within a content domain to help them know which parts of the rich information pool available are significant for teaching and which parts are irrelevant. She agrees with Newmann (1987) in emphasizing the need for **indepth** experiences in a content area, so that students come to understand not only the apparent subject matter but also the kinds of mental processes and operations that constitute a complex domain (Shulman, 1987). Material in such a curriculum needs to be selected to be influential on the learner because it transfers and transforms, leads to "grounded knowing," and captivates and inspires (Oliver, 1990; Perkins & Salomon, 1988; Schama, 1991).

The problem of data in an information-rich age raises another issue of curriculum integration. Exactly how should a classroom teacher blend the thinking processes of cognition and the concepts of a knowledge domain in a student's course of study? Some researchers, and many textbook publishers, maintain these two information bases need only be commonly presented or mutually infused into subject matter (Ennis, 1989;

Swartz, 1987). Others call for interdisciplinary or multidisciplinary reconceptualizations (Fogarty, 1991; Jacobs, 1991). Obviously, articulation among subject teachers and a debated scope and sequence of appropriate topics, agreed across grade levels, follow from this position. But what is most essential, according to either position, is that mastering thinking operations and not mere content converge lies at the heart of understanding content disciplines. These operations are also basic to generating student meaning (Ammon & Hutcheson, 1989). This challenge leads to the concern for teachability and student response in learning (Bereiter & Scardamalia, 1992).

Managing tasks. In the limited hours students attend school, a finite number of activities or specific lessons can be included in the curriculum. How can teachers assure that these activities lead to the meaningful outcomes a cognitive experience requires? Shulman (1987) suggests that one of the most important aspects of pedagogical expertise involves knowing what problems to present in a course, when to present them, and how to relate them to student activity in a lesson design that challenges student thinking and motivates student interest and activity. Vygotsky's (1978) cognitive theory emphasizes the concept of "tools" in human learning, concentrating on the connections between material and psychological instruments that influence conception, on one hand, and lively social interaction, on the other. The problems of content presentation focused on "toolness" lie at the center of task management in a curriculum, addressing issues of cognition and content representation, as well as providing mechanisms for conveying meaning in the teaching-learning act (Kozulin, 1990).

What are the major material tools of a given discipline? What problems and problem formations do students need to be prepared to solve? What documents or key products represent the best display of expertise or beauty in a particular domain? These are questions that form the foundation of curriculum decision making. They are the heart of what a teacher needs to determine before the specific tasks of classroom work can be prepared. In short, concrete tasks need to be designed consistent with the standards of excellence implied or explicated in a content domain. At the same time, educators must consider what is most elemental for learning a particular content, as well as the skills, attitudes, and knowledge that make that subject intellectually come alive (Presseisen, 1988b).

The current task concerns of curriculum focus on student activity and appropriate designs to accommodate various developmental levels of conceptualization. Science teaching in the middle grades, for example, is very involved with "hands-on" experimentation and authentic activity presentation (North Central Regional Educational Laboratory, 1991). Mathematical reasoning, under the new professional guidelines of the National Council of Teachers of Mathematics, seeks real world applications of theorems and axioms, and still recognizes that not all of the variables in a given problem can be responded to by every student in any one lesson (Black, 1989; Lockwood, 1991). Language arts programs emphasize more "holistic" experiences across the various genres of expression, leading to greater comprehension and more creative understanding of complex ideas (Palincsar & Brown, 1989; Scardamalia & Bereiter, 1985; Shanahan, 1991). Such classroom tasks need to be carefully positioned for any given population of students.

> The student becomes intellectually engaged in learning by relating what is already known to what might be.

An underlying problem of the curricular task is the question of "bridging the gap," that is, to help students move from their initial conception of what is in the curriculum to something further along the increasingly sophisticated sequence of ideas in the subject matter (Rogoff, 1990). How do students internalize what is presented in class? How do they come to understand the qualities of curricular content spontaneously and with a commitment to resolve discrepancies? The restructured classroom conceives of this problem as one of **strategic** learning (Belmont, 1989). For Collins, Brown, and Holum (1991) this constitutes the central issue of cognitive apprenticeship. Based on Vygotsky's (1978) notion of the "zone of proximal development" (ZPD), apprenticeship requires that classroom tasks not only present information to the student, but also provide experience by which he/she is able to go beyond what is presented. The student becomes intellectually engaged in learning by relating what is already known to what might be. Every student's potential for learning becomes mutually involved in the real experience of a specific lesson. The curriculum must account for this learner awareness of both his/her own role in the instructional process, and the influence of others in the classroom. This conative dimension of the essential elements suggests a third major concern of curriculum.

Managing self. In order to achieve optimal student experience, the curriculum in a restructured classroom environment must actively engage every student in his/her own learning and knowledge building. Self-regulation and metacognitive skill acquisition are two vital aspects of student involvement in learning. The development of self-regulation is a cornerstone of learner autonomy and lifelong learning. It involves the students' "awareness of the variables that are important to learning and their ability to take control of their learning environment" (Palincsar & Brown, 1989, p. 19). Metacognitive skill development relates to strategies for learning particular content and heightened awareness of the cognitive demands of specified classroom tasks.

McCombs and Marzano (1989) conceptualized **self-as-agent** as a central phenomenon that brings together both a student's "skill" and "will" in the development of thoughtful behavior. They theorize that such integration makes possible the development of personal expertise in a particular task or subject, driven initially by the will or motivation of the learner, and subsequently by instructional intervention that assists in the delineation of task and the self-regulated development of competencies. The meshing of the learner and the learning is central to a restructured classroom. To be educated is to be **personally** involved, as well as cognitively engaged, in the community of thinking that is fundamental to a learning environment.

Given these requisites for the restructured classroom, how can a curriculum contribute to developing a student's self-regulatory behavior and metacognitive awareness? Teachers need to focus on materials and activities that arouse student curiosity and engage their interest. Providing roles for student choice and voluntary association at the outset of a classroom assignment are important initial concerns. Casting problems and activities in novel and challenging ways are additional considerations. After students are involved in an assignment, relating the curricular materials to strategic skill development becomes a major concern of pedagogy. For example, Palincsar and Brown (1989) identify six strategies that are central to the student's ability to monitor and foster reading comprehension. These strategies then become the scaffold, or lattice, upon which particular reading activities are made meaningful.

In addition to developing strategic abilities within the specific content, students must learn self-regulatory procedures that enable them to efficiently accomplish specific learning tasks embedded in a particular curriculum. Sternberg (1990a) cites executive monitoring skills, accessed through an individual student's development of personal style, as important for knowledge development. He and his associates (Sternberg, Okagaki & Jackson, 1990) maintain that the student, while simultaneously learning content controls, needs to consciously improve his/her own learning techniques. The use of prior knowledge, visualizing contents, recognizing a point of view, looking for effective learning strategies, listening for meaning, and learning by doing are examples of such techniques. The curricular problem for student advancement is to create classroom activities and a learning environment in which these dual improvements can take place.

McCombs and Marzano's (1989) concept of the self-system in cognitive development also raises the issue of what is unconscious in the student's awareness. They see the emerging self in holistic terms, a "consciousness that directs more unconscious processes" (McCombs & Marzano, 1989, p. 3). This highlights the question of how a curriculum can foster a student's **indepth** perspective of subject matter—mindful of the time constraints on instruction and learning. Perkins (1991a) sees this concern as part of the problem of developing insight about a particular subject; he ties this to goals of teaching for transfer and building an integrated curriculum. Suhor (1992) suggests that a whole range of semiotic functions are introduced with this problem. How can the classroom teacher help students "go beyond the information given" (Bruner, 1964) and make creative connections to other knowledge? The curriculum must be used to help students trust their own minds, to build connections to what they know and do beyond the classroom, and to consider their own and their classmates' ways of thinking. Through such elaborative experience, the learner-as-self becomes defined, cognitive competence becomes owned, and commitment to learning is enjoined. Thus, Anne Frank and Romeo and Juliet will emerge from the pages of literature and extend a student's understanding to his/her own consciousness.

Cooperation in learning. The interactive, social nature of the restructured classroom puts a high premium on cooperative activity as a curricular requisite of learning. Students need to work on mutually challenging tasks that build complementary roles and perspectives, and which engender respect for diversity and variation. Cooperative learning methods assume that students can learn **from** as well as **with** their peers, that work can be pursued by collaborative teams, and that, with some well-thought-out, group-based assignments, prepared by sensitive teachers, different youngsters with varying abilities can meaningfully contribute to a unified assignment (Slavin, Karweit & Wasik, 1991). In such cooperative learning, the talent of every youngster can be bolstered and the meaning of the shared task internalized (Presseisen, 1992).

> Students need to work on mutually challenging tasks that build complementary roles and perspectives, and which engender respect for diversity and variation.

The social context of the classroom is also important to Vygotsky (1978), who viewed learning as embedded in experiences in bound by communication and exchange. Vygotsky maintained that the student becomes aware of his/her own cognitive operations only **after** they are practiced and endorsed by others. Further, he proposed that scientific concepts in that exchange need to be both built into the formal context of a body of knowledge or subject matter and systematized through **everyday use** by the learner and his/her peers (Kozulin, 1990).

The role of the teacher as mediator in the learning exchange is a critical link between the student and the curriculum. Good teachers serve as both interpreters and questioners who assist students' construction of knowledge and finely tune classroom exchange for maximum meaning and student benefit (Feuerstein, 1990). Such teaching establishes where a student is in the ZPD and determines the most productive activity for both the individual learner and for groups of learners in a classroom (Brown & Ferrara, 1985; Bruner, 1984). Similarly,

Feuerstein's "mediated learning experience" (MLE) relates the learner's needs to the concepts that ought to be known by the student in the interactive exchange. The teacher is both a tool of instruction and a creator of additional classroom tools. Through such a mediational approach, social interaction is the essence of the environmental exchange. The teacher provides the "bridge" to student transfer and the actual subject learning.

Cooperating with others, then, raises the need for building a social presence in the course of schooling (Brophy & Alleman, 1991). Making choices, building on social networks, figuring out and applying rules, and extending various relationships among people and ideas are as much a part of a particular curriculum as the technical components (Sternberg, Okagaki, & Jackson, 1990). How individual students master such social requisites of group learning must be a significant concern of both curricular focus and teacher attention. Such a social dimension is part of the full interpretation of a learner's construction of meaning at school. It remains to be seen how such a curriculum blends with instruction in the classroom.

Instruction in the Restructured Classroom Environment

While curriculum is the subject matter taught in the classroom, instruction is the interaction of the teacher and students with the subject matter (Erickson & Schultz, 1992). Unfortunately, teaching in schools today is mainly recitation, consisting of unrelated teacher questions chiefly aimed at having students deliver a correct answers (Kamii, 1984; Tharp & Gallimore, 1988). Since traditionally learning is seen as linear and sequential, students are required to master surface-level information and discrete, decontextualized skills—often using drill and practice—before moving on to more advanced or complex tasks (Gagné 1970; Popham, 1987). As proposed in the eight essential elements, the cognitive agenda is profoundly at odds with these premises and begins with different assumptions about student learning.

The aim of instruction in a restructured classroom environment is to change the teacher's instructional role from information provider to assistor or facilitator of student performance (Brown, 1991b; Tharp & Gallimore, 1988). When students respond to open-ended questions and are encouraged to develop multiple solutions to a single problem, the teacher acts as a coach or co-learner, a pedagogue who selects and develops meaningful learning activities (Wood, Cobb & Yackel, 1991). When more indepth explanations are required, the teacher becomes a mediator who provides students with additional guidance, supportive modeling and practice, and interactions with others (Haywood, 1990). Key to all these roles is the teacher's ability to ask more provocative questions and to know the exemplary steps of a youngster's cognitive development (Case, 1992).

What types of instructional experiences should teachers select to enable students successfully to process the school's curriculum?

As with curriculum, teachers in a restructured classroom must design instruction in concert with the four learner-centered concerns of managing information, managing tasks, managing self, and cooperation in learning. Therefore, another important question of this study asks: What types of instructional experiences should teachers select to enable students successfully to process the school's curriculum?

Managing information. Since learners continuously interact and interpret the world, the process of information acquisition in the restructured classroom is viewed as the learner's successive development of structures which are assessed, revised, or replaced in ways that facilitate learning and accommodate the learner's background and purposes (Case, 1992; Hiebert, 1991). When students lack an efficient way of organizing and storing information, teachers should directly supply a beginning knowledge structure to support the development of specific content domains (Beyer, 1987). Information organizers and concept attainment are two examples of instructional approaches which assist students' understanding and recall of information.

Advanced organizers are generally introduced prior to new learning tasks to provide relevant anchoring ideas for more differentiated and detailed material to follow (Ausubel, 1977; Mayer, 1989). While the exact design of the organizer depends upon the characteristics of the learner and material to be mastered, advanced organizers are generally short sets of verbal or visual information that provide a means for generating logical relationships. Beyer (1987) has extended this strategy to his program for teaching critical thinking. Furthermore, post-organizers also appear to be effective in facilitating learning and retention of information, even after it is introduced (Alexander, Frankiewicz & Williams, 1979).

By tradition, teachers have taught linear outlining as the primary verbal representation of information. But today, graphic organizers or conceptual models—matrices, webs, cycles, and sequences—are used to reflect better the structure of ideas and, hence, make information more meaningful and memorable (Jones, Pierce & Hunter, 1988-89; Mayer, 1989). Such visual cues become the "tools" of instruction in Vygotsky's sense, and are thus transformational instruments of thinking (McTighe & Lyman, 1988). Further, student learning is more positively affected when students construct their own graphic organizers, preferably in collaboration with other students, or complete those begun by the teacher (Alvermann, 1988; Moore & Readance, 1984).

Similarly, in a restructured classroom environment, learners should be assisted to construct and refine concepts, preferably with metacognitive awareness of goals and strategies (Schroeder & Lester, 1989; Wood, Cobb & Yackel, 1991). In an effort to solve a problem or make a decision, students' concept understanding is enhanced when they engage in "instructional conversation" (Tharp & Gallimore, 1988) or "substantive conversation" (Newmann, 1991). An instructional conversation is characterized by authentic, open-ended teacher questions; teacher questions that build on previous student answers, or "uptake" (Collins, 1982); and sustained discussions in which student engagement is substantive, not just procedural (Nystrand, 1992). Also, as part of this substantive discussion, conceptual change is facilitated when the learner is encouraged to differentiate relevant from irrelevant concept attributes, distinguish examples from nonexamples, hypothesize the hierarchical relationships among concept clusters, and create their own representative exemplars (Barth, 1991). By participating in such experiences, students begin to expand their understanding of a concept, and gain more flexibility in their own thinking. (Nickerson, 1989).

Overcoming resistance to conceptual change can be a difficult cognitive struggle (Bransford & Vye, 1989; Gardner, 1990).
Researchers have found that misconceptions are so powerful
and entrenched that they survive years of formal education
(Resnick, 1985). If these inaccurate ideas are
allowed to go undetected or unchallenged,
the misconceptions can continue to interfere with the students' understanding of important subject matter. Thus, Sternberg
(1990a) cites the need to use information to
create doubt, whet the learner's curiosity,
and challenge the constructs that exist.
Similarly, Vygotsky's theory cites the useful
contrast between scientific ideas (concepts)
and "everyday thinking" (Presseisen & Kozulin, 1992).

> A mediational teaching style is one promising approach for assisting unskilled learners to adapt to their expanded task manager role.

Managing tasks. The central element of teaching is the way
a teacher translates curriculum into student tasks or assignments. The teacher's choice of task influences student learning
by directing the learner's attention to particular aspects of content (e.g., facts, concepts, principles, solutions) and by specify-
ing ways for processing information (e.g., memorizing, classify-
ing, inferring, analyzing) (Knapp & Shields, 1990). These effects
on learning are clearly apparent in the contrast between the
outmoded behavioral emphasis on accumulating isolated facts
and the constructivist's goal of meaning construction.

In the restructured classroom environment, the student is
expected to assume more responsibility for task-management.
While such a goal is laudable, Perkins (1991b) cautions that
throwing unprepared students suddenly into complex cognitive
problem-solving situations may actually be a prescription for
student failure. Obviously, coping strategies need to be carefully
interrelated with the classroom content and the assigned tasks
closely aligned to what students already know. Several intervention models of instruction exist that purport to do this.

A mediational teaching style is one promising approach for
assisting unskilled learners to adapt to their expanded task
manager role. In MLE, Feuerstein and his colleagues (1980,
1985) refer to the unique interactions by which adults intentionally interpose themselves between the student and an external stimulus to alter the stimulus prior to the learner's percep-

tion. As part of this process, the mediator selects, frames, and filters the lesson presented, interpreting it for the learner. In addition, mediators interpose themselves between the student and the student's response to the stimuli, thus helping learners be aware of their own metacognitive functioning and their ability to self-regulate (McCombs & Marzano, 1989). No longer do students interpret stimuli as accidental occurrences, but rather as contextually bound problems, about which an array of reactions are potentially effective (Brown, Collins & Duguid, 1989).

According to Feuerstein's theory, intentionality (and reciprocity), transcendence, and meaning are the three essential characteristics of every mediated interaction (Feuerstein, 1990; Presseisen & Kozulin, 1992). The intentionality of the mediator, which is shared by the learner, produces a sense of vigilance that is evidenced by greater attentiveness, focus, and acuity of perception. The transcendence of the mediation interaction refers to going beyond the specific situation or need, and reaching out or "bridging" to goals that may be only slightly, or not apparently, related to the original situation. Finally, MLE is characterized by an affective, motivational, or value-oriented event or experience that leads the student to become meaningfully involved in the learning. According to Feuerstein (1990) and his associates (Haywood, 1990; Link, 1985), these three mediational characteristics—intentionality, transcendence, and meaning—interact and form the universal, necessary conditions for every successful teaching-learning experience.

The cognitive apprenticeship approach to instruction—aimed at making thinking explicit and visible—is another innovative intervention to help students deal with cognitively complex problems (Collins, Brown & Holum, 1991; Means & Knapp, 1991). Built on a Vygotskian basis, and similar to Feuerstein's MLE, apprenticeship is designed to assist students in acquiring an integrated set of skills through the processes of observation and guided practice (Rogoff, 1990). The apprenticeship approach seeks to promote the development of expertise through the three core instructional methods of modeling, scaffolding, and coaching. Modeling requires the teacher to externalize the usually internal processes and activities, specifically heuristics and control processes, by which the teacher applies conceptual knowledge. Scaffolding seeks to aid the learner in the ZPD, providing just enough support or guidance for student cognitive advancement (Brown & Ferrara, 1985). In this context, the teacher's relationship with students involves the accurate diagnosis of the student's current skill or ability level, and the implementation of intermediate steps of instruction at an appropriate level of difficulty (Rosenshine & Meister, 1992). Finally, coaching—the general process of overseeing student learning—involves observing students as they carry out a learning task and facilitating the enhancement of their cognitive activity (Collins, Brown & Holum, 1991).

> In all of these models of mediational instruction, the key to a reflective classroom dialogue is how the teacher talks, listens to students, and encourages student-to-student discourse.

Palincsar and Brown's (1984) reciprocal teaching method offers a third instructional model for developing better thinkers and learners. While similar to both Feuerstein's MLE and the cognitive apprenticeship approach, the Palincsar and Brown intervention centers on modeling, scaffolding, and coaching students in four strategic reading skills: formulating questions, summarizing, predicting, and clarifying. Briefly, the procedure begins when the teacher models these four strategies in the context of understanding written passages. After silently reading the text, the students each take turns playing the role of instructor and leading the other students through the four strategies. Initially, the teacher provides sufficient support to allow students to take on whatever portion of the task they are able to do. Gradually, however, the prompts fade until the students can perform independently (Brown, Palincsar & Purcell, 1986; Palincsar, 1992; Palincsar & Brown, 1984).

In all of these models of mediational instruction, the key to a reflective classroom dialogue is how the teacher talks, listens to students, and encourages student-to-student discourse (Englert, Raphael, Anderson, Anthony, & Stephens, 1991). In the traditional classroom, student talk and shared understanding occur minimally (Pogrow, 1991; Tharp & Gallimore, 1988). But in the restructured classroom environment, the teacher acts extensively and responsively to aid student comprehension through a dialogue, or "instructional conversation" (Goldenberg, 1991). A clear focus on the task is the initial step in such a conversation; elaborating that task is the next pedagogical link in the instructional exchange (Stigler & Stevenson, 1991). Charged with the task of assisting students to construct their own context, the teacher listens carefully, and adjusts the immediate response to meet the learner's emergent understanding (Brown & Campione, 1986; Englert et al., 1991; Tharp & Gallimore, 1988, 1991). Teacher questioning also leads students through appropriate post-activity reflection, sharing insights about what they have learned through the task (Brophy & Alleman, 1991).

Managing self. Not only is teaching the process of truly conversing, it is also the act of facilitating the students' capability to assume full responsibility for their own learning. Nearly two decades ago, Maxine Green (1973) wrote that teaching "happens" when students can do certain things on their own— for example, when the learner extends him/herself to find answers he/she has posed, when students give reasons and see connections within their experiences, and when they recognize their own or someone else's errors and propose appropriate corrections. Thus, teaching is ultimately assisting students to self-manage and to actualize the concept of self-as-agent.

Using the mediational teaching style based on Feuerstein's theory of cognitive modifiability, the teacher can promote student awareness of feelings of competence, using a dual process: first, structuring tasks for student success; and, second, interpreting even minimal signs of student success as an indication of increased competence (Clark & Peterson, 1990; Feuerstein & Hoffman, 1990; Haywood, 1990). Moreover, mediational dialogues can enhance the student's conception of him/herself as a thinker by providing immediate feedback, especially on process-oriented responses, and making the student aware of the precise aspect of thoughts and behaviors that led to success. Thus, rather than saying "Good job!", the teacher might reply, "Good! You developed a plan and now you know how to proceed." Mediation of a sense of competence enhances a student's motivation to persevere on increasingly difficult tasks, and is necessary to secure the development of autonomous functioning (Feuerstein, 1990; Markus & Wurf, 1987; McCombs & Marzano, 1989; McTighe & Clemson, 1991).

Just as mediational teachers reinforce the student's self-concept as a successful performer, teachers must also assist students—especially younger and low-achieving students

(Palincsar & Brown, 1989; Smey-Richman, 1988; Zimmerman & Martinez-Pons, 1990)—to self-evaluate, and to control their own cognition and behavior (Feuerstein, 1990; Smith & Nelson, 1992). Sometimes, self-regulation means the students seek to improve their ability to attend, become more precise and accurate, or inhibit their impulsivity (Feuerstein, 1980; Wittrock, 1990); at other times, self-regulation for academic tasks means setting goals, self-reinforcement, and self-instruction (Smith & Nelson, 1992; Zimmerman & Martinez-Pons, 1990). Critical to the success of student self-regulation is the teacher's ability to maintain a nonthreatening classroom environment conducive to good thinking—one in which challenge and risk-taking are promoted, and where originality, independent thought, and differences of opinions are welcome (Barell, Liebmann & Sigel, 1988; Caine & Caine, 1991; Marzano et al., 1988).

> Metacognition—a component of self-regulated learning occurs when students become more strategic in planning, monitoring, and evaluating their mental performance.

Metacognition—a component of self-regulated learning (Pintrich & de Groot, 1990)—occurs when students become more strategic in planning, monitoring, and evaluating their mental performance (Barell, Liebmann & Sigel, 1988; Costa, 1991; Flavell, 1976; Palincsar & Brown, 1989). Students experience metacognition when they use their inner voice or self-talk—"language turned inward" which has it origins in social dialogue (Vygotsky, 1978)—to monologue with themselves about their own writing (Englert et al., 1991). In composition classes, scaffolding tools—for example, cue cards, think sheets, or self-checking lists—can be designed to reduce the burden of information processing and to support student attempts to plan, elaborate, and revise their drafts (Englert, Raphael, & Anderson, 1992; Rosenshine & Meister, 1992; Scardamalia & Bereiter, 1983). Similarly, thinking aloud and concrete prompts aimed at metacognitive functioning are used as part of the cognitive apprenticeship model (Palincsar & Brown, 1984; Schoenfeld, 1985; Singer & Donlan, 1982). As students accept more responsibility for cognitive and metacognitive thinking, the use of scaffolding tools gradually is diminished.

Cooperation in learning. In a restructured classroom environment, students working cooperatively to accomplish shared goals is the context within which managing information, tasks, and self best occurs. Unfortunately, contemporary learning processes in American schools tend to focus on the individual and, too often, remove students from interpersonal contexts which support and provide meaning to learning (Tharp & Gallimore, 1988). Unlike learning in society at large, classroom instruction seldom involves sufficient group efforts to achieve understanding or to solve problems (Resnick, 1987b; Tharp & Gallimore, 1988).

In practice, providing for social construction of knowledge means moving from strictly whole-class instruction, sometimes followed by individual seatwork, to a greater reliance on interactive, small-group activities. Theoretically, pair and small-group collaboration can sharply increase the rate of social dialogue and improve the quality of assisted performance by teachers and peers (Englert et al., 1991; Rosenshine & Meister, 1992; Tharp & Gallimore, 1991). During small-group activities, the learner can benefit from peers who model complex cognitive processes, and from classmates at different levels of understanding (Collins, Brown & Holum, 1991; Schroeder & Lester, 1989). Practically, small-group activities can help eliminate students' requests for immediate help, and can provide teachers with opportunities to observe students' thinking and to make interventions when appropriate (Good, Reys, Grouws & Mulryan, 1989-90; Wood, Cobb & Yackel, 1991).

Collaborative peer editing or peer response groups is another strategy based on the understanding that writing involves an interaction between readers and writers in a literate community (Englert et al., 1991; Freedman, 1987; Rosenshine & Meister, 1992; Sealey, 1986). Peer editing groups—usually organized in pairs or small groups of three or four students—confer at various stages of the writing process, i.e, pre-writing, drafting, revising, editing, and publishing (Sealey, 1986), and provide opportunities for students to dialogue about the content, form, and creation of their text (Barrett, 1989; Beyer, 1992; Englert et al., 1991). Asking advice and peer feedback, especially at the initial stages of writing (Olson, 1990), helps students develop a sense of audience beyond that of the teacher-examiner, and an awareness of how revision through collaboration extends and elaborates one's ideas (Barrett, 1989; Brown, 1989; Brown & Campione, 1986).

Peer and cross-age tutoring are additional strategies for students to share not only the "answer," but the processes used to solve a problem. Those tutored generally benefit because they identify easily with peer models, and they receive more immediate feedback and clarification (Ashley, Jones, Zahniser & Inks, 1986). Furthermore, peer tutors learn through the act of teaching: they reinforce their own knowledge and skills, and gain in social maturity factors including self-confidence, sense of responsibility, and self-esteem (Ashley et al., 1986; Jenkins & Jenkins, 1987; Reisman, 1988).

> To promote cognitive change, teachers must facilitate cooperation in learning as well as to instructional concern for curriculum, task, and student self-development.

The emergence of "real" conversation about academic matters is an important feature of cooperative learning (Davidson & Worsham, 1992). In this approach to instruction, heterogeneous groups of four or five students work "together to maximize their own and each other's learning" (Johnson & Johnson, 1991, p. 298). Slavin (1983, 1991) suggests that group goals, often in the form of group rewards or recognition, and individual accountability must be present for cooperative learning tasks to promote academic learning. Moreover, interactions within groups must have certain qualities—helping, ensuring all do a fair share, giving constructive feedback, challenging other's reasoning without engaging in personal criticism, sharing resources, being openminded, and promoting safety so members feel free to share their thoughts (Johnson & Johnson, 1989; Presseisen, 1992). Thus, to promote cognitive change, teachers must facilitate cooperation in learning as well as to instructional concern for curriculum, task, and student self-development.

Assessment in the Restructured Classroom Environment

Just as our understanding of how children develop and learn challenges our curriculum and teaching practices, it forces us to reexamine how we assess student learning, as well. Conventional tests of educational progress are designed to quantify indirectly, in a single setting, whether or not the student possesses or recalls factual knowledge or discrete skills, irrespective of the context. Students work individually within a specified time frame to select the one "right" or "best" answer for each test item. These traditional tests are based on the empiricist approach to cognitive development, which first views learning as sequential and linear, and then sees complex learning as composed of smaller prerequisite elements (Shepard, 1991). Resnick and Resnick (1992) use the terms "decomposability" and "decontextualization" to refer to the underlying assumptions of such a theory, where higher-order skills occur only after component skills are independently mastered. Shepard (1991) further describes the relationship between assessment and instruction as a "teach-test-teach" mode in which, at each learning juncture, tests are used for the purpose of measuring specific behavioral outcomes of instruction.

The limitations of conventional testing are frequently cited in school reform literature (Linn, Baker & Dunbar, 1991). Chief among them is that paper-and-pencil tests are proxies rather than examples of the actual performances we want students to master (Wiggins, 1989a). Moreover, evidence suggests that standardized achievement tests foster segregating students by ability, lower expectations for some students, lead to student disengagement in learning and thinking, and neglect the application of learning in the real world (Paris, Lawton & Turner, 1992). Further, these tests provide little diagnostic information on the quality of student understanding (Fleming & Chambers, 1983). Conventional testing can also negatively impact instruction, when teachers focus on limited content and simplistic format (Brown, 1989; Nolen, Haladyna & Haas, 1990). As a result, these tests are not only poorly serving students, teachers, and parents, but their validity is diminished (Frederiksen & Collins, 1989). Test scores themselves become meaningless, a concept which Messick (1984) refers to as "test score pollution."

If the primary goal of the restructured classroom environment is to foster **authentic** student achievement—the demonstrated performance of an accomplished mind—then the assessment goal is to develop high quality measures of this valued achievement. The alternative or direct assessments being proposed are performance-based measures that require students to demonstrate specific performances or abilities that are valued as educational outcomes (Archbald & Newmann, 1988). Emphasis is placed on students demonstrating thought-fulness, making judgments, applying new understandings, and making connections in a variety of ways. Moreover, these alternative assessments are referred to as authentic when performance is assessed in "real," life-relevant rather than contrived, conditions (Newmann, 1991). Although basic skills and knowledge are obviously important to a thinking person, in the new assessments the mere reproduction of subject matter is not valued as authentic achievement. Rather, thinking is considered an on-going process, not something concluded after the acquisition of facts (Shepard, 1991). Examples of these "rediscovered modes of assessment" (Wolf, Bixbey, Glenn & Gardner, 1991) include portfolios of work products and performance-based tasks, such as extended projects and presentations, and what Sizer (1992) refers to as "exhibitions" which thoughtfully demonstrate accumulated knowledge.

The alignment and integration of curriculum, instruction, and assessment are critical in the restructured classroom environment. But how should this alignment come about and what is the appropriate role for assessment? To some, assessment can be a vehicle to redirect instruction toward the conscious pursuit of authentic achievement (Shepard, 1991; Wiggins, 1989a). When assessment shapes instruction, "teaching to the test" is an educationally effective strategy (Resnick & Resnick, 1992). It allows student and teacher to focus on higher-order, cognitive functioning and other valued standards of performance. It provides a bridge for students to understand the bases of instruction from a perspective of assessing their own performance, a major metacognitive and self-regulating goal (Garcia & Montes, 1992). To others, assessment and instruction need to be well integrated and dynamic (Feuerstein, 1980), and, in Vygotskian terms, allow for continual movement between the two processes and constant regrouping to reach goals. For example, Feuerstein (1979) and others look at a child in the process of learning to determine his/her potential for change. Such an assessment of cognitive potential reflects two types of measures, an existing level of competence, and a measure of "responsivity to instruction" (Short, Cuddy, Friebert & Schatschneider, 1990) which provides qualitative information regarding cognitive change. However, regardless of the proposed degree of integration of assessment and instruction, there is general agreement that the static results and outcome-orientation of traditional tests provide insufficient measures of competence or ability, particularly for low-achieving or at-risk students, where **qualitative** information concerning processing strategies is critical.

Will a teacher's use of alternative or performance-based assessments facilitate a better learning environment for students at-risk? The following discussion describes how use of such assessments can, when combined with meaningful classroom activities and carefully selected curricula, transform the classroom to allow the eight essential elements of a restructured classroom environment to operate and support learning and development. The discussion is organized in two sections: first, the major rules which guide assessment in a restructured classroom environment are described; and second, the role changes required of teachers in developing and implementing these rules are presented.

There are at least three basic rules, or principles, which must guide the development and implementation of authentic classroom assessment.

Rules guiding assessment in a restructured classroom. Educational restructuring, as with any genuine reform effort, implies altering existing rules to facilitate adaptation to major change. A central theme of the current reform movement is that these alterations will achieve "a different order of results" (Corbett, 1990). How should progress toward these newly-defined outcomes of high performance be measured? There are at least three basic rules, or principles, which must guide the development and implementation of authentic classroom assessment. These rules concern the development of standards, the construction of knowledge, and the role of collaboration in fostering autonomy.

Central to authentic assessments in the restructured classroom environment is the development of a set of standards excellence for **all** students; that is, clear, explicit definitions of the particular performances and understandings that must be mastered by all students as outcomes of instruction (Wiggins, 1992). Such standards include tangible goal statements for both the academic content areas and the higher-level cognitive operations. Implied here is a view of thinking as a type of performance to be sampled and assessed, just as in auditions, athletic competitions, and driving tests (Wiggins, 1989b). Thinking as a performance shares a number of characteristics with other performances, including a balance of humility or quality and risk, a non-linear development progression over time, and interpretation of information and beliefs (Wolf et al., 1991).

High expectations for all students is based on the premise that intelligence is not a fixed trait—all children have the ability to learn at their own rate and style, Also, with this paradigm, the goal of schooling is to maximize each individual student's achievement and mastery of standards. Evidence suggests the negative effects of ability grouping and other special placements for lower-achieving students (Oakes, 1992; Slavin, 1987). Providing these students with a watered-down curriculum denies them the opportunity to master complex performance and reinforces their placements through the provision of boring, static tasks. Having high expectations for all students implies teachers need not assess student readiness to participate in a thoughtful task by assessing whether they possess the independent skills involved in task performance. In a restructured classroom, the preferred approach is to have all children focus on the task, thus permitting students who need to develop specific skills to see their relevance, in context, and providing all students an opportunity to engage in understanding and thinking. Moreover, providing all students with high quality assessment tasks communicates a shared understanding of high expectations. In this way, assessment provides an opportunity for students to learn valuable skills, rather than to merely produce "right" answers.

Related to this view of intelligence is a new understanding of cognitive development. This understanding reflects a change from an early Piagetian view of cognitive development, that is, the development of basic processes which apply to all contexts, to a view of development as gradual advances in skills and domain-specific knowledge (Rogoff, 1990). The implication here for assessment, as well as for curriculum and instruction, is that children will display different abilities and skills depending on the specific purpose and context of the task (Beyer & Nodine, 1985; Fischer, 1980; Siegler, 1989). Rogoff (1990) emphasizes the significance of microgenetic development when she includes in her definition of development "transformations in thinking that occur with successive attempts to handle a problem, even in time spans of minutes" (p.11). Authentic assessment recognizes the significance of context and task demands by proposing tasks that are longitudinal, that involve students and teachers working together, and that allow students to use resources, such as books and calculators. In short, these are tasks that model serious adult work and reflect the mediational quality of the classroom.

Recently, based on the dynamic view of intelligence, a number of clinical programs have been developed which have implications for classroom instruction and student assessment (Budoff, 1987; Feuerstein, 1980). Although educators have known for some time that children who do not spontaneously exhibit certain abilities may, in fact, respond with cues, suggestions, or prompts (e.g., Flavell, 1976; Freeman, 1980), it is only recently the researchers have begun to examine the educational implications of these findings (Lidz, 1987). In contrast to the traditional diagnostic use of tests to determine a child's "readiness," or instructional level, the **Learning Potential Assessment Device** (Feuerstein, 1979), for example, assesses the child's performance by identifying a range of skills, as in the ZPD, bound at one end by an existing level of competence and at the other end by a **potential**, developmental level. This potential level can be reached by gradually developing learner responsibility through mediation, metacognition, and self-regulating activities, as described in mediational pedagogical strategies (Brown & Campione, 1986; Brown & Ferrara, 1985; Campione, Brown, Ferrara & Bryant, 1984). In the restructured classroom, assessment becomes a central dimension of cognitive transfer with both curriculum and instruction.

> Unlike conventional assessments, alternative assessments inform students and involve them in meaningful discussion about what is valued and intended.

Unlike conventional assessments, alternative assessments inform students and involve them in meaningful discussion about what is valued and intended. This in itself can be a learning process for both students and teachers. Some even go so far as to define a goal of assessment to be to "promote intense discussion of standards and evidence among all of the parties who are affected (Wolf et al., 1991, p. 59). Exemplars of levels of performance that set the standards must also be communicated to students, so it is clear as to how their performance is to be judged; students can monitor their own performance (Wiggins, 1989a). The dramatic change is from conventional testing, where students are passive and the teacher has all the answers, to empowering students to actively "assess their own performance reliably and thus develop clear goals to strive for in their learning" (Frederiksen & Collins, 1989, p. 30). Ultimately, such assessments foster student autonomy and self-regulation. Rather than just receiving a score on a test, students can measure their own achievement against a standard of excellence.

Assessment, then, is a means for monitoring a student's performance in comparison to some agreed-upon standards. The purpose is not to compare or rank students based on some quantitative score (e.g., Wiggins' "gatekeeping"), by requiring students to provide answers from which it is impossible to determine underlying strategies, but rather to provide the student and teacher with qualitative information, over time and across situations, about student cognitive functioning. This does not mean that qualitative information, such as the use of grammatical rules in producing a composition, are irrelevant. It does mean, however, that what is valued is the application of basic information in authentic ways to facilitate the development and enhance the quality of student thinking. If high standards and expectations are not developed, and student performance in relation to these standards monitored and assessed over time, many students, particularly those at risk, will not be challenged to become self-regulated learners.

The second and third rules guiding assessment in the restructured classroom environment follow from what we know about the nature of knowledge and understanding. First, that teachers need to provide all students with experiences that require the active construction of knowledge; the goal is for students to demonstrate their thinking and learning **potential** by actually "doing" (as opposed to transmitting or acquiring) science, for example. This doing, according to Greeno (1989), is the student's elaboration and reorganization of his/her knowledge and understanding. Implied here is the significance of context, which is known to profoundly influence children's cognitive functioning (Bronfenbrenner, 1991; Ceci, Ramey & Ramey,

1990) and test performance. Interestingly, although research focusing on the use of such assessment practices in the classroom is scarce (Nickerson, 1989; Stiggins, 1985, 1991), and more general issues of quality remain unaddressed (Linn, Baker & Dunbar, 1991), subjective reports of their powerful motivating and engaging qualities are abundant in educational literature and the current popular press (Mezzacappa, 1992b; Wiggins, 1992). Further, it appears that new, inviting assessment activities can be powerful and meaningful learning experiences for both students and teachers (Wolf, LeMahieu & Eresh, 1992).

Viewing knowledge as socially-constructed gives rise to the third rule guiding assessment in the restructured classroom environment, which is that teachers in such a classroom must construct social environments for both learning and assessment. This follows from the new understanding of the social nature of cognition. Thinking, according to Vygotsky (1978), is an activity which is dependent on speech and which is developed and maintained through interpersonal experiences. In terms of classroom assessment, this interpersonal experience is two-fold: first, it stresses the importance of teacher-student relationship to provide experience necessary for advancing skills and understanding. Teachers need to guide students to internalize their "tools" for thinking and thus transform to higher levels of competence (Brown & Ferrara, 1985). The second interpersonal context of assessment refers to collaboration and interaction among peers and others. Included here are group projects and presentations which provide occasions for modeling thinking strategies and scaffolding complex performances in order to share and learn from others (Resnick & Klopfer, 1989). In addition, there are ways for presenting assessment tasks to individual and groups of students, parents, school staff, and community members.

Alternative assessment and teacher role changes. What is required of teachers in developing and implementing the rules guiding assessment in the restructured classroom environment? Are teachers well prepared for and receptive of this new evaluative role? The answers to these questions involve building an environment that supports at least three types of teacher change. First, teachers need a new belief system based on the current research, referenced throughout this chapter, on cognitive development and how students learn. Understanding this new paradigm means providing **all** students with equal opportunities to use new information, through meaningful problem-solving situations, to achieve meaningful goals; it means understanding that there are many ways to solve problems rather than one simple, correct solution; it means being sensitive to each student's context and mindful that "the way we tend to construct our world is only one construction among many" (Brown & Langer, 1990, p. 332). It also means understanding the range of strategies that students may use to solve particular problems and the circumstances and advantages of each (Siegler, 1989). For example, does a particular solution to a mathematical problem reflect a mechanical computation or a conceptual understanding? Also critical is that teachers develop an open and collaborative atmosphere where beliefs such as reconceptualized understandings about learning and testing, along with goals and standards, are clearly communi- cated to students. Obviously, what and how a teacher chooses to assess learning in the classroom sends important messages to students (Wolf, et al., 1992).

> **Teachers must also be open to students having a more active and responsive role in classroom assessment.**

A second understanding required of teachers concerns the purpose and characteristics of "good" classroom assessments. Assessment in the restructured classroom are designed to directly inform both teacher and student on the skills and understandings of the individual student. Thus, they support both teachers in their instructional planning and students in the development of their cognitive capacity. As authentic measures, they have value beyond evaluation, and are relevant, foster disciplined inquiry, and require the integration of knowledge (Archbald & Newmann, 1988). To develop these assessments means, after establishing standards, that teachers must identify a range of performance levels within these standards to monitor and facilitate student progress. If teachers do not select good tasks and measures and establish criteria for what to value, the reliability and validity of these new assessments will be in serious doubt. Teachers must also be open to students having a more active and responsive role in classroom assessment, through participating in the development of tasks and standards, through self- and peer-evaluation, and through collaborative work with others.

Third, teachers need practical knowledge and experience in designing and scoring these new measures and in using the findings. In order to determine initially what they want students to know and be able to do at the end of the academic year, teachers need a new understanding of "literacy" within their content areas of expertise, the fluidity of knowledge, and connections among disciplines, as opposed to the traditional use of text-as-curriculum (Brown, 1991b; Eisner, 1982). Teachers need opportunities to develop, use, and score the three basic types of assessments—paper-and-pencil assessments (e.g., teacher and text tests, quizzes, homework), performance assessments (e.g., observations of student behaviors, judgments of student products), and direct personal communication with students (e.g., student interviews and conversations, teacher intuitions and feelings about students) (Stiggins, 1991). Teachers must learn to be cautious in developing and using these new measures. Before jumping on the portfolio "bandwagon," they need to understand that a portfolio is more than just a file crammed full of student products. Rather, a portfolio is a purposeful collection of student work with criteria established for both selecting and judging the merit of the pieces included (Camp, 1990). It is a metacognitive tool of learning. Finally, teachers need support and encouragement in the development and use of these new measures.

Following from this new belief system is the proposition that knowledge about how students learn must similarly guide a teacher's curricular, instructional, and assessment practices. Thus, the teacher's challenge is to adopt a mindful, flexible perspective (Brown & Langer, 1990)—to create appropriate, meaningful apprenticeship experiences for students—by modeling tasks, scaffolding or supporting the student, coaching through the student's entire learning process (Collins, Brown & Holum, 1991), and being a "reflective practitioner" (Zessoules & Gardner, 1991). What needs to be addressed is much more than just "assessment literacy." Although currently this knowledge seems to be available to only a select group of educational researchers and scholars (Stiggins, 1991), it is the implications that a coordinated effort has for all school decision-making that is so important for the restructured classroom. Indeed, it is these interrelationships of curriculum, instruction, and assessment which ought to be the center of teacher education in general, as well as the focus of preparation of all those involved in changing schools. These interrelation- ship should also be the bases of conversations and collaboration within grade levels, school buildings, districts, and even states. Without the support of school values and regulations in the context of these interrelationships, the new vision of learning and assessment in the restructured classroom environment is not likely to be fulfilled. It must be pointed out once again that it is in the classroom itself—Pauly's (1991) crucible of education—where the new paradigm for schooling in the 21st century begins.

> At-risk youngsters have all too often been viewed as learners outside the regular classroom.

IMPLICATIONS FOR AT-RISK STUDENTS

Designing the restructured classroom environment for all students assumes the essential elements are functional for students at risk of school failure as well as those for whom success seems relatively assured. In fact, the movement to radically transform American education calls for a redefinition of education in this country and "normed thinking"—where students are seen as either successes or failures—is no longer a viable option (Jones & Pierce, 1992).

But what does a restructured learning environment seek to accomplish in terms of the cognitive capacity of youngsters who have historically been poorly served by schooling, and who are "locked-in" to educational communities in crisis? There appear to be at least four major implications of restructured schooling for students at risk. These include: (1) the need for inclusion in the classroom and the larger school community; (2) the emphasis on the development of student potential; (3) the focus on thinking as key to intelligent performance; and (4) the search for more explicit intercultural relationships. These implications are herein discussed relative to the eight essential elements.

Need for Inclusion in the School Community

At-risk youngsters have all too often been viewed as learners outside the regular classroom. Often forged into groups labeled by handicap or deficit, these students rarely escape such categorical treatment and generally fail to see the higher-order thinking they so badly need. Although tracking students is a complex and dynamic process, research shows that after more than seventy years of study, homogeneous sorting in elementary schools fails to foster the desired achievement outcomes (Oakes, 1992). In terms of social placement, Oakes proposes, negative effects result from the influences of tracking, especially for African-American and Latino youngsters who are disproportionately represented in low-track academic classes.

The restructured classroom needs to be a user-friendly workplace in which all students are warmly welcomed to full-right membership and feel they are significant contributors to the learning exchange (Jones & Hixson, 1991). Cushman (1992) calls for heterogeneous grouping in secondary schools, too, modeling the larger, democratic society and challenging educators to initiate de-tracking procedures. Alternative grouping, special projects and apprenticeships, and cooperative learning assignments are only a handful of the activities that teachers can design on a continuous progress path to challenge differing student abilities and to stretch each learner's mental accomplishments. While more collaborative work is called for among teachers to create these growth opportunities, the expectation of success makes the additional effort worthwhile.

Inclusion in the regular educational community enables at-risk students to join in the exchange of academic problem resolution. Sometimes the give-and-take is with a "wiser" adult; sometimes it is with classmates. What is underlined in such instructional conversations, so important to every learner's development—and even more so to youngsters with limited experience—are the differing means by which the teacher can both appreciate and intervene in a student's thought processing (e.g., modeling, feeding back, contingency managing, directing, questioning, explaining, task structuring) (Ballenger, 1992; Tharp & Gallimore, 1991). By contrast, to be sorted out, to be given a watered-down curriculum, and to be expected to perform according to less stringent standards are aspects of built-in-failure. For America's at-risk students, this is not legitimate membership in a learning community.

Inclusion needs to be extended to at-risk students' lives beyond school. Parents and caregivers, potential mentors and assisters in the community, all need to be apprised of the at-risk student's higher-level experience in learning. As these students begin to formulate real meanings concerning their work in classrooms, they can share these meanings with friends, family, and others. While there may be tensions between academic experience and the actual lives of urban youngsters, such tensions need to be surfaced and dealt with to insure valid instructional success (Palincsar, 1992).

Emphasis on the Development of Student Potential

The developmental nature of the learner, which underlies many of the essential elements, is primarily a dynamic view of learning. At-risk students need to be viewed the same as their more able peers. They should not be measured for **how much** of a given ability they possess, but seen as potentially moving along a similar sequence of thought development—only at a differing **rate** (Elkind, 1989). Kaniel and Feuerstein (1989) call for students with learning difficulties to become candidates for "cognitive modifiability," conscious educational efforts to change their ways of thinking, to challenge them with new learning, to be creative, to build their own innovative concep- tions of reality.

For at-risk students to share in the restructured learning environment, their circumstances and diverse cultural backgrounds need to be carefully considered and appreciated by the classroom instructor (Means, Chelemer & Knapp, 1991; Moll, 1992). Moreover, such characteristics do not mean that these students formulate fundamental knowledge in ways inferior to other learners; Gardner's (1983) multiple intelligences are equally attainable across culture and sub-cultures (Elkind, 1989). What is apparently different is their inability to focus on understanding and its generalizability (Pogrow, 1992). Paris & Winograd (1990) maintain that a heightened appreciation of metacognition is what is called for in the instruction of at-risk students. They propose that metacognition helps these students in at least three ways: to understand their own thinking and learning, to become aware of and to begin to deal with "bugs" or difficulties in a particular problem solution, and to relate to instructional situations with better comprehension and more positive affect. Thus, these researchers see potential for both cognitive and conative change in students whose learning once was considered marginal.

The message of student modifiability needs to be carried beyond the classroom and school, as well. Strategic learning that is concomitant with metacognitive behavior must be recognized in the larger community in which at-risk students reside (Jones & Pierce, 1992). Feuerstein (1990) calls this the need to mediate for an optimistic alternative. Other researchers see the possibility that through such transfer student resilience can be enhanced (Benard, 1991). Ultimately, to carry the learning of the restructured classroom to the real world experienced by at-risk students means to see their lives, their problems, and the constraints they face on a daily basis in a different perspective.

> Strategic learning that is concomitant with metacognitive behavior must be recognized in the larger community in which at-risk students reside.

Focus on Thinking as Key to Intelligent Performance

The restructured classroom casts cognitive development as central to teaching and learning, and key to the assessment of performance. Such expectations should be no different for at-risk learners. Some researchers see these relationships as closely aligned with principles for creating powerful apprenticeship opportunities in the classroom: content, method, sequencing, and sociology (Collins, Hawkins & Carver, 1991). Content must aim for student expertise development; method focuses on ways to develop that expertise, sequencing prepares orderly advancement to better and more complex performance; and sociology demands positive situations which can interrelate the individual with the group. But the most telling aspect of such learning for at-risk students lies in their ability to **internalize** the cognitive aspects of instruction, to **self-regulate**, build on personal strengths, and become spontaneous thinkers. By contrast, this is exactly what Kaniel and Feuerstein (1989) suggest is the missing ingredient of the outmoded "passive-acceptance approach" to teaching students with learning difficulties. Without restructured education, these youngsters are kept busy with minimal, rote tasks and alienated from serious, cognitive learning.

Self-regulation as an authentic educational goal is particularly important for long-range development of low-achieving and disadvantaged students (Au, 1980; Brown & Ferrara, 1985). Unfortunately, this goal is ignored in some of the major educational platforms set for America's schools. Uphoff (1991) notes the national misreading of the concept of "readiness" in early childhood, highlighting the current expectation that it is the child who must bend to meet the institution. Is that authentic? Where in the national program are the evaluation strategies that facilitate the gradual development of metacognitive abilities, including self-regulation, in children who may not be members of the mainstream population nor fluently speak standard English?

... the demand for effective teachers who can relate to students of many backgrounds and varied personal histories will only increase in the coming decade.

Assessments are available to diagnose at-risk students' learning potential and to identify their appropriate levels of instruction, but they are rarely found in actual practice. Consider the "think aloud technique" used in studies of problem-solving strategies (Newall & Simon, 1972), in diagnosing learning disabilities (Short et al., 1990), and in remediating problem-solving deficiencies (Bereiter & Bird, 1985). Few are the schools that are aware of dynamic assessment programs, such as those developed by Feuerstein (1979) and others (Lidz, 1987). A similar testing strategy has been noted as highly successful in the reciprocal teaching approach (Palincsar & Brown, 1984), but rare are the school systems in which such implementations are being conducted and researched (Campione, 1992). In terms of innovative evaluation of at-risk learners in the current reform period, unless assessment policies and procedures are adjusted to match new curricula and instructional goals in the classroom, Oakes' negative conclusion on tracking is likely to be repeated.

Search for More Explicit Intercultural Relationships
The need for education to respect the learner and the learning process are important implications of the restructured classroom's influence on at-risk populations. Good teachers are rare. Those instructors who hold the belief that poor and mi-

nority youngsters have little knowledge to contribute to a classroom's dialogue should not be teachers at all (Brown & Langer, 1990; Jones & Hixson, 1991). Considering the cultural diversity evident in America's changing demographics, the demand for effective teachers who can relate to students of many backgrounds and varied personal histories will only increase in the coming decade (Moll, 1990; Vobejda, 1992). These are the instructors with the positive belief systems called for in restructured classrooms.

A salient finding of the cognitive revolution is the acknowledgment that to understand how something works, it is necessary to experience it directly (Goldenberg & Gallimore, 1991). Such experience creates local knowledge-building: it is that which is proximal in the ZPD (Goldenberg, 1991). Feuerstein (1990) maintains it is teachers who can mediate the various needs youngsters bring to the classroom who really engage students in their learning space. Mediated learning, then, must be an objective with regard to intercultural relationships in the classroom of current America (Presseisen & Kozulin, 1992). Teachers need to maximize such mediation for all students, but especially for those who are not members of the mainstream culture. Tharp (1989) proposes that such instruction delivers the significant, universalistic teaching/learning strategies that are embedded in the foundation of current educational reform: "varied activity settings, language development activities, varied sensory modalities in instruction, responsive instructional conversations, increased cooperative and group responsive instructional conversations, increased cooperative and group activities, and a respectful and accommo- dating sensitivity to students' knowledge, experience, values, and tastes" (p. 356). In contrast to majority students, if these students do not have the opportunity for such learning at school, it very well may never occur.

Fundamental to education in a restructured classroom, then, is the opportunity to examine simultaneously one's own culture and that of one's neighbors, as well. With the new literacies of the cognitive revolution, every at-risk student's curriculum must seek intercultural exchanges, reflected in every subject area, and constantly revised with use (Hiebert, 1991). Constructing new meanings at school, in cooperation with teachers and classmates, will enable autonomous learners to brave the vexing problems they face beyond the school's confines.

IN CONCLUSION

The overall goal of this chapter has been to address the problem of creating a learning environment for all students that makes possible the achievement of restructured purpose in American education. In terms of the three questions that guided this examination (see pp. 11–12), what has been learned and what still needs to be pursued?

Restructured Schooling and the Cognitive Paradigm

Perhaps the clearest finding of this study is the importance of cognition to the restructuring goals of the current reform effort. Whether conscious or not, the major redesign of American education hinges on making real the higher-order processes involved in the development of competent students. This factor emphasizes that the thinking required for work and study in the world today is neither simplistic nor easy. Educators need to understand the complexity of developing minds; they need to review and know the research of nearly a century of theorizing and experimentation. They need to become active learners themselves in applying the principles of cognition to the practice of education.

Cognitive matters relate to the global marketplace as well as to the nation's schools. Teaching for thinking or inquiry should not be glibly presented as a "silver bullet" for American policy makers (Eisner, 1992). Rather, the country needs to understand that success in both education and work, ultimately, is characterized by the ability to analyze and manipulate symbolic images—words, numbers, visual representations—in dynamic problem solving (Reich, 1991). Schools need to ask themselves what this type of performance requires of the learning process, not just when exit examinations are given but throughout a student's academic career from early childhood to graduation. As Tharp and Gallimore (1989) apply their research, the issue is not only of "rousing minds to life," but rousing entire schools, as well, and connecting these institutions to the larger community and workplace.

An emphasis on cognition is not to focus on logic or reasoning as the sole definition of thinking, but to see the broader dimensions of a new, interdisciplinary science. Conation and metacognition, creativity as well as critical analysis, are called for in education's new understandings of the development of multiple thinking abilities. The importance of teacher education is underscored here, as well as the need to re-evaluate how schooling defines "intelligences" and how it assesses the existence and performance of intelligent behaviors (Gardner, 1990). Further, the integration of curriculum, instruction, and assessment calls for a serious re-organization of traditional teacher roles (Cuban, 1992; Schlechty & Cole, 1991).

> For too long, American schools have not advanced the cognitive development of students considered "at-risk" of failure and dropping out.

At-Risk Students and Thinking

We believe that developing the thinking ability of all students is a challenge to be confronted. For too long, American schools have not advanced the cognitive development of students considered "at-risk" of failure and dropping out. Considering the recent census report on dropout rates (Mezzacappa, 1992b), the need to include these populations in a restructured approach to education is critical and immediate. Unfortunately, to date, it has not been an issue energetically addressed in either local or national political platforms.

The eight essential elements of a restructured classroom environment which form the basis of this study must underlie the learning experience of all students, while recognizing and respecting differences in background, ability, and perspective of each learner. Some of these differences reflect developmental concerns; educators must work on what is appropriate for the experience of each youngster to spark learning and understanding. Some reflect individual circumstances; educators must be cognizant of the diverse personal backgrounds of students, more varied now than classrooms have been since the beginning of this century. While other differences reflect group dimensions, educators must analyze the particular circumstances of populations isolated by history and cultural experience. Today, the importance of fulfilling all of the essential elements may be one way of seeking a kind of "standard" for student learning in an era when standardization does not so readily fit reality (Eisner, 1992).

To bring about the integration of curriculum, instruction, and assessment within the restructured classroom environment is not an easy task. For at-risk students, the question of appropriate tools for learning is matched by the need to understand the workings of a student's ZPD. Exploring the potential role of technology as a "tool" may also facilitate learning for these students. While some researchers reviewed in this study stress the primary importance of human interaction and mediation (Feuerstein, 1990; Kozulin, 1990), there are others who maintain that a parallel use of computers and electronic media can enhance learners' understanding and elaborate on meaningful classroom contexts (Collins, 1991; Polin, 1991; Salomon, Perkins & Globerson, 1991; Scott, Cole & Engel, 1992). These applications need to be researched further and their effects carefully documented. Also, impact on cognition depends on how technology is used by teachers and students (Shavelson & Salomon, 1985). It should not be forgotten that the most important aspect of restructuring American education is to bring at-risk students into a meaningful exchange of ideas as full members of a learning community (Thurow, 1991). The role of higher thought development versus remediation in efforts such as Chapter 1 programming is a particular case in point that deserves serious examination (Jones & Pierce, 1992; Lewis, 1992).

Diversity and Learning

The social context of learning is a condition that has been shown to be unique in the formation of reflective thought (Hiebert, 1991; Moll, 1982). The dynamism of a restructured classroom environment rests on the liveliness of classroom dialogue and the teacher's ability to create innovative curricular experiences, tied to cognitive development, which students can share and extend. An important aspect of restructured education yet to be examined is the balance between the purview of the individual and the collective vision required by knowledge in a particular domain. Experiments in current curriculum development and alternative assessment techniques have begun, yet they need to be monitored and assessed. It must not be forgotten that the goal of the current reform effort is to give every generation and every student a chance to become mindful.

Finally, the role of constructivism in the restructured classroom environment suggests that every student builds knowledge and understanding in his/her own way. The single "uniformity" to be pursued, within the cultural pluralism evidenced in America's classrooms today, is the need for each learner to become self-regulatively inventive and, simul- taneously, able to analyze carefully. As Piaget (1964) suggested nearly three decades ago:

> The accent must be an auto-regulation, on active assimilation—the accent must be on the activity of the subject. Failing this there is no possible didactic or pedagogy which significantly transforms the subject. (p. i).

In short, there is no substitute for thinking something through on your own. In the current reform era, providing all students an environment in which this can happen is the essence of radical change in America's schools.

NOTE

1. Various published descriptions of restructured learning environments were reviewed in conjunction with determining the model of eight essential elements. In particular, **The Nine Common Principles of Essential Schools** of the Coalition of Essential Schools (Coalition of Essential Schools, 1991) and the **Learner-Centered Psychological Principles: Guidelines for School Redesign and Reform** (APA Task Force, 1992) were drawn upon for this study.

REFERENCES

APA Task Force on Psychology in Education. (1992). *Learner-centered psychological principles: Guidelines for school redesign and reform* (Second revision). Washington, DC: American Psychological Association.

Adey, P. (1990, May-June). Thinking science. *Teaching Thinking and Problem Solving, 12*(3), 1–5.

Adler, M. J. (1982). *The Paideia proposal: An educational manifesto.* New York: Macmillan.

Alexander, L., Frankiewicz, R. G., & Williams, R. E. (1979). Facilitation of learning and retention of oral instruction using advance and post-organizers. *Journal of Educational Psychology, 71*, 701–707.

Alvermann, D. E. (1988). Effects of spontaneous and induced lookbacks on self perceived high and low-ability comprehenders. *Journal of Educational Research, 81,* 325–331.

Ammon, P., & Hutcheson, B. P. (1989). Promoting the development of teachers' pedagogical conceptions. *Genetic Epistemologist, 17*(4), 25–29.

Archbald, D. A., & Newmann, F. M. (1988). *Beyond standardized testing: Assessing authentic acadeic achievement in the secondary school.* Reston, VA: National Association of Secondary School Principals.

Ashley, W., Jones, J., Zahniser, G., & Inks, L. (1986). *Peer tutoring: A guide to program design* (Research and Development Series No. 260). Columbus, OH: Ohio State University, Center for Research in Vocational Education. (ERIC Document Reproduction Service No. ED 268 372).

Au, K.H. (1980). Participation structures in a reading lesson with Hawaiian children: Analysis of a culturally appropriate instructional event. *Anthropology and Education Quarterly, 11*(2), 91–115.

Ausubel, D. (1977). The facilitation of meaningful verbal learning in the classroom. *Educational Psychologist, 12,* 162–178.

Baars, B. J. (1986). *The cognitive revolution in psychology.* New York: Guilford Press.

Ballenger, C. (1992). Because you like us: The language of control. *Harvard Educational Review, 62*(2), 199–207.

Barell, J., Liebmann, R., & Sigel, J. (1988). Fostering thoughtful self-direction in students. *Educational Leadership, 45*(7), 14–17.

Baron, J. B., & Sternberg, R. J. (Eds.). (1987). *Teaching thinking skills: Theory and practice.* New York: W. H. Freeman.

Barrett, P. A. (1989). Finding their own voices: Children learning together. *Doubts and certainties, (The Mastery in Learning Project), 4*(4), 1–5.

Barth, R. S. (1991). Restructuring schools: Some questions for teachers and principals. *Phi Delta Kappan, 73*(2), 123–128.

Belmont, J. M. (1989). Cognitive strategies and strategic learning: The socio-instructional approach. *American Psychologist, 44*(2), 142–148.

Benard, B. (1991). *Fostering resilience in kids: Protective factors in the family, school, and community.* Portland, OR: Northwest Regional Educational Laboratory.

Bereiter, C., & Bird, M. (1985). Use of thinking aloud in identification and teaching of reading comprehension strategies. *Cognition and Instruction, 2,* 131–156.

Bereiter, C., & Scardamalia, M. (1992). Cognition and curriculum. In P. W. Jackson (Ed.), *Handbook of research on curriculum* (pp. 517–542). New York: Macmillan.

Beyer, B. K. (1988). *Developing a thinking skills program.* Boston: Allyn & Bacon.

Beyer, B. K. (1987). *Practical strategies for the teaching of thinking.* Boston: Allyn & Bacon.

Beyer, F. S. (1992, April). *Impact of computers on middle-level student writing skills.* Paper presented at the annual meeting of the American Educational Research Association, San Francisco, CA.

Beyer, F. S., & Nodine, C. F. (1985). Familiarity influences how children draw what they see. *Visual Arts Research, 11*(2), 60–68.

Beyer, F. S. & Smey-Richman, B. (1988, April). *Addressing the "at-risk" challenge in the nonurban setting.* Paper presented at the annual meeting of the American Educational Research Association, New Orleans, LA.

Black, A. (1989). Developmental teacher education: Preparing teachers to apply developmental principles across the curriculum. *Genetic Epistemologist, 17*(4), 5–14.

Boden, M. A. (1990). Cognitive science. *Radcliffe Quarterly, 76*(2), 8–9.

Brandt, R. S. (1986). On improving achievement of minority children: A conversation with James Comer. *Educational Leadership, 43*(5), 13–17.

Bransford, J. D. & Vye, N. J. (1989). A perspective on cognitive research and its implications for instruction. In L. B. Resnick & L. E. Klopfer (Eds.), *Toward the thinking curriculum: Current cognitive research (1989 Yearbook)* (pp. 173–205). Alexandria, VA: Association for Supervision and Curriculum Development.

Bronfenbrenner, U. (1991). What do families do? *Family Affairs, 4*(1–2), 1–6.

Brophy, J., & Alleman, J. (1991). A caveat: Curriculum integration isn't always a good idea. *Educational Leadership, 49*(2), 66.

Brown, A. L., & Campione, J. C. (1986). Psychological theory and the study of learning disabilities. *American Psychologist, 14*(10), 1059–1068.

Brown, A. L., & Ferrara, R. A. (1985). Diagnosing zones of proximal development. In J. V. Wertsch (Ed.), *Culture, communication and cognition: Vygotskian perspectives* (pp. 273—305). New York: Cambridge University Press.

Brown, A. L., Palincsar, A. S., & Purcell, L. (1986). Poor readers: Teach, don't label. In U. Neisser (Eds.), *The school achievement of minority children: New perspectives* (pp. 105–143). Hillsdale, NJ: Lawrence Erlbaum.

Brown, J., & Langer, E. (1990). Mindfulness and intelligence: A comparison. *Educational Psychologist, 25*(3 & 4), 305–335.

Brown, J. S., Collins, A., & Duguid, P. (1980). Situated cognition and the culture of learning. *Educational Researcher, 18*(1), 32–42.

Brown, R. G. (1991a). *Schools of thought.* San Francisco: Jossey-Bass.

Brown, R. G. (1991b). The one-literacy schoolhouse in the age of multiple literacies. *Educational Horizons, 69*(3), 141–145.

Brown, R. G. (1989). Testing and thoughtfulness. *Educational Leadership, 46*(7), 31–33.

Bruner, J. S. (1984). Vygotsky's zone of proximal development: The hidden agenda. In B. Rogoff & J. V. Wertsch (Eds.), *Children's learning in the "zone of proximal development"* (pp. 93–97). San Francisco: Jossey-Bass.

Bruner, J. S. (1964). On going beyond the information given. In R. J. C. Harper, C. C. Anderson, C. M. Christenson, & S. M. Hunka (Eds.), *The cognitive processes: Readings* (pp. 293–311). Englewood Cliffs, NJ: Prentice Hall.

Bruner, J. S. (1960). *The process of education.* New York: Vintage Books.

Budoff, M. (1987). Measures for assessing learning potential. In C. S. Lidz (Ed.), *Dynamic assessment: An interactional approach to evaluating learning potential* (pp. 173–195). New York: Guilford Press.

Caine, R. N., & Caine, G. (1991). *Making connections: Teaching and the human brain.* Alexandria, VA: Association for Supervision and Curriculum Development.

Camp, R. (1990, October). *Portfolio approaches to instruction and assessment in writing.* A workshop presented at Research for Better Schools, Philadelphia, PA (photocopy).

Campione, J. (1992, February). *Assessment and cognition.* Paper presented at the Third International Conference on Cognitive Education, University of California, Riverside, CA.

Campione, J. C., Brown, A. L., Ferrara, R. A., & Bryant, N. R. (1984). The zone of proximal development: Implications for individual differences and learning. In B. Rogoff & J. V. Wertsch (Eds.), *Children's learning in the "zone of proximal development"* (pp. 77–91). San Francisco: Jossey-Bass.

Carnevale, A. P. (1991). *America and the new economy.* Washington: U.S. Department of Labor, Employment and Training Administration.

Case, R. (1992). *The mind's staircase: Exploring the conceptual underpinnings of children's thought and knowledge.* Hillsdale, NJ: Lawrence Erlbaum.

Ceci, S. J., Ramey, S. L., & Ramey, C. T. (1990). Framing intellectual assessment in terms of a person-process-context model. *Educational Pyschologist, 25*(3 & 4), 269–291.

Chance, P. (1986). *Thinking in the classroom: A survey of programs.* New York: Teachers College Press, Columbia University.

Clark, C. M., & Peterson, P. L. (1990). *Teachers' thought processes.* (Research in Teaching and Learning, Volume 3). New York: Macmillan.

Coalition of Essential Schools. (1991). The nine common principles of essential schools. *Horace, 8*(2), 8.

Collins, A. (1991). The role of computer technology in restructuring schools. *Phi Delta Kappan, 73*(1), 28–36.

Collins, A., Brown, J. S., & Holum, A. (1991). Cognitive apprenticeship: Making thinking visible. *American Educator, 15*(3), 6–11, 38–46.

Collins, A., Hawkins, J., & Carver, S. M. (1991). *A cognitive apprenticeship for disadvantaged students* (Technical Report No. 10). New York: Center for Technology in Education, Bank Street College of Education.

Collins, J. (1982). Discourse style, classroom interaction and differential treatment. *Journal of Reading Behavior, 14*, 429–437.

Comer, J. P. (1988). Educating poor minority children. *Scientific American, 259*(5), 42–48.

Comer, J. P. (1980). *School power: Implications of an intervention project.* New York: Free Press.

Commission on the Skills of the American Workforce. (1990). *America's choice: High skills or low wages.* Rochester, NY: National Center on Education and the Economy.

Conley, D. T. (1991, February). Restructuring schools: Educators adapt to a changing world. *Trends & Issues.* Eugene, OR: ERIC Clearinghouse on Educational Management.

Corbett, H. D. (1990). *On the meaning of restructuring.* Philadelphia, PA: Research for Better Schools.

Costa, A. L. (1991). *The school as a home for the mind.* Palatine, IL: Skylight Publishing.

Council of Chief State School Officers. (1991). Restructuring learning to improve the teaching of thinking and reasoning for all students. *Concerns, 32*, 1–8. Washington, DC: Author.

Council of Chief State School Officers. (1989). *Success for all in a new century: A report of the Council of Chief State School Officers on restructuring education.* Washington, DC: Author.

Cuban, L. (1992, March 11). Please, no more facts; just better teaching. *Education Week, 11*(25), 40, 30.

Cushman, K. (1992). Essential schools' "universal goals": How can heterogeneous grouping help? *Horace, 8*(5), 1–8.

Darling-Hammond, L. (1990). Achieving our goals: Superficial or structural reforms? *Phi Delta Kappan, 72*(4), 286–295.

David, J. L. with Purkey, S., & White, P. (1987). *Restructuring in progress: Lessons from pioneering districts.* (Results in Education Series). Washington, DC: National Governors' Association, Center for Policy Research.

Davidson, N., & Worsham, T. (Eds.). (1992). *Enhancing thinking through cooperative learning.* New York: Teachers College Press.

Detterman, D. K. & Sternberg, R. J. (Eds.). (1982). *How and how much can intelligence be increased.* Norwood, NJ: Ablex.

Dewey, J. (1964). *Democracy and education* (4th printing). New York: Macmillan.

Diamon, M. C. (1988). *Enriching heredity: The impact of the environment on the anatomy of the brain.* New York: Free Press.

Dickinson, D. (1991). *Positive trends in learning: Meeting the needs of a rapidly changing world.* Atlanta, GA: IBM Educational Systems.

Dillon, R. F., & Sternberg, R. J. (Eds.). (1986). *Cognition and instruction.* Orlando, FL: Academic Press.

Educational Testing Service. (1990). *The education reform decade.* Princeton, NJ: Author, Policy Information Center.

Eisner, E. W. (1992). The federal reform of schools: Looking for the silver bullet. *Phi Delta Kappan, 73*(9), 722–723.

Eisner, E. W. (1982). *Cognition and curriculum: A basis for deciding what to teach.* New York: Longman.

Elkind, D. (1989). Developmentally appropriate practice: Philosophical and practical applications. *Phi Delta Kappan, 71*(2), 113–117.

Elkind, D. (1979). *The child and society: Essays in applied child development.* New York: Oxford University Press.

Elmore, R. F. (1991). *Restructuring schools: The next generation of educational reform.* San Francisco: Jossey-Bass.

Elmore, R. F. (1988). *Early experience in restructuring schools: Voices from the field.* (Results in Education Series). Washington, DC: National Governors' Association, Center for Policy Research.

Englert, C. S., Raphael, T. E., & Anderson, L. M. (1992). Socially mediated instruction: Improving students' knowledge and talk about writing. *The Elementary School Journal, 92*(4), 411–449.

Englert, C. S., Raphael, T. E., Anderson, L. M., Anthony, H. M., & Stevens, D. D. (1991). Making strategies and self-talk visible: Writing instruction in regular and special education classrooms. *American Educational Research Journal, 28*(2), 337–372.

Ennis, R. H. (1991, April). *Critical thinking: A streamlined conception.* Paper presented at annual meeting of American Educational Research Association, Chicago, IL (photocopy).

Ennis, R. H. (1989). Critical thinking and subject specificity: Clarification and needed research. *Educational Researcher, 18*(3), 4–10.

Ennis, R. H. (1986). A taxonomy of critical thinking dispositions and abilities. In J. B. Baron & R. J. Sternberg (Eds.), *Teaching thinking skills: Theory and practice* (pp. 9–26). New York: W. H. Freeman.

Erickson, F., & Schultz, J. (1992). Students' experience of the curriculum. In P. W. Jackson (Ed.), *Handbook of research on curriculum: A project of the American Educational Research Association* (pp. 465–485). New York: Macmillan.

Feldman, S. (1992). Children in crisis: The tragedy of under-funded schools and the students they serve. *American Educator, 16*(1), 8–17, 46.

Feuerstein, R. (1990). The theory of structural cognitive modifiability. In B. Z. Presseisen, R. J. Sternberg, K. W. Fischer, C. C. Knight, & R. Feuerstein, *Learning and thinking styles: Classroom interaction* (pp. 68–134). Washington, DC: National Education Association.

Feuerstein, R., with Rand, Y., & Hoffman, M. B. (1979). *The dynamic assessment of retarded performers: The learning potential assessment device, theory, instruments, and techniques.* Glenview, IL: Scott, Foresman.

Feuerstein, R., with Rand, Y., Hoffman, M. B., & Miller, R. (1980). *Instrumental Enrichment: An intervention program for cognitive modifiability.* Baltimore, MD: University Park Press.

Feuerstein, R., & Hoffman, M. B. (1990). Mediating cognitive processes to the retarded performer: Rationale, goals, and nature of intervention. In M. Schwebel, C. A. Maher, & N. S. Fagley (eds.), *Promoting cognitive growth over the life span* (pp. 115–136). Hillsdale, NJ: Lawrence Erlbaum.

Feuerstein, R., Hoffman, M. B., Jensen, M. R., & Rand. Y. (1985). Instrumental Enrichment, and intervention program for structural cognitive modifiability. In J. W. Segal, S. F. Chipman, & R. Glaser (Eds.), *Thinking and learning skills (Vol. 1): Relating instruction to research* (pp. 43–82). Hillsdale, NJ: Lawrence Erlbaum.

Fischer, K. (1980). A theory of cognitive development: The control and construction of hierarchies of skills. *Psychological Review, 57,* 477–531.

Flavell, J. H. (1976). Metacognitive aspects of problem solving. In L. B. Resnick (Ed.), *The nature of intelligence* (pp. 231–235). Hillsdale, NJ: Lawrence Erlbaum.

Fleming, M., & Chambers, B. (1983). Teacher-made tests: Windows to the classroom. In W. E. Hathaway (Ed.), *New directions for testing and measurement: Testing in the schools* (pp. 29–38), San Francisco: Jossey-Bass.

Fogarty, R. (1991). Ten ways to integrate the curriculum. *Educational Leadership, 49*(2), 61–65.

Fosnot, C. T. (1989). *Enquiring teachers, enquiring learners: A constructivist approach for teaching.* New York: Teachers College Press.

Frederiksen, J. R., & Collins, A. (1989). A systems approach to educational testing. *Educational Researcher, 18*(9), 27-32.

Freedman, S. W. (1987). *Peer response groups in two ninth grade classrooms.* (Technical Report No. 12). Berkeley, CA: University of California, Center for the Study of Writing.

Freeman, N. H. (1980). *Strategies of representation in young children.* New York: Academic Press.

Gagné, R. M. (1979). *The conditions of learning.* New York: Holt, Rinehart & Winston.

Garcia, Y., & Montes, F. (1992). Authentic assessments for limited English-proficient students. *Intercultural Development Research Association (IDRA) Newsletter, 19*(4), 9–11.

Gardner, H. (1991). *The unschooled mind: How children think and how schools should teach.* New York: Basic Books.

Gardner, H. (1990, December). *The proper assessment of multiple intelligences.* Paper presented at the Second National Conference on Assessing Thinking, Baltimore, MD (photocopy).

Gardner, H. (1985). *The mind's new science: A history of the cognitive revolution.* New York: Basic Books.

Gardner, H. (1983). *Frames of mind: The theory of multiple intelligences.* New York: Basic Books.

Glickman, C. (1991). Pretending not to know what we know. *Educational Leadership, 48*(8), 4–10.

Goldenberg, C. (1991). *Instructional conversations and their classroom application.* Washington, DC: National Center for Research on Cultural Diversity and Second Language Learning.

Goldenberg, C., & Gallimore, R. (1991). Local knowledge, research knowledge, and educational change: A case study of early Spanish reading improvement. *Educational Researcher, 20*(8), 2–14.

Good, T. L., Reys, B. J., Grouws, D. A., & Mulryan, C. M. (1989-90). Using work-groups in mathematics instruction. *Educational Leadership, 47*(4), 56–62.

Goodlad, J. I. (1984). *A place called school: Prospects for the future.* New York: McGraw Hill.

Green, M. (1973). *Teacher as stranger: Educational philosophy for the modern age.* Belmont, CA: Wadsworth Publishing.

Greeno, J. G. (1989). A perspective on thinking. *American Psychologist, 44*(2), 134–141.

Haller, E. P., Child, D. A., & Walberg, H. J. (1988). Can comprehension be taught? *Educational Researcher, 17*(9), 5–8.

Harvey, G., & Crandall, D. P. (1988). *A beginning look at the what and how of restructuring.* Andover, MA: The Regional Laboratory for Educational Improvement of the Northeast and Islands.

Haywood, H. C. (1990, July). *A total cognitive approach in education: Enough bits and pieces.* Presidential address presented at the Second International Conference of the International Association for Cognitive Education, Mons, Belgium.

Hiebert, E. H. (1991). *Literacy for a diverse society: Perspectives, practice, and policies.* New York: Teachers College Press, Columbia University.

Hilliard, A., III. (1991). Do we have the will to educate all the children? *Educational Leadership, 49*(1), 31–36.

Hodgkinson, H. (1991). Reform versus reality. *Phi Delta Kappan, 73*(1), 9–16.

Hodgkinson, H. L. (1985). *All one system: Demographics of education, kindergarten through graduate school.* Washington, DC: Institute for Educational Leadership.

Jacobs, H. H. (1991). Planning for curriculum integration. *Educational Leadership, 49*(2), 27–28.

Jenkins, J. R., & Jenkins, L. M. (1987). Making peer tutoring work. *Educational Leadership, 44*(6), 64–68.

Johnson, D. W., & Johnson, R. T. (1991). Collaboration and cognition. In A. L. Costa (Ed.), *Developing Minds* (Vol. I, pp. 298–301). Alexandria, VA: Association for Supervision and Curriculum Development.

Johnson, D. W., & Johnson, R. T. (1989). *Cooperation and competition: Theory and research.* Edina, MN: Interaction Book Company.

Jones, B. F., & Hixson, J. (1991). Breaking out of boundaries into a learner-friendly world. *Educational Horizons, 69* (2), 97–103.

Jones, B. F., & Pierce, J. (1992). Restructuring educational reform for students at risk. In A. Costa, J. Bellanca, & R. Fogarty (Eds.), *If minds matter: A foreword to the future* (Vol. 1, pp. 63–82). Palatine, IL: Skylight Publishing.

Jones, B. F., Pierce, J., & Hunter, B. (1988-1989). Teaching students to construct graphic organizers. *Educational Leadership, 46*(4), 20–25.

Kamii, C. (1984). Autonomy: The aim of education envisioned by Piaget. *Phi Delta Kappan, 65*(6), 410–415.

Kaniel, S., & Feuerstein, R. (1989). Special needs of children with learning difficulties. *Oxford Review of Education, 15*(2), 165–179.

Knapp, S., & Shields, P. M. (1990). *Better schooling for the children of poverty: Alternatives to conventional wisdom* (Vol. 2). Menlo Park, CA: SRI International.

Kozulin, A. (1990). *Vygotsky's psychology: A biography of ideas.* Cambridge, MA: Harvard University Press.

Leinhardt, G. (1990). Capturing craft knowledge in teaching. *Educational Researcher, 19*(2), 18–25.

Lewis, A. C. (1992). Previews of Chapter 1 changes. *Phi Delta Kappan, 73*(10), 740–741.

Lidz, C. S. (Ed.). (1987). *Dynamic assessment: An interactional approach to evaluating learning potential.* New York: Guilford Press.

Link, F. R. (1985). Instrumental Enrichment: A strategy for cognitive and academic improvement. In F. R. Link (Ed.), *Essays on intellect* (pp. 89–106). Alexandria, VA: Association for Supervision and Curriculum Development.

Linn, R. L., Baker, E. L., & Dunbar, S. B. (1991). Complex, performance-based assessment: Expectations and validation criteria. *Educational Researcher, 20*(8), 15–21.

Lipman, M. (1991). Squaring Soviet theory with American practice. *Educational Leadership, 48*(8), 72–76.

Lipman, M., Sharp, A. M., & Oscanyan, F. S. (1980). *Philosophy in the classroom.* Philadelphia, PA: Temple University Press.

Lockwood, A. T. (1991). Mathematics for the information age. *Focus in change, 5,* 3–7. Madison, WI: National Center for Effective Schools Research and Development.

Markus, H., & Worf, E. (1987). The dynamic self-concept: A social psychological perspective. *Annual Review of Psychology, 38,* 299–337.

Martinello, M. L., & Cook, G. E. (1992). Interweaving the threads of learning: Interdisciplinary curriculum and teaching. *Curriculum Report, 21*(3), 1–6.

Marzano, R. J., Brandt, R. S., Hughes, C. S., Jones, B. F., Presseisen, B. Z., Rankin, S. C., & Suhor, C. (1988). *Dimensions of thinking: A framework for curriculum and instruction.* Alexandria, VA: Association for Supervision and Curriculum Development.

Mayer, R. E. (1989). Models for understanding. *Review of Educational Research, 59*(1), 43–64.

McCombs, B., & Marzano, R. (1989). Integrating skill and will in self-regulation: Putting the self as agent in strategic training. *Teaching Thinking and Problem Solving, 11*(5), 1–4.

McDonnell, L. M. (1989). *Restructuring American schools: The promise and the pitfall* (Conference paper No. 12). New York: Teachers College Press, Columbia University, Institute on Education and the Economy.

McTighe, J., & Clemson, R. (1991). Making connections: Toward a unifying instructional framework. In A. L. Costa (Ed.), *Developing minds* (Vol. 1, pp. 304–311). Alexandria, VA: Association for Supervision and Curriculum Development.

McTighe, J., & Lyman, F. T., Jr. (1988). Cueing thinking in the classroom: The promise of theory-embedded tools. *Educational Leadership, 45*(7), 18-24.

Means, B., Chelemer, C., & Knapp, M. S. (1991). *Teaching advanced skills to at-risk students: Views from research and practice.* San Francisco: Jossey-Bass.

Means, B., & Knapp, M. S. (1991). Cognitive approaches to teaching advanced skills to educationally disadvantaged students. *Phi Delta Kappan, 73*(4), 282–289.

Messick, S. (1984). Abilities and knowledge in educational achievement testing: An assessment of dynamic cognitive structures. In B. S. Plake (Ed.), *Social and technical issues in testing: Implications for test construction and usage* (pp. 152–172). Hillsdale, NJ: Lawrence Erlbaum.

Mezzacappa, D. (1992a, June 2). Crossroads: A new testing method is getting a tryout: What you know, how you use it. *Philadelphia Inquirer,* pp. A1, A5.

Mezzacappa, D. (1992b, June 5). Bleak report on dropout rates for minorities. *Phildelphia Inquirer*, p. A19.

Miller, G. (1989). Two foundations contribute $12 million for mind-brain research. *McConnell-Pew program in cognitive neuroscience* (News Release). Princeton, NJ: Princeton University.

Mirman, J. A., Swartz, R. J., & Barell, J. (1988). Strategies to help teachers empower at-risk students. In B. Z. Presseisen (Ed.), *At-risk students and thinking: Perspectives from research* (pp. 138–156). Washington, DC: National Education Association.

Moll, L. C. (Ed.). (1992). *Vygotsky and education: Instructional implications and applications of sociohistorical psychology.* New York: Cambridge University Press.

Moll, L. C. (1990). Social and instructional issues in educating "disadvantaged" students. In M. S. Knapp & P. M. Shields (Eds.), *Better schooling for children of poverty: Alternatives to conventional wisdom* (Vol 2, pp. III–3–III–22). Washington: U.S. Department of Education.

Moore, D. W., & Readance, J. E. (1984). A quantitative and qualitative review of graphic organizer researcher. *Journal of Educational Research, 78*(1), 11–17.

National Center for Education Statistics (1991). *The nation's report card: The state of mathematics achievement in Pennsylvania* (Report 21–ST–02). Washington, DC: Office of Educational Research, U.S. Department of Education.

National Coalition of Advocates for Students. (1991). *The good common school: Making the vision work for all students.* Boston: Author.

National Commission on Excellence in Education. (1983). *A nation at risk: The imperative for educational reform.* Washington, DC: Government Printing Office.

Newall, A., & Simon, H. A. (1972). *Human problem solving.* Englewood Cliffs, NJ: Prentice-Hall.

Newmann, F. M. (1991). Linking restructuring to authentic student achievement. *Phi Delta Kappan, 72*(6), 458–463.

Newmann, F. M. (1987). *Higher order thinking in the high school curriculum.* Paper presented at the annual meeting of the National Association of Secondary School Principals, San Antonio, TX. Madison, WI: National Center on Effective Secondary Schools, University of Wisconsin (photocopy).

Nickerson, R. S. (1989). New directions in educational assessment. *Educational Researcher, 18*(9), 3–7.

Nickerson, R. S. (1986). Reflections on reasoning. Hillsdale, NJ: Lawrence Erlbaum.

Nolen, S. B., Haladyna, T. M., & Haas, N. S. (1990, April). *A survey of actual and perceived users, test preparation activities, and effects of standardized achievement tests.* Paper presented at the annual meeting of the American Educational Research Association, Boston.

North Central Regional Educational Laboratory & PBS Elementary/Secondary Service. (1991). *Schools that work: The research advantage* (Guidebook 3: Children as explorers). Oak Brook, IL: Author.

Nystrand, M. (1992, April). *Dialogic instruction and conceptual change.* Paper presented at the annual meeting of the American Educational Research Association, San Francisco (photocopy).

Oakes, J. (1992). Can tracking research inform practice? Technical, normative, and political considerations. *Educational Researcher, 21*(4), 12–21.

Oliver, D. (1990). Grounded knowing: A postmodern perspective on teaching and learning. *Educational Leadership, 48*(1), 64–69.

Olson, V. L. P. (1990). The revising process of sixth-grade writers with and without peer feedback. *Journal of Educational Research, 84*(1), 22–29.

Palincsar, A. S. (1992, April). *Beyond reciprocal teaching: A retrospective and prospective view.* Cattell Talk presented at the annual meeting of the American Educational Research Association, San Francisco, CA. (photocopy).

Palincsar, A. S., & Brown, A. L. (1989). Instruction for self-regulated reading. In L. B. Resnick & L. D. Klopfer (Eds.), *Toward the thinking curriculum: Current cognitive research* (1989 Yearbook, pp. 19–39). Alexandria, VA: Association for Supervision and Curriculum Development.

Palincsar, A. S., & Brown, A. L. (1984). Reciprocal teaching and comprehension-fostering and comprehension-monitoring activities. *Cognition and Instruction, 1*(2), 117–175.

Paris, S. G., Lawton, T. A., & Turner, J. C. (1992). Reforming achievement testing to promote student learning. In C. Collins & J. M. Mangieri (Eds.), *Teaching thinking: An agenda for the 21st century* (223–241). Hillsdale, NJ: Lawrence Erlbaum.

Paris, S. G., & Winograd, P. (1990). Promoting metacognition and motivation of exceptional children. *Remedial and Special Education, 11*(6), 7–15.

Passow, A. H. (1991). Urban schools a second (?) or third (?) time around: Priorities for curricular and instructional reform. *Education and Urban Society, 23*(3), 243–255.

Paul, R. W. (1987). Dialogical thinking: Critical thought essential to the acquisition of rational knowledge and passions. In J. B. Baron & R. J. Sternberg (Eds.), *Teaching thinking skills: Theory and practice* (pp. 127–148). New York: W. H. Freeman.

Pauly, E. (1991). *The classroom crucible: What really works, what doesn't, and why.* New York: Basic Books.

Penrose, R. (1989). *The emperor's new mind: Concerning computers, minds, and the laws of physics.* New York: Oxford University Press.

Perkins, D. N. (1991a). Educating for insight. *Educational Leadership, 49*(2), 4–8.

Perkins, D. N. (1991b). What constructivism demands of the learner. *Educational Technology, 31*(9), 19–21.

Perkins, D. N., & Salomon, G. (1989). Are cognitive skills context-bound? *Educational Researcher, 18*(1), 16–25.

Perkins, D. N., & Salomon, G. (1988). Teaching for transfer. *Educational Leadership, 46*(1), 22–32.

Piaget, J. (1964). Dedication. In R. E. Ripple & V. N. Rockcastle (Eds.), *Piaget rediscovered: A report of the conference on cognitive studies and curriculum development* (p. i). Ithaca, NY: School of Education, Cornell University.

Pintrich, P. R., & de Groot, E. V. (1990). Motivational and self-regulated learning components of classroom academic performance. *Journal of Educational Psychology, 82*(1), 33–40.

Pogrow, S. (1992). Converting at-risk students into reflective learners. In A. L. Costa, J. Bellanca, & R. Fogarty (Eds.), *If minds matter: A foreword to the future* (Vol. 2, 117–125). Palatine, IL: Skylight Publishing.

Polin, L. (1991). Vygotsky at the computer: A Soviet view of "tools for learning." *The Computing Teacher, 19*(1), 25–27.

Popham, W. J. (1987). The merits of measurement-driven instruction. *Phi Delta Kappan, 68*(9), 679-682.

Presseisen, B. Z. (1992, February). *Implementing thinking in the school's curriculum.* Paper presented at the third annual meeting of the International Association for Cognitive Education, University of California, Riverside.

Presseisen, B. Z. (1991). Thinking skills: Meanings and models revisited. In A. L. Costa (Ed.), *Developing minds: A resource book for teaching thinking* (Vol. 1, rev. ed., pp. 56–62). Alexandria, VA: Association for Supervision and Curriculum Development.

Presseisen, B. Z. (1990). Important questions. In B. Z. Presseisen, R. J. Sternberg, K. W. Fischer, C. C. Knight, & R. Feuerstein. *Learning and thinking styles: Classroom interaction.* Washington, DC: National Education Association.

Presseisen, B. Z. (1988a). *At-risk students and thinking: Perspectives from research.* Washington, DC: National Education Association.

Presseisen, B. Z. (1988b). Avoiding battle at curriculum gulch: Teaching thinking AND content. *Educational Leadership, 45*(7), 7–8.

Presseisen, B. Z. (1987). Thinking skills throughout the curriculum: A conceptual design. Bloomington, IN: Pi Lambda Theta.

Presseisen, B. Z., & Kozulin, A. (1992, April). *Mediated learning: The contributions of Vygotsky and Feuerstein in theory and practice.* Paper presented at the annual meeting of the American Educational Research Association, San Francisco.

Reich, R. B. (1991, January 20). Secession of the successful. *New York Times Magazine,* pp. 16–17, 42–45.

Report on Education Research. (1992). *Rural children worse off than urban, suburban peers, 24*(1), 1–2. Washington, DC: Capitol Publications.

Resnick, L. B. (1987a). *Education and learning to think.* Washington: National Academy Press.

Resnick, L. B. (1987b). Learning in school and out. *Educational Researcher, 16*(9), 13–20.

Resnick, L. B. (1985). *Cognitive science and instruction.* Pittsburgh, PA: Learning Research and Development Center, University of Pittsburgh (photocopy).

Resnick, L. B., & Klopfer, L. E. (Eds.). (1989). *Toward the thinking curriculum: Current cognitive research* (1989 Yearbook). Alexandria, VA: Association for Supervision and Curriculum Development.

Resnick, L. B., & Resnick, D. P. (1992). Assessing the thinking curriculum: New tools for educational reform. In B. R. Gifford & M. C. O'Connor (Eds.), *Changing assessments: Alternative views of aptitude, achievement and instruction* (pp. 37–75). Boston: Kluwer.

Riessman, F. (1988). Transforming the schools: A new paradigm. *Social Policy, 19*(1), 2–4.

Rogoff, B. (1990). *Apprenticeship in thinking: cognitive development in social context.* New York: Oxford University Press.

Rosenshine, B., & Meister, C. (1992). The use of scaffolding for teaching higher-level cognitive strategies. *Educational Leadership, 49*(7), 26–33.

Salomon, G., Perkins, D. N., & Globerson, T. (1991). Partners in cognition: Extending human intelligence with intelligent technologies. *Educational Researcher, 20*(3), 2–9.

Scardamalia, M., & Bereiter, C. (1985). Fostering the development of self-regulation in children's knowledge. In S. F. Chipman, J. W. Segal, & R. Glaser (Eds.), *Thinking and learning skills: Research and open questions* (Vol. 2, pp. 563–577). Hillsdale, NJ: Lawrence Erlbaum.

Scardamalia, M., & Bereiter, C. (1983). The development of evaluative, diagnostic and remedial capabilities in children's composing. In M. Martlew (Ed.), *The psychology of written language: A developmental approach* (pp. 67–95). London: Wiley.

Schama, S. (1991, September 8). Clio has a problem. *New York Times Magazine,* pp. 30–34.

Schlechty, P. C. (1990). *Schools for the 21st century: Leadership imperatives for educational reform.* San Francisco: Jossey-Bass.

Schlechty, P. c. (1989). *Creating the infrastructure for reform.* Washington, DC: Council of Chief State School Officers.

Schlechty, P., & Cole, B. (1991). Creating a system that supports change. *Educational Horizons, 69*(2), 78–82.

Schoenfeld, A. H. (1985). *Mathematical problem solving.* New York: Academic Press.

Schroeder, T., & Lester, F. (1989). Developing understanding in mathematics via problem solving. In P. T. Trafton (Ed.), *1989 Yearbook of the National Council of Teachers of Mathematics* (pp. 31–42). Reston, VA: National Council of Teachers of Mathematics.

Scott, T., Cole, M., & Engel, M. (1992). Computers and education: A cultural constructivist perspective. In G. Grant (Ed.), *Review of Research in Education* (*Vol. 18*, pp. 191–251). Washington, DC: American Educational Research Association.

Sealey, J. (1986). *Peer edition groups.* R. & D Interpretation Service Bulletin on Oral and Written Communication. Charleston, WV: Appalachia Educational Laboratory.

Secretary's Commission on Achieving Necessary Skills. (1991). *What work requires of schools: A Scans report for America 2000.* Washington, DC: U. S. Department of Labor.

Shanahan, T. (1991). New literacy goes to school: Whole language in the classroom. *Educational Horizons, 69*(3), 146–151.

Sharron, H. (1987). *Changing children's minds: Feuerstein's revolution in the teaching of intelligence.* London: Souvenir Press.

Shavelson, R., J., & Salomon, G. (1985). Information technology: Tool and teacher of the mind. *Educational Researcher, 14*(5), 4.

Shepard, L. (1991). Psychometrician's beliefs about learning. *Educational Researcher, 20*(6), 2–16.

Short, E. J., Cuddy, C. L., Friebert, S. E., & Schatschneider, C. W. (1990). The diagnostic and educational utility of thinking aloud during problem solving. In H. L. Swanson & B. Keogh (Eds.), *Learning disabilities: Theoretical and research issues* (pp. 93–109). Hillsdale, NJ: Lawrence Erlbaum.

Shulman, L. S. (1987). Knowledge and teaching: Foundations of the new reform. *Harvard Educational Review, 57*(1), 1–22.

Siegler, R. S. (1989). Strategy diversity and cognitive assessment. *Educational Researcher, 18*(9), 15–19.

Singer, H., & Donlan, D. (1982). Active comprehension: Problem-solving schema with question generation of complex, short stories. *Reading Researcher Quarterly, 17*(2), 166-186.

Sizer, T. R. (1992). *Horace's school: Redesigning the American high school.* Boston: Houghton Mifflin.

Sizer, T. R. (1984). *Horace's compromise: The dilemma of the American high school.* Boston: Houghtoin Mifflin.

Slavin, R. E. (1991). Synthesis of research on cooperative learning. *Educational Leadership, 48*(5), 71–82.

Slavin, R. E. (1987). Cooperative learning and the cooperative school. *Educational Leadership, 45*(3), 7–13.

Slavin, R. E. (1983). When does cooperative learning increase student achievement? *Psychological Bulletin, 94*, 429–445.

Slavin, R. E., Karweit, N. L., & Wasik, B. A. (1991). *Preventing early school failure: What works* (Report No. 26). Baltimore, MD: Center for Research on Effective Schools for Disadvantaged Students.

Smey-Richman, B. S. (1991). *School climate and restructuring for low-achieving students.* Philadelphia, PA: Research for Better Schools.

Smey-Richman, B. S. (1988). *Involvement in learning for low-achieving students.* Philadelphia, PA: Research for Better Schools.

Smith, D. J., & Nelson, J. R. (1992). The effect of a self-management procedure on the classroom and academic behavior of students with mild handicaps. *School Psychology Review, 21*(1), 59–72.

Sparks, D. (1991, September). Restructuring schools through staff development: An interview with Phil Schlechty. *The Developer*, pp. 1, 5–7.

Sternberg, R. J. (1990a). Intellectual styles: Theory and classroom applications. In B. Z. Presseisen, R. J. Sternberg, K. W. Fischer, C. C. Knight, & R. Feuerstein, *Learning and thinking styles: Classroom interaction* (pp. 18–42). Washington, DC: National Education Association.

Sternberg, R. J. (1990b). *Metaphors of mind: Conceptions of the nature of intelligence.* New York: Cambridge University Press.

Sternberg, R. J. (1982). Who's Intelligent? *Psychology Today, 16* (4), 30–39.

Sternberg, R. J., & Bhana, K. (1986). Synthesis of research on the effectiveness of intellectual skills programs: Snake-oil remedies or miracle cures? *Educational Leadership, 44*(2), 60–67.

Sternberg, R. J., Okagaki, L., & Jackson, A. S. (1990). Practical intelligence for success in school. *Educational Leadership, 48*(1), 35–39.

Stiggins, R. (1991). Assessment literacy. *Phi Delta Kappan, 72*(7), 534–539.

Stiggins, R. J. (1985). Improving assessment where it means the most: In the classroom. *Educational Leadership, 43*(2), 69–74.

Stiggins, R. J., Rubel, E., & Quellmalz, E. (1988). *Measuring thinking skills in the classroom* (rev. ed.). Washington, DC: National Education Association.

Stigler, J. W., & Stevenson, H. W. (1991). How Asian teachers polish each lesson to perfection. *American Educator, 15*(1), 12–20, 43–47.

Suhor, C. (1992). Semiotics and the teaching of thinking. *Teaching Thinking and Problem Solving, 14*(1), 1, 3–6.

Swartz, R. (1991). *New ways to assess learning in science.* Andover, MA: The NETWORK (photocopy).

Swartz, R. (1987, August). *Structured teaching for critical thinking and reasoning in standard subject-area instruction.* Paper presented at a Conference on Informal Reasoning, Learning Research and Development Center, University of Pittsburgh, Pittsburgh, PA.

Tanner, D. (1989). A brief historical perspective of the struggle for an integrative curriculum. *Educational Horizons, 68*(1), 7–11.

Tharp, R. G. (1989). Psychocultural variables and constants: Effects on teaching and learning in schools. *American Psychologist, 44*(2), 349–359.

Tharp, R. G., & Gallimore, R. (1991). *The instructional conversation: Teaching and learning in social activity* (Research Report No. 2). Washington, DC: National Center for Research on Cultural Diversity and Second Language Learning.

Tharp, R. G., & Gallimore, R. (1989). Rousing schools to life. *American Educator, 13*(2), 20–25, 46–51.

Tharp, R. G., & Gallimore, R. (1988). *Rousing minds to life.* New York: Cambridge University Press.

Thurow, L. (1991). The centennial essay. *The American School Board Journal, 178*(9), 41–43.

Uphoff, J. K. (1991). School readiness issues: Conflicting claims confuse and confound. *Teaching Thinking and Problem Solving, 13*(6), 1, 4–5.

Valencia, S. (1990). A portfolio approach to classroom reading assessment: The whys, whats, and how. *The Reading Teacher, 43*(4), 338–341.

Vobejda, B. (1992, June 1). A diverse U. S. seen in census. *Philadelphia Inquirer,* pp. A1, A7.

Vygotsky, L. S. (1978). *Mind in society: The development of higher pscyhological processes.* Edited by M. Cole, V. John-Steiner, S. Scribner, & E. Souberman. Cambridge, MA: Harvard University Press.

Wehlage, G. G., Rutter, R. A., Smith, G. A., Lesko, N., & Fernandez, R. R. (1989). *Reducing the risk: Schools as communities of support.* London: Falmar Press.

Wertsch, J. V. (Ed.). (1985). *Culture, communication, and cognition: Vygotskian perspectives.* New York: Cambridge University Press.

Wiggins, G. (1992). Creating tests worth taking. *Educational Leadership, 49*(8), 26–33.

Wiggins, G. (1990). Reconsidering standards and assessment. *Education Week, 9*(18), pp. 36, 25.

Wiggins, G. (1989a). A true test: Toward more authentic and equitable assessment. *Phi Delta Kappan, 70*(9), 703–713.

Wiggins, G. (1989b). Teaching to the (authentic) test. *Educational Leadership, 46*(7), 41–47.

Wilson, E. K. (1971). *Sociology: Rules, roles and relationships.* Homewood, IL: Dorsey.

Winocur, S. L. (1986). *IMPACT: Improve minimal proficiencies by activating critical thinking.* Bloomington, IN: Phi Delta Kappa.

Wittrock, M. C. (Ed.). (1990). Students' thought process. In American Educational Research Association, *Research on teaching and learning* (Vol. 3, pp. 4–49). New York: Macmillan.

Wittrock, M. C. (1987). Teaching and student learning. *Journal of Teacher Education, 38*(6), 30–33.

Wolf, D., Bixby, J., Glenn III, J., & Gardner, H. (1991). To use their minds well: Investigating new forms of student assessment. In G. Grant (Ed.), *Review of Research in Education* (Vol. 17, pp. 31–74). Washington, DC: American Educational Research Association.

Wolf, D. B., LeMahieu, P. G., & Eresh, J. (1992). Good measure: Assessment as a tool for educational reform. *Educational Leadership, 49*(8), 8–13.

Wood, T., Cobb, P., & Yackel, E. (1991). Change in teaching mathematics: A case study. *American Educational Research Journal, 28*(3), 587–616.

Zessoules, R., & Gardner, H. (1991). Authentic assessment: Beyond the buzzword and into the classroom. In V. Perrone (Ed.), *Expanding student assessment* (pp. 47–71). Alexandria, VA: Association for Supervision and Curriculum Assessment.

Zimmerman, B. J., & Martinez-Pons, M. (1990). Student differences in self-regulated learning: Relating grade, sex, giftedness to self-efficacy and strategy use. *Journal of Educational Psychology, 82*(1), 51–59.

Zuboff, S. (1988). *In the age of the smart machine: The future of work and power.* New York: Basic Books.

Implementation of Instrumental Enrichment and Cognitive Modifiability in the Taunton Public Schools: A Model for Systemic Implementation in U.S. Schools

by Jane R. Williams and William L. Kopp

I NTRODUCTION
The plight of low-socioeconomic minority students must be addressed. The decreasing economic competitiveness and increasing poor and minority populations have added a new dimension to the vision of future schooling in America. The residual effect is that the achievement of those students we educate poorly, will become increasingly more problematic. Disconcerting statistics reported by the Massachusetts Department of Youth Services (Boston Globe; July 1991:26) state school dropout rates, rates of sexually transmitted diseases, murders, and serious injury all reflect disproportionate suffering among youngsters from minority groups. Although 79% of the juvenile population in Massachusetts is white, 56% of the youth committed to the State's Department of Youth Services (DYS) are Black or Hispanic. DYS commitments for drug trafficking are eleven times more frequent for Blacks and Hispanics than for Whites.

Over the past ten years the Taunton School System has been involved, on a grass roots level, in a system wide implementation of Feuerstein's methods in the City of Taunton. One

From a paper submitted in partial fulfillment of the Level II Trainer Certification Requirements at Hadassah - Wizo - Canada - Research Institute, July 1993. Reprinted with permission.

hundred teachers have been trained in, and are teaching Instrumental Enrichment (IE). More than eighteen hundred students from the gifted to the retarded performer, monolingual and bilingual, from the exceptional to the average, currently receive IE in our integrated classrooms. Psychologists and teachers have been trained, and now use the LPAD to determine students' cognitive deficits and to suggest methods of cognitive modification. There is a salaried position in the School System for a Coordinator of Instrumental Enrichment. The Superintendent of Schools is totally involved and committed to this process. The School Committee has mandated that IE be an integral part of the fourth, fifth, and sixth grade curricula be taught during the prime learning time of the students' day. An analytical account of this odyssey follows. It reveals the successes and failures we encountered in the process and suggests a model for future implementation efforts. As we continue to learn, the experience described below provides only a mile-stone.

OUR STUDENTS

The City of Taunton, a community of blue collar workers, is located approximately 35 miles south of Boston. From 1980 to 1990, Taunton's population climbed 11% from 45,000 to 49,832 and the city experienced significant growth due to the number of high-tech firms that settled here. However, this economic boom missed its language-minority population.

The Portuguese and Spanish constitute the largest ethnic groups in the city, with 12,000 and 2,362 people, respectively (an increase of 82.2% over the past ten years). They immigrated from a society that was primarily agrarian, to an area which offers mainly high tech jobs. Lacking the required entry level skills, they depend on the few menial jobs that still exist for work.

The average unemployment rate in Taunton is 10.6%. About ten percent of the population here earn below the US designated poverty level. Single parents head 12% of family households. The number of school-age children in Taunton receiving AFDC subsidy has grown from 786 children in FY 1990 to 1,035 children in FY 1992. Valuable learning opportunities are lost due to poor attendance, high truancy, and suspension rates.

In conjunction with these facts, there are presently 308 students with limited English proficiency in separate bilingual classrooms throughout the Taunton School System. Additionally, there are 1,565 diagnosed special needs students, 673 of whom are in substantially separate resource room settings for most of the day.

Failure rates on basic skill tests and high-school drop out rates here are reported to increase for poor, minority, and non-English speaking students, as well as students with parents who did not finish high school (Massachusetts Department of Education, February, 1991:1). Additionally, the trend shows the highest drop out rates occur in the second and third year of high school with more males dropping out than females.

> **Failure rates on basic skill tests and high-school dropout rates here are reported to increase for poor, minority, and non-English speaking students, as well as students with parents who did not finish high school.**

During the past several years, our school district has made a concerted effort to meet the needs of our poor and language-minority students. It has moved away from the traditional practice of homogeneous grouping; implemented an English and native languages program; offered learning experiences that are aimed at raising students' cognitive skills; and established comprehensive staff development programs.

The Taunton School System became involved in cognitive education through a bilingual grant in 1983. At that time the District was attempting to develop a culture-free, non-biased assessment approach to bilingual children. The school psychologist was introduced to IE by a bilingual consultant, and upon further investigation, became intrigued with the concept. Some of the qualities he found appealing were: (1) IE has a strong theoretical base, delineating the cognitive processes to be taught, as well as the methodology to achieve, maintain, and transfer these skills; (2) it is content free, providing an ethnically diverse student population with equal footing; (3) it provides explicit training both in the mental processes used to perform tasks and in self-management strategies; (4) it has a unique motivational format; (5) it is explicitly linked with the "real world," and 6) it has demonstrated significant success.

CHRONOLOGY

In 1987, after staff members had attended state-sponsored workshops, the first workshop was held in Taunton. This grant-funded workshop was designed to train twenty psychologists and educators how to use the Learning Potential Assessment Device. It was held on two extended weekends and the participants volunteered their time on Saturdays and Sundays.

Although the workshop was very well received, the LPAD was not implemented in the schools. In 1988, the first I.E. workshop was held in the district with twenty teachers, funded by grant money. This workshop was held in March and implementation began with enthusiastic and eager teachers in September of the same year.

We realized that for the program to be effective it had to be accepted as part of the school curriculum by the School Committee. The coordinator of the program, along with a group of students from IE pilot classrooms, presented their arguments for the implementation of IE to the School Committee. The coordinator also presented preliminary results from the pilot study as well as anecdotal reports about student's excitement and renewed vigor in teaching as a result of the experience with IE. Along with the support of the superintendent, the School Committee recommended that Level I Instrumental Enrichment be introduced to all fifth grades with Level II to follow the next year in grade six and finally, for Level III to be implemented in grade seven. The School Superintendent invited committee members to observe an IE lesson and interview students. Consequently, their vote of support was unanimous.

The second task the Superintendent had to complete to guarantee successful system wide implementation was create a position of Instrumental Enrichment Coordinator. A job description was written and a person chosen from among the middle school teachers. The position was offered to a dynamic, intelligent, personable, and respected teacher who is a strong believer in IE and committed to its success. At this point the Instrumental Enrichment project surged forward.

Another factor in the successful implementation of IE did not come about by design. A psychologist who studied the theory of Cognitive Modifiability was promoted to a central office position. Consequently, we had easy access to the office of the Superintendent of Schools. Requests were made and arguments presented on the basis of personal knowledge and experience, not secondhand information. It was also found that, in all presentations, inservice workshops, demonstrations, etc., a team approach was more effective than one person presenting information by himself or herself.

Voluntary participation of teachers was a key factor in the implementation process. The teachers who participated in the initial workshops were dedicated and committed. They were open, flexible, and willing to give extra of themselves and their time. Once these teachers were "hooked" they began to enthusiastically spread the message. This group increased with each passing year. The point was finally reached where the relatively few resistant teachers were mandated to participate.

> Voluntary participation of teachers was a key factor in the implementation process. The teachers who participated in the initial workshops were dedicated and committed.

Principals were also invited to participate in the training workshops. In schools where principals participated in the workshop alongside their staff, IE was implemented best. Taunton has principals who understand and are as enthusiastic about IE as their teachers. An added benefit to their participation is that the principal is able to engage parents in the program.

Scheduling of IE classes had to be dealt with immediately. Since Instrumental Enrichment serves as a vehicle for cognitive development rather than offering subject matter, teachers and the community were uncomfortable with taking time away from the curriculum. Our policy has been to help them understand that IE improved children's learning, and that the time lost in the process is "gained" by the fact that the children are enabled to learn the academics more efficiently.

The IE goals represent a monumental task indeed. These goals can only be achieved through a systematic, enduring training effort. The majority of our teachers became enthused and excited during the course of their training. The first group of twenty teachers was carefully selected from the ranks of regular classroom teachers, bilingual teachers, special education teachers, and specialists. All of these teachers were dedicated professionals who we felt would welcome this new approach. Colleagues became intrigued about what the IE teachers were doing and began to inquire about the program. This approach created a general feeling of acceptance within the school system.

Once the teachers were trained, it was essential not to leave them on their own. The coordinator of the program was assigned to provide IE teachers with follow-up support. She made regular visitations to classrooms to ensure that the principles of mediated learning were being followed. Any teacher who experienced difficulties in teaching an instrument, or a particular group of students, simply had to call the coordinator to receive help. It is our feeling that the integration of IE into the school curriculum would not be accomplished without the support offered by the coordinator.

We have also established a monthly session of inservice training. This inservice training has not only dealt with the mechanics of teaching IE, but, more importantly, mediating the teachers' understanding of the concepts and theory of structural cognitive modification. We believed that understanding the conceptual base of the program will help improve the teaching and diagnostic skills in the classroom. We are pleased with this practice and will continue it in the future.

BARRIERS

It is important to indicate the four major barriers which challenged the implementation process. First, the initial cost of the program was substantial. The fiscal year 1990 budget allocated for the program, including workshops, materials and consultant expenses totaled $34,209. This figure did not include the salary of the coordinator. Second, contractual problems arose over the assignment of additional teaching periods to the teacher's course load. Third, initially, the IE classes were scheduled during supplementary period, which is a non-teaching period at the end of the day. This schedule had to be changed because it is the poorest quality teaching period of the day and also because it excluded IE students from participating in optional activities such as band, chorus, newspaper, intramural, etc., Fourth, the instability of the teaching force in Taunton makes training and continuity problematic.

The cost related problem was partly solved by the use of grant funds to support our initial training efforts with the help of consultants. Now we have our in-house training personnel and support team. The problem was partly solved by changing priorities, which we did with the support from the district office. The contractual and scheduling problems were solved by the integration of Instrumental Enrichment into the curriculum supported by the School Committee. The first teaching period of days 1, 3, and 5 is scheduled for the teaching of IE. Each period lasts fifty minutes, giving each student two and one half hours of IE instruction per week.

> **We reviewed the effects on Instrumental Enrichment on reading comprehension scores on the Stanford Achievement Test for Reading (SAT-R), at attendance, and at the way participating teachers view the program.**

In spite of the difficulties, the IE program has been introduced to all grade four, five, and six students in the Taunton Public Schools. The program is currently being taught in all elementary and middle schools through heterogeneous groupings. There are some 1,800 students receiving Instrumental Enrichment in forty-seven different classrooms. The population in these rooms is diverse, including students in regular and bilingual education, Chapter 1, and the gifted and talented programs.

THE PILOT PROJECT

We first designed a pilot IE project. It was conducted in our public school setting by a staff that continued to perform their daily work. It also included input from studies done by graduate education students in local colleges and universities. It was not as scientific as we would have liked it to be, but it was a reasonable and manageable attempt to evaluate the efficacy of our efforts.

During the first year of implementation, all sixth grade students in one school were assigned to experimental and control groups. The experimental group received IE classes for three, forty-five minute sessions each week. The instruction was conducted cooperatively by the I.E. Coordinator and the psychologist. The control group received the regular curriculum. Experimental and control subjects were tested twice in September and June of each of three consecutive academic years (until the students graduated from the eighth grade), starting in 1988.

We reviewed the effects of IE on reading comprehension scores on the Stanford Achievement Test for Reading (SAT-R), at attendance, and at the way participating teachers view the program. The results were positive and are briefly reported. Rather than reporting the results of our evaluation, our main concern here is to emphasize the important function a pilot effort plays in the successful implementation of IE.

At the end of the first year, the experimental group mean increased by 28% in the SAT-R comprehension subsection and by 25% in the SAT-R total reading, while the control group mean increased only by 8% in comprehension and by 10% in total reading. The mean difference in favor of the experimental group was 14% on the total SAT-R 20% on the comprehension SAT-R. The second year the experimental group mean increased by 10% in comprehension and by 20% in total reading while the control group mean increased by 3% in comprehension and by 5% in total reading. During the final year of the study, the experimental group mean increased by 42% in comprehension and by 5% in total reading while the control group mean increased by 2% in comprehension and by 7% in total reading. We considered these results to be profound because of the heterogeneity of the students' cognitive and language abilities.

In 1988-89, the aggregate daily attendance for the experimental group was 93% and 91% for the control group. In 1989-90, the experimental group's average attendance was 92% while the control group's was 89%. In 1990-91, the final year of the study, the experimental group's attendance was 92% and the control group's was 87%. Over the three-year period of the study, the aggregate daily attendance of the experimental group was 4% higher than that of the control group. We were pleased with these figures and believed that they resulted from the fact that the I.E. students felt more confident in their abilities and more positive toward school.

Teachers' responses were generally favorable. They reported transfer of strategies learned in Instrumental Enrichment classes; increased participation of the IE subjects in other classes; and increased tolerance of individual differences among students as indicated by their willingness to help fellow classmates.

In addition to the data we collected, we reviewed academic achievements as measured by standardized test. Last year, the State of Massachusetts conducted assessment tests throughout the state for grades four, eight, and twelve. Our students in the eighth and twelfth grades had not received IE, and their test scores were below the norm. Our fourth grade students had received one year of IE and their test scores were the best scores the City of Taunton has ever had. When our test scores were compared with those of other urban centers, our results were outstanding. This year's district wide testing of the Iowa Test of Basic Skills for the fourth and seventh grade (both have been exposed to IE) indicate that our students' scores in reading, mathematics, social studies and science are on the rise.

> The integration of children from special education, bilingual education, the gifted/talented program and regular education in the same classroom was made possible and meaningful with the implementation of IE.

This pilot impacted the system as a whole and the program grew with new-found excitement and conviction. We have acquired a shared belief that practices that make IE successful— the concept of Mediated Learning, are sound. Our teachers now see that subject matter is merely the vehicle to enhance our students' thinking skills and problem solving abilities. We will follow our pilot groups through high-school to establish the true value of this effort.

INTEGRATION OF EDUCATIONAL SERVICES

The integration of children from special education, bilingual education, the gifted/talented program and regular education in the same classroom was made possible and meaningful with the implementation of IE. We also found it helpful in enhancing the cooperative work of regular and special educators, school psychologists and social workers. We matched special education teachers with regular education teachers to team teach Instrumental Enrichment.

In the past year we have made inroads in one of our special populations. It was of interest and surprise to us that the greatest amount of resistance we encountered came from those teachers who work with the very children for whom this approach was developed and is most effective. We have a separate program for the moderate to severely retarded learners. One of our psychologists has worked successfully with selected children from that program on a pull-out basis. It took two years for the teacher to be convinced that IE can help her students. Next year, the psychologist will team teach with the teacher to conduct IE with her students. On the high school level, the same approach has yielded similar results with retarded adolescents.

> From the very beginning, parents should be introduced to the nature and purpose of the program. When ready, parents could be trained to continue the mediation process at home with their children.

THE NEW ROLE OF SCHOOL PSYCHOLOGY

As soon as the implementation of I.E. was complete it became clear that we were engaging in a long-term effort. It was now totally unacceptable to our teachers to discuss the progress, or lack thereof, of the children in traditional terms. It was now necessary to change the language and thinking of the entire school district. This would take time and we were determined not to be discouraged or overwhelmed by the enormity of the undertaking.

We felt that the key personnel in this regard were the psychologists, guidance counselors, and specialists who evaluate children for special education services; for this reason, we organized two workshops for these staff members. A third such workshop was also arranged and attended by the same mix of specialists. As a result of these workshops, the specialists began to use Feuerstein's Learning Propensity Assessment Device (LPAD) (formerly named Learning Potential Assessment) and to report their findings at special education team meetings. These personnel, in turn, conducted inservice sessions for the guidance counselors and special education educators to discuss the terminology and the implications of the LPAD findings.

As an outgrowth of these meetings during the past year, a psychologist and a speech therapist developed a pre-referral system based upon the language and principles of Structural Cognitive Modifiability. It is our hope that this approach will help reduce the number of children referred to special education. We are now ready to extend this approach system wide. All teachers will be trained in our new pre-referral process.

PARENT INVOLVEMENT

Parent education must be included in the implementation process. From the very beginning, parents should be introduced to the nature and purpose of the program. When ready, parents could be trained to continue the mediation process at home with their children. Every year since the inception of IE, we organized meetings with parent/teacher organizations, parent advisory groups, and the parents of Chapter 1 students. Parents have been extremely receptive and very supportive of the program. We are now ready to offer training to parents as mediators. We hope this will add great value to our educational process.

SUMMARY

As a result of this effort, our entire school district is in the process of reform. Much has been accomplished in Taunton since the first LPAD workshop. However, much remains to be done until IE is fully implemented. The process continues. Today, teachers feel comfortable with IE and with the idea that all children are capable of learning. At special education meetings the results of the LPAD are discussed, either along with, or in place of, traditional testing. Before children are referred for special education, a process is in place whereby more attempts are made to educate the children in regular education classrooms. Teachers are being evaluated according to the principles of mediated learning. Children feel better about themselves. Test scores have risen in all academic areas. Attendance at school is improving and children are actively engaged in the classroom. There are anecdotal reports from children, years after they have received IE, stating that they attribute some successes in their schooling to their exposure to the program.

Acknowledgments

Grateful acknowledgment is made to the following authors and agents for their permission to reprint copyrighted materials.

Lawrence Erlbaum Associates, Inc., Publishers for "Intervention Programs for Retarded [Low] Perfomers: Goals, Means, and Expected Outcomes" by Reuven Feuerstein, Ya'acov Rand, Mildred B. Hoffman, Moshe Egozi, and Nilly Ben Shachar-Segev. From *Educational Values and Cognitive Instruction: Implications for Reform* edited by Lorna Idol and Beau Fly Jones, p. 139–178, 1991. Reprinted with permission of *Lawrence Elrbaum Associates, Publishers*, Hillsdale, NJ. Copyright 1991 by *Lawrence Erlbaum Associates, publishers*. All rights reserved.

Barbara Presseisen and Alex Kozulin for "Mediated Learning: The Contributions of Vygotsky and Feuerstein in Theory and Practice" by Barbara Presseisen and Alex Kozulin, 1992. Reprinted with permission. All rights reserved.

American Educational Research Association for "Empirical Status of Feuerstein's Instrumental Enrichment (FIE) Technique as a Method of Teaching Thinking Skills" by Joel M. Savell, Paul T. Twohig, and Douglas L. Rachford. From *Review of Educational Research*, vol. 56, no. 4, p. 381–409, Winter 1986. Reprinted with permission of the *American Educational Research Association*. Copyright 1986 by *American Education Research Association*. All rights reseved.

Minister of Education, Government of Alberta, Canada for "Cognitive Education Project" by Robert Mulcahy and Associates, University of Alberta, from *Project Highlights*, p. 1–8. Reprinted with permission of *Minister of Education, Government of Alberta*. All rights reserved.

International Journal of Cognitive Education and Mediated Learning for "Reviving Thought Processes in Pre-adolescents. Towards a Dynamic Conception of Intelligence: Is it Possible to Learn How to Think?" by Rosine Debray. Vol. 1, no. 3, p. 211–219, 1990. Reprinted with permission of *International Journal of Cognitive Education and Mediated Learning*. Copyright 1990 by *International Journal of Cognitive Education and Mediated Learning*. All rights reserved.

Index

Learn from Our Books *and* from Our Authors!

Bring Our Author/Trainers to Your District

At IRI/SkyLight, we have assembled a unique team of outstanding author/trainers with international reputations for quality work. Each has designed high-impact programs that translate powerful new research into successful learning strategies for every student. We design each program to fit your school's or district's special needs.

1 Training Programs

IRI/SkyLight's training programs extend the renewal process by helping educators move from content-centered to mind-centered classrooms. In our highly interactive workshops, participants learn foundational, research-based information and teaching strategies in an instructional area that they can immediately transfer to the classroom setting. With IRI/SkyLight's specially prepared materials, participants learn how to teach their students to learn for a lifetime.

2 Network for Systemic Change

Through a partnership with Phi Delta Kappa, IRI/SkyLight offers a Network for site-based systemic change: *The Network of Mindful Schools.* The Network is designed to promote systemic school change as possible and practical when starting with a renewed vision that centers on *what* and *how* each student learns. To help accomplish this goal, Network consultants work with member schools to develop an annual tactical plan and then implement that plan at the classroom level.

3 Training of Trainers

The Training of Trainers programs train your best teachers, those who provide the highest quality instruction, to coach other teachers. This not only increases the number of teachers you can afford to train in each program, but also increases the amount of coaching and follow-up that each teacher can receive from a resident expert. Our Training of Trainers programs will help you make a systemic improvement in your staff development program.

To receive a FREE COPY of the IRI/SkyLight catalog or more information about trainings offered through IRI/SkyLight, contact CLIENT SERVICES at

TRAINING AND PUBLISHING, INC.
2626 S. Clearbrook Dr., Arlington Heights, IL 60005
800-348-4474 • 847-290-6600 • FAX 847-290-6609

There are

one-story intellects,

two-story intellects, and three-story

intellects with skylights. All fact collectors, who

have no aim beyond their facts, are one-story men. Two-story men

compare, reason, generalize, using the labors of the fact collectors as

well as their own. Three-story men idealize, imagine,

predict—their best illumination comes from

above, through the skylight.

—*Oliver Wendell*

Holmes

TRAINING AND PUBLISHING, INC.

Arlington Heights, Illinois